Jesus Freaks

StORies of REvolutionaries
WHO Changed their World:

FEARing GOD, Not Man.

REVOLUTIONARIES

dc Talk
and the Voice of the Martyrs

BETHANY HOUSE PUBLISHERS
MINNEAPOLIS, MINNESOTA

Jesus Freaks: Revolutionaries

Stories of Revolutionaries Who Changed Their World: Fearing God, Not Man

by dc Talk

Previously published as *Jesus Freaks Vol II*

Copyright © 2002 by Bethany House Publishers

Design by Thurber Creative Services, Tulsa, Oklahoma

Manuscript prepared by Rick Killian, Boulder, Colorado.

Scripture credits and permissions are on page 383.

Published by Bethany House Publishers
11400 Hampshire Avenue South
Bloomington, MN 55438

Bethany House Publishers is a Division of
Baker Publishing Group, Grand Rapids, Michigan

Printed in the United States of America

ISBN 978-0-7642-0084-7

The Library of Congress has catalogued the original edition as follows:

Jesus freaks. Vol. II : stories of revolutionaries who changed their world :
fearing God, not man / by DC Talk.
p. cm.
Includes bibliographical references and index.
ISBN 0-7642-2746-7 (pbk. with flaps)
1. Persecution. 2. Christian martyrs. I. DC Talk (Musical group)
BR1601.3 .J54 2002
272'.9—dc21
2002010012

Dedicated to...

the memory and work of
RICHARD (1909–2001)
and SABINA (1913–2000)
Wurmbrand
and those like them
who USED THEIR LIVES
to make a difference
for Jesus.

Your faith was not in vain.

We would also like to express
our continued gratitude to

The VOICe of the Martyrs
for providing the
contemporary STORIES
for this book and for their ministry
to those in the
Persecuted Church.

www.persecution.com

"You have heard it said unto you ... but I say unto you ..."

From the beginnings of His public ministry, Jesus set the record straight: *"I have come to change the world."* He had come to change people's thinking. He had come to revolutionize their paradigm—the way they saw the world and had comfortably settled into it, following their own desires, ignoring those around them who needed help, and figuring that was the way to do it because everyone else was doing pretty much the same thing.

Then came Jesus. *"You have heard it said ... but I say unto you ..."*

We often think we have arrived spiritually because we have memorized a bunch of rules and regulations, or a list of do's and don'ts, and built them into our culture and lifestyle. If you just wear your Christian T-shirt once a week, always have your radio tuned to the local Christian music station, don't do drugs or drink, go to church on Sundays and Bible study one night a week, take part in the summer missions trip, and don't have sex until you are married, then you are a real witness to those around you.

But Jesus came and shattered man's perception of the world. He taught about a kingdom that was more powerful than man could ever comprehend. This kingdom, however, didn't always make common sense. He taught that the kingdom of heaven is more than clothes, music, Bible studies, and what you do on the outside. The kingdom of heaven is spiritual. The kingdom of heaven is peace. The kingdom of heaven is the narrow road of following Jesus day by day. You can't be like everyone else and follow Him. His sheep hear His voice and chase after Him; they don't just roam with the rest of the herd and think that is going to save them.

The path He has for you is very different, very special; it is unique in all of humankind. He came to change the world. How can those who truly follow Him have any less of a goal in life?

Jesus came to comfort the afflicted, but He also came to afflict the comfortable.

Throughout history true followers of Christ have been revolutionaries. As the trends of society have been dictated by the herd mentality, these men and women of God have stood up and said, "Hey, wait a minute. That's not right!" They reached out their hands to people the rest of the world walked by without a glance, they spoke out when shutting up may have saved their lives, they distributed Bibles when others were passing out ammunition, they took God places others called "God-forsaken," they picked up their crosses and followed Christ when others cried "Lord, Lord" but did nothing. And for this they were called "Freaks."

People often look up to us because we are in the public eye, but the people in this book are the *true* heroes. They are the ones people should look up to.

The freedoms we have today to own a Bible, believe what seems right to us, go to the church we want, and follow God as completely as we want are all because of the Jesus Freaks who came before us. If only we had yet done enough to earn such an honored title among the rest of these "Freaks."

Proverbs 1:32 NIV tells us "the complacency of fools will destroy them." Are we too comfortable in our lifestyles to truly be following Christ?

• • •

The world was shocked when those who called themselves fundamentalist believers in God killed 3,023 people on September 11, 2001, by crashing planeloads of people into the World Trade Center, into the ground in Pennsylvania, and into the Pentagon. In the United States in recent years, those who have called themselves fundamentalist believers in God have bombed abortion clinics, assassinated doctors who performed abortions, holed themselves up within compounds and shot it out with the FBI, or committed mass suicides thinking that their "martyrdoms" would change the way people think. In the Middle Ages those who called themselves fundamentalist believers in God went on "crusades" to "free" Israel and left a wake of pillaging, looting, and rape in their wake. They felt themselves revolutionaries for the cause of God, but they were deluded. They died thinking they were heroes and martyrs.

We hear the word *martyr* a lot these days. People who feel sorry for themselves because others have been inconsiderate to them are said to be "playing the martyr" to get the attention of their friends. People are called "martyrs" on the evening news because they have suffered even slightly for some cause. People use the word as a political tool to try to spark a revolution and conform others to their way of thinking. They try to manipulate others with this word to get what they want.

All true martyrs are revolutionaries, but not all revolutionaries are true martyrs.

Those who rise up and kill themselves to kill others are not martyrs at all. They have lost sight of the truth and have been sucked into a lie. They have never experienced the true power of love. The kind of love God is. The love that cannot be defeated, though you beat it, you torture it, or you shoot it with guns or stab it with knives. They try to accomplish their goals through fear and intimidation. They do not understand that true martyrdom is being a witness of the Truth. It is not defined simply by dying for some cause; it is defined by living for the freedom of others. Freedom from fear. Freedom from prejudice and persecution. Freedom from hatred, bitterness, and jealousy. Freedom to be forgiven and to forgive.

Martyrs die because they refuse to deny the Truth, they are unwilling to force their ways upon others, and they are unwilling to fight back when fighting back would deny the Love they are trying to show those hurting them. This is how martyrdom changes things: It stands up as a witness of the One who is Truth and Love, and the One who is Truth and Love can do little else but stand up and surround them with His presence. And His presence changes things.

These are the true revolutionaries that have existed throughout history, starting at the Cross. These are the great cloud of martyrs—*witnesses*—that are seated in heaven watching the revolution for true freedom—spiritual freedom—rage on the earth. It is a revolution of words and hearts and helping hands. It is a revolution that turns the world upside right and lets God touch the earth with His love wherever the revolutionaries go, whether it be across the street, across the ocean, into a prison cell, or to the grave. These are the revolutionaries who were not willing to set aside the Truth for the convenience of being accepted or the privilege of living only by their own desires. These are the revolutionaries who fight for the spiritual freedom that is only found in Jesus and are unwilling to let that freedom go for anything.

We have much to learn from such revolutionaries. We also have much to carry on for them—much to carry on for Him.

That's why doing a second book on Jesus Freaks makes sense. In the first book a lot of people read about what was happening in the world and were surprised and shocked and never knew they had it so good. But what do we do with that knowledge? *Jesus Freaks: Revolutionaries* is not just about those who stood up for Jesus, but those who were willing to make their lives a difference for Jesus. That is the call today as well: When you read JF1, you may have decided that you were willing to die for Jesus, but will you be with those in JF2 who made the decision to live for Him and have that life make a difference for Him?

A MESSAGE FROM TOM WHITE

Fearing GOD, Not Man

Many revolutionaries for Jesus have influenced my life. Richard and Sabina Wurmbrand are two of them. They were fearless Christian leaders in Romania. When the Russian tanks were rolling into their country, many were trying to run the other way, but Richard and Sabina stood beside the road and handed gospel booklets in Russian to the tank commanders. This Lutheran pastor and his wife did not see problems. They saw opportunities.

When trains full of Russian troops would move through the main station, Hebrew Christians from their congregation would place gospels through the windows and into the hands of eager soldiers before the political KGB officer could reach them.

Richard and Sabina spent years in prison for their courageous stand, ministering even behind bars. They founded the mission I represent: The Voice of the Martyrs.

Many revolutionaries for Jesus cannot read or write, but all of us are willing to be used by God, who opens our mouths to share the Good News. In Bangladesh one man told us about a fanatical Muslim attack on his home: "They burned my house. They burned my wife's clothes. But they cannot burn Jesus from our hearts." Another Bangladeshi Christian rides his bicycle through villages, even though they threaten to cut off his feet. He cannot read the tracts he gives to others, but his son reads them to him each morning before he goes out.

DIRECTOR OF THE VOICE OF THE MARTYRS

It is characteristic of revolutionaries for Jesus to view our mission as more important than our possessions. My friend Pastor Li Di Xian, who lives in China, has been arrested eighteen times in the past few years. He preaches in house churches, which are "illegal." (The Chinese official church generally follows government policy by not allowing anyone under the age of eighteen to attend church.) I visited one of Pastor Li's groups where many children attended. More than four hundred Christians were sitting on the ground. Li keeps a small cloth suitcase ready so he will have a change of clothes when he is arrested again.

A similar situation exists in Vietnam, where there are hundreds of thousands of new Christians but no church buildings are allowed. Evangelist To Dinh Trung was in the Quang Ngai prison when nervous officials told him that he could go home several months early. He had received thousands of letters from Christians around the world. Brother Trung refused to go home early to his wife and two children, because he was leading many prisoners to Christ!

We revolutionaries for Jesus strive to keep our eyes on the Cross.

I was honored to spend eighteen months in prison in Cuba with those who love Jesus. I was sentenced to twenty-four years for distributing Christian literature. There I met Pastor Noble Alexander, who remained in prison more than twenty years. Pastor Noble baptized more than three hundred men in different prisons while the guards were looking the other way. Many times the prisoners were dunked under hot dishwater.

Revolutionaries for Jesus understand that eternity is worth everything.

Wearing the badge of courage for Christ does not require us to live in an area that is openly hostile to Christians. Someone influenced all of these Christian leaders who at one time in their lives were lost, without God. Someone courageously sacrificed time to pray, to teach, to read Bible stories, and to model the love and mercy of Christ over and over and over again. To do this consistently takes a Holy Spirit–revolutionized mind and spirit.

Revolutionaries for Christ are not swayed by opinions and reactions from the world. We must always be gracious as we present the Good News of our Redeemer, but we must remember that the cross of Christ, His Way, will threaten and be an offense to some (Galatians 5:10–11; 1 Peter 2:7–8). This must not deter us from our mission.

When religious leaders, merchants selling idols, and ignorant mobs attacked the disciples, the accusation was, "They have turned our world upside-down" (Acts 17:6, paraphrased). It is easy to forget that the Christless values and religions of the world are upside-down. They will not lead us to eternity.

Revolutionaries for Jesus, while sharing the forgiveness of Christ in a loving way, are not blunted by the desire to always be accepted or loved by others. We must respect the beliefs of others but not allow this gracious response to silence us from sharing the Truth. Christians and only Christians are able to offer the key to eternity, the key to the Door, Jesus Christ, who revolutionizes and redeems us into His world, the world that is right-side-up.

rev·o·lu·tion·ar·y

(rev-★-lü-sh★n-er-ē)n.

[from Latin *revolvere*: to revolve, or turn around]

1) A person who brings about (a) a sudden, radical, or complete change; (b) a fundamental change in political, social, or cultural organization; (c) a fundamental change in the way of thinking about or visualizing something: a change of paradigm <the Copernican *revolution*> 2) One engaged in a revolution. 3) An advocate or adherent of revolutionary doctrines, doctrines that are a complete turnaround from the cultural, economic, and political norms of the day. 4) A disciple of Christ; a Jesus Freak.

11

These who have turned the world upside down have come here too ... and these are all acting contrary to the decrees of Caesar, saying there is another king—Jesus.

SPOKEN OF PAUL AND SILAS BY THOSE WHO OPPOSED THEM IN THESSALONICA

(ACTS 17:6–7 NKJV)

What this means is that those who become Christians become new persons. They are not the same anymore, for the old life is gone. A new life has begun!

PAUL, SPEAKING ABOUT THE PERSONAL REVOLUTION OF BECOMING A CHRISTIAN

(2 CORINTHIANS 5:17 NLT)

"LORD, Show Me the Truth"

By 1967 it was as if a whole generation had detached itself from the conventional values of their society and converged on the Haight-Ashbury district of San Francisco looking for answers. Yet what was touted as a haven for free thinking and countercultural renewal had instead become a viper's pit of hard drugs, rape, abuse of innocence, organized crime, and the recruiting ground for every religious persuasion imaginable.

Into this walked a young man named Kent Philpott, who felt compelled of God to go there with the Gospel. In April of 1967, he met another young man, David Hoyt, who had devoted himself to Hinduism and preached the world of Krishna Consciousness. They began months of debating back and forth the nature of truth and spirituality that brought in many friends and supporters on both sides.

Kent's open-minded dialogue and David's sincere search for truth soon had David reeling in doubt about what he had previously held as true. Then one night in desperation, he called out to God: "Lord, show me the Truth. Jesus Christ, if you are the Son of God, come into my life! Forgive and heal me!"

In what was to David a blinding burst of light like what Paul experienced on the road to Damascus came the realization that Jesus was God's Son, sent to the world to free him. Jesus was alive and the true Savior of humanity! Jesus was the only one who could truly set people free! David became a Christian on the spot.

Soon after this, Kent and David teamed up to become among the first to establish a mission in the Haight-Ashbury district and reach out to those coming there for new answers. From their efforts and others that sprang up around the same time began the revival that became known as the Jesus Movement. They were among the first revolutionaries to be called "Jesus Freaks."

Why Search for Truth?

The personal revolution of becoming a Christian has always been the only basis of true freedom and real change. Though the truths of God's Word and His kingdom are eternal and unchanging, they are continually made new to every person who encounters them. Throughout history great change has only been made by those hungriest for Truth and those not content to simply follow the beliefs of others, but who instead demand the genuine revelation of coming to know God personally. Those who will accept no less than that are the ones who become world changers.

"And how about you? Who do you say I am?" Simon Peter said, "You're the Christ, the Messiah, the Son of the living God."
Jesus came back, "God bless you, Simon, son of Jonah! You didn't get that answer out of books or from teachers. My Father in heaven, God himself, let you in on this secret of who I really am. And now I'm going to tell you who you are, really are. You are Peter, a rock. This is the rock on which I will put together my church, a church so expansive with energy that not even the gates of hell will be able to keep it out."

Jesus and Peter
(Matthew 16:15–18 THE MESSAGE)

The rock Jesus spoke of here was the revelation of Jesus as the Christ that Peter expressed: Jesus as God's anointed Son, and Jesus as one's personal Lord and Savior. It is upon that rock that Jesus has always built His church. And it is without this revelation that people are led astray, even people of the established church, who seek power and position because they don't know the wealth that exists in the Truth of the Gospel.

What Is TRUth?

Jesus answered, "You say that I am a king. I was born and came into the world for this one purpose, to speak about the truth. Whoever belongs to the truth listens to me." "And what is truth?" Pilate asked. Then Pilate went back outside to the people and said to them, "I cannot find any reason to condemn him."

Jesus and Pilate
(John 18:37–38 TEV)

In this exchange is the summary of preaching the Gospel to the blind world.

"Here is the Truth, right in front of you!"

"What truth?"

Those who would be blind don't see it. Yet those who hunger for truth will. Many don't know they are hungry for it. Others have searched their whole lives for it and never find it until someone exposes them to it. But that is always the exchange: Those who know the truth must share it with others; those who don't know it have to decide whether or not they will receive it. If they will receive it, then God will reveal it to their hearts if they will hunger and thirst for it.

Why is Truth so elusive? Because Truth is not a list of beliefs or statements or mathematical formulas that can simply be memorized. It is not a philosophical system or the end of a journey where you can arrive and then be done. Truth is a Person—Jesus Christ—and knowing the Truth is a relationship. Just as getting to know a person takes time, getting to know Jesus can happen no faster. It happens day by day, meeting with Him, walking with Him, talking with Him, listening to Him, being with Him, and obeying Him.

Even if it takes all of eternity to get to know Him, there can

never be a better use of our time. Where is the time for bitterness, hatred, depression, power mongering, judging others, and drawing lines between people if we are consumed with getting to know Jesus? If we are all busy searching for Truth and loving others as Jesus told us to, there are worlds of problems we will never get into, and there are worlds of problems we will help solve.

For by whom has truth ever been discovered without God? By whom has God ever been found without Christ? By whom has Christ ever been explored without the Holy Spirit? By whom has the Holy Spirit ever been attained without the mysterious gift of faith?

Tertullian
Christian father and apologist
c. A.D. 150–229

I am the way, and the truth, and the life. The only way to the Father is through me.

Jesus
(John 14:6 NCV)

THOSE Who LOVe the TRUTH Are Always Revolutionary

The cross is God's truth to us, and therefore it is the only power which can make us truthful. When we know the cross, we are no longer afraid of truth. We need no more oaths to confirm the truth of our utterance, for we live the perfect truth of God.

There is no truth toward Jesus without truth toward man. Untruthfulness destroys fellowship, but truth cuts false fellowship to pieces and establishes genuine brotherhood. We cannot follow Christ unless we live in revealed truth before God and man.

Dietrich Bonhoeffer
Hung for resisting the Nazis
Flossenburg, Germany
1945

Being truthful—always telling the truth—is revolutionary. Those who know the Truth can't help but stand up for Him and tell others about Him. They can't help but make a difference for Him.

If those who say they know the Truth—that they know Jesus—don't share Him, do they really know the Truth? Probably not. Those who know Him can't deny Him. Knowing Him is just too life-altering to go long without talking about Him.

Knowing Jesus changes things so that a person can't just sit back in a comfortable lifestyle and do nothing while others swallow lies or are persecuted. Knowing Him means being a constant witness of the Truth and a constant catalyst of change for a better world. Whether it is on a large scale or a small scale, those who belong to Jesus make a difference.

Do you know Jesus?

This book is filled with stories of those who do and were

willing to give everything to make a difference for Him.

Learn from them.

Be like them.

Make your life make a difference for the Truth!

Here are THEIR

Stories:

If any of you
wants to be MY follower,
you M U S T put aside your
selfish ambition,
SHOULDER YOUR Cross,
and follow ME.

If you try to keep y o u r l i f e
for yourself, YOU WILL LOSE it.
But if you **GIVe UP your life**
for MY sake
and for the sake OF THE
GOOD NEWS,
you will find
True Life.

Jesus
(Mark 8:34–35 NLT)

From a Friend's Last Look

"Kim"	North Korea	2001

Kim had come home, unable to speak. His mother could tell he was in shock and sat with him, soothing him and trying to find out what had happened. Finally he began to open up to her.

"I was with one of my best friends today when two police officers approached us. They grabbed my friend and accused him of being a Christian. One of the officers knocked him to the ground while the other took out his gun. My friend didn't get angry or curse anyone. He ... he didn't even try to defend himself.

"Even as the gun was pointed directly at him, his face remained peaceful. He looked straight into my eyes, and without speaking a word, I knew exactly what he was saying. He wanted me to believe the same thing he did. And then he just said, 'Bless them.'

"He was executed right in front of me—because he was a Christian. I do not even know what a Christian is. I don't understand any of this."

Kim's mother held his head in her hands. There were tears in her eyes. Now it was she who was in shock. She then told him simply, "I understand."

"How could you possibly understand why they would kill my friend?"

She slowly began to tell her son about her Lord Jesus Christ, how He had miraculously been born of a virgin and crucified on a cross to save all those who would believe in Him. As she continued sharing with her eldest son, she began to sob. Now it was she who couldn't go on. She felt the pain of never daring to tell her son about Jesus Christ, lest his fate would be like that of his friend. She also felt the overwhelming joy of knowing that God had not forgotten her son, but allowed someone else to bring him the Gospel.

Finally she told him, "God allowed you to witness the martyrdom of one of His brave children. As those bullets hit his heart, a seed of hope was planted in yours."

The son prayed that night and received Jesus Christ into his heart. He was filled with joy as he embraced his mother and thanked her for telling him the truth. But suddenly he began to weep again and appeared distraught. Confused, the mother asked, "Now what's wrong?"

"My brothers," Kim cried, "they do not know Jesus. We must tell them!"

His three brothers soon came home and discovered their older brother and mother crying together. Their first thought was that something terrible had happened to their father, and they quickly knelt down beside their mother, asking what was wrong.

With unnatural boldness the eldest son stood up and responded, "You should also receive Jesus Christ." Before the evening had passed, all three had done exactly that.

The mother was filled with joy. Although she had never dared to speak to her children about her Christian faith, she had diligently prayed for them every day. Now that her children had accepted Jesus, she began cautiously looking for a Bible so they could learn more of God's Word. But she could not find any.

Eventually her oldest son secretly crossed the Yalu River into China in search of Bibles. You can imagine the look on his face when he finally came across a miniature Bible in the Korean language. He pleaded with the Christians in China, asking how he could obtain some of these Bibles. Regrettably no more were available. Refusing to admit defeat, he told the Christians the dramatic story of how he had witnessed his friend's death and how he and his brothers had learned of Jesus Christ. Before departing for North Korea, he said, "I am in need of five thousand of these Bibles to share with my family and others in North Korea. I will be back in one month to pick them up."

Hearing of the request, some Christian workers hurriedly printed five thousand copies of the miniature Korean Bibles. Over the next year or so, Kim returned on several occasions to smuggle the Bibles back across the border. All four of these brothers are now actively sharing their faith, knowing firsthand the consequences if they are discovered. Since their last pickup of these Bibles some months ago, no one has heard further news of them.

• • •

Transformation. Change. In an instant, by the touch of God, a life can be changed. There is nothing more miraculous in the world. One minute a person can be walking down the street, and then something happens to make that person realize they don't know it all. There is more to life than they had ever imagined. They are not alone. There is a God who loves them and He is Truth. In a moment, in a twinkling of an eye, the world is different. It is like everything just went from black and white to color, like suddenly they can see when they were blind before, like they were in prison and now have been set free.

Such change is both instant and incremental; it is this that makes a person a revolutionary for Christ—someone willing to risk it all for the Truth. While change often comes in leaps, as it did for Kim and his family, it will also take them a lifetime to work out what has happened in their hearts. They will do this by becoming revolutionaries in their society, smuggling the Truth to as many as they can, working a "resistance" of the world system to find those whose hearts are ready for the Gospel, and working against those who would control how they think, behave, and believe.

People who aren't convinced that what they believe is the Truth don't do such things.

The secret police greatly persecuted the underground church, because they recognized in it the only effective resistance left. It was just the kind of resistance (a spiritual resistance) which, if left unhindered, would

undermine their atheistic power. They recognized, as only the devil can, an immediate threat to them. They knew if a man believed in Christ he would never be a mindless, willing subject. They knew they could imprison the physical body, but they couldn't imprison a person's spirit—their faith in God. And so they fought very hard.

Richard Wurmbrand
Founder of The Voice of the Martyrs
Spent fourteen years in a Communist prison
Romania
1940s, '50s, and '60s

23

"If the Son sets you free, you will be free indeed."

Jesus
(John 8:36 NIV)

The Son of Consolation

Barnabas	Salamina, Cyprus	A.D. 64

"Don't be a fool, Joses. The man is a murderer and a spy! He only wants to come to us so that he can gather names to give to the council and bring us all to trial as he did Stephen. He will stop at nothing to see that every person who preaches in the name of Jesus is executed. No, we cannot let him come here, no matter what he claims. Brother Barnabas, we know you mean well as always, but you must see the reason in protecting ourselves. We cannot let Saul come to meet with us. Brother Peter, I turn to your leadership as always in this matter; please tell Barnabas that we would be exposing ourselves to unnecessary risk."

Peter looked from the speaker to Joses, whom the members of the first church had nicknamed Barnabas, the "son of consolation," because of his constant encouragement to the brethren. Barnabas looked troubled by the words, but Peter could tell he wasn't finished pleading his case. "Brother Barnabas, you have something else to add?"

"Only that I know the change that came to my life from accepting Jesus as the Messiah. And I know the change that came to your life, Brother Peter. And yours, Brother Isaac, and the change that came to the rest of you here today. Didn't Jesus preach that all who call upon His name would be saved? Well, Saul has called on that name. He also met with the risen Jesus on the road to Damascus. I know the man who held the coats of those who stoned Stephen as we stood by helplessly, and I know the man who reasoned with the Jewish brethren and Greeks in Damascus that Jesus is the Messiah. He is the same man on the outside, but not the same man on the inside. Saul is no longer a persecutor, but a brother in Christ. In fact, he left Damascus in fear for his own life because of the boldness of his testimony. What good is Jesus' sacrifice and Stephen's forgiveness of those who killed him if we cannot look past the flesh of a man and accept what Jesus has done to change his heart?"

Those in the room grew quiet for a moment, then Peter spoke for all of them. "As always, Barnabas, your words have spoken straight to my heart. I cannot refuse fellowship to any who will call upon His name, as Jesus himself said He would not. Can any of the rest of you?"

As Peter looked around the room, no eyes met his gaze, but many nodded their heads in agreement with him. They knew the danger of rejecting Jesus' words was greater than any threat to their lives.

It was in such a way that Saul, who was destined to become Paul the apostle, was admitted as a brother to the church in Jerusalem by Barnabas, "the encourager."

Barnabas continued to travel with and encourage Saul for some time after that. They journeyed together to Antioch in Syria, where they taught and argued the cause of Christ so well that the members of the church in Antioch were the first to call themselves "Christians." He also supported Paul as he returned to Jerusalem to persuade the brethren there that Christianity was not to be a sect of Judaism—following all the laws of the Old Testament and just adding Jesus—but it was a transformation of their covenant with God into something new through Christ, surpassing the law to a life in the Spirit made possible by Jesus' death and resurrection.

Barnabas was such an eloquent speaker and preached with such passion and convincing doctrine that he was the chosen speaker over Paul on their first missionary journey. However, when God began to bring Paul to the forefront, Barnabas the encourager took the lesser place without complaint. He was not worried about position as much as seeing the call of God fulfilled in Paul's life.

John Mark, Barnabas's nephew, had deserted Paul and Barnabas on their first missionary journey when things looked like they were getting rough, but he repented and asked to go along with them on their second journey to the north. Paul refused to let him come along because of his earlier desertion, but Barnabas stuck with John Mark much as he had stuck with Paul before the brethren in Jerusalem years earlier.

Thus Barnabas and Paul went separate ways. Paul took Silas and headed to Syria and Cilicia, and Barnabas and John Mark went to Cyprus. Barnabas eventually encouraged John Mark to travel with Peter.

Being originally from Cyprus, Barnabas stayed on there preaching Christ to all who came across his path. Such a following rose up that he fell into contention with a Jewish sorcerer who was losing business because the things Barnabas taught freed the people from their fear of him and what his "magic" could do to them. Because of this, the sorcerer stirred the non-Christians of the city against Barnabas. They soon falsely accused Barnabas of some crime and had him thrown into prison.

When a time was set for Barnabas to come before a judge in Salamina, fearing the judge would discover his innocence and release him, a mob led by the sorcerer raided the jail, put a rope around Barnabas's neck, dragged him outside the city, and burned him.

• • •

Barnabas was not swayed by the views of the mainstream. When everyone else flowed idly with the currents of fear or popular opinion, he took his paddle in hand and fought hard to get their boat back into God's flow of love and acceptance, even if he was the only one paddling. He judged people by the confessions of their hearts and how they lined up with the Word of God, not by their pasts or what they looked like. Where others saw a lost cause or an enemy, Barnabas saw great potential and a brother or sister in the Lord that needed the support of an encourager. He stood by those others rejected, and by doing so he helped them to realize greater things in their own lives than he did in his own.

In a world where self-promotion seems to be a key to success, there are not too many like Barnabas. How many of us would be willing to help those around us go on to accomplish greater things than we do ourselves or befriend the unpopular because they claim they belong to Christ?

> Now you can have sincere love for each other as brothers and sisters because you were cleansed from your sins when you accepted the truth of the Good News. So see to it that you really do love each other intensely with all your hearts.

Peter
(1 Peter 1:22 NLT)

27

Jesus promised his disciples three things—that they would be completely fearless, absurdly happy, and in constant trouble.

G. K. CHESTERTON
BRITISH WRITER AND CHRISTIAN APOLOGIST
1874–1936

"How Could I Not Have an Interest?"

"Asif"	Pakistan	2001

"Asif" was carefree as he sped his motorcycle down the street of his Pakistani town. He enjoyed being noticed by the young women as he sped by. In the traditional Muslim culture of Pakistan, overt glances would have been very inappropriate, but still Asif could tell when he had been seen. He was young, and he felt powerful as he drove past, relishing the murmur of the motorcycle's engine in his ears and the feel of the tires gripping the road. He smiled to himself and twisted the accelerator to give the bike a quick burst of speed.

Suddenly where the beautiful sky had been he saw only dirt, and where his motorcycle had raced along beneath him, it now felt like it was flying over his head. For the next few seconds all was clouds of dust and spinning. The next thing he knew he was lying on his back with his motorcycle next to him on the ground, its engine coughing and then dying. He heard the echo of the squealing tires as the car that hit him sped away. He had never even seen it.

Then he noticed the splitting pain shooting up his leg. When he looked at it, he could tell from the way his foot lay off to the wrong side that it was broken. He tried to stay calm, but panic was gripping his heart and he wanted to scream.

Before he lost his composure, though, he felt a reassuring hand upon him. A woman had come out of the crowd of passers-by and knelt beside him, laying her hand on his leg. He was calmed for the moment and surprised as she began to pray.

Through the pain, Asif heard the name of Jesus in her prayer. Despite his immediate thankfulness that someone had stopped to help, a wave of anger came over him at the mention of that name. *How can this woman pray to Jesus, a mere prophet? Doesn't she*

know that I am a Muslim, a follower of Mohammed, the greatest prophet? Why isn't she praying to Allah?

Yet Asif was suddenly distracted from his anger by an energy he felt running through his body as she prayed. It was different from anything he had ever felt before. His anger began to fade as his leg straightened itself and the bone came back into place. Eventually he sat up and carefully examined his leg. It was completely whole.

As he stood, he noticed that there was no more pain either. He picked up his bike and walked it home.

Some time later, the same woman brought him a Bible. He never saw her again after that.

Hungry to know more about this prophet who had healed his leg, he began to read the Bible, especially the New Testament and the miracles of Jesus. Asif's question weighed heavier: *If Jesus was truly only one of many prophets, how could he perform such amazing works?* As Asif lay on his bed, he wondered, *Who is Jesus? I know many prophets have come to earth, but none has had the power of Jesus.*

Asif was so perplexed by how a minor prophet such as Jesus could heal him two thousand years after His death that he took his questions to the *mulvi* (religious leader) at his mosque.

"Why are you talking about Jesus?" the mulvi sneered. "Do you have an interest in him?"

"How could I *not* have an interest?" Asif responded incredulously. "He healed me."

The mulvi and others at the mosque took Asif and locked him in a room. They forced poison down his throat thinking that if he died before fully accepting Christ, he would still make it to Paradise. They left him there overnight for the poison to do its work. Asif felt sick and thought he was dying. He vomited repeatedly and threw up blood.

However, around midnight Asif found himself still barely alive and lying in the dust, caked with his own blood and vomit. The room was dark and he didn't have the strength to get up. He didn't know what else to do, so he prayed. He called out to Jesus and told Him he wanted to see Him before he died.

Before he knew what had happened, a bright light had filled the dusty room. Asif suddenly felt a little better and forced himself up to see what was causing the light. Before him stood Jesus. It was at that moment that Asif surrendered the rest of his life to the Lord, saying, "God, this life is for you; as long as I am on earth, I will work for you."

Sometime before dawn, Asif managed to escape and made his way home.

When he tried to tell his parents of his experience the next morning, they were not impressed. "You are a Muslim," his parents told him. "If you accept Jesus, you must leave this house."

So Asif had no choice. He took his Bible and left. He went to a larger city where he met a pastor at a Christian bookstore. The pastor discipled Asif and later baptized him. From the first moments of his newfound faith, Asif felt a strong desire to share who Jesus was and what He had done for him with those around him, regardless of their religious backgrounds. Because of this, his troubles with the police and city leaders began almost immediately.

"A landlord [city leader] came to me and said, 'Where are you going? And why are you preaching this "gospel"? These are Muslim people. Why are they accepting Jesus?' "

Seeing that Asif was undeterred, this landlord and some other Muslims took him and beat him with heavy sugarcane stalks. They stomped on his leg and broke it again. As they pounded his body, they shouted, "You dog! You low-class scum! Why did you come here and make our people Christians?" They ordered Asif to leave the city immediately.

Despite their further threats, he refused.

As they were beating him, he prayed for them, "Please, God, change their minds and their hearts." Then he cried out to God to help him and give him strength.

Many weeks later, after Asif had recovered from his injuries, the landlords and the police closed down a meeting where Asif was sharing about Jesus again. Asif was taken to the police station, where he was severely beaten.

When Asif was asked how he could endure this and not be discouraged, he quoted Philippians 1:29 (NAS), "For to you it has been granted for Christ's sake, not only to believe in Him, but also to suffer for His sake."

Asif continues to evangelize whenever and wherever he has the opportunity.

• • •

In the largest sense of the word, a revolutionary changes his country or culture; but in a smaller sense, what changes the individual from a bystander to a revolutionary?

In the best of cases, a worldly revolutionary fights for an ideal such as freedom or independence. The revolutionary takes up arms to eliminate the oppressors and to spread privilege among all the classes. When revolutionaries are convinced of the truth that a better life is possible for all under another government or system, then they are willing to fight to the death to make that government or system possible.

Yet a true revolutionary revolts even against this system of revolution. As Christ refused to free himself from the cross, throwing himself totally into the will of His Father and placing His life in the hands of Pilate and Herod, Christian revolutionaries' main wars are within themselves—between walking in their own will or in Christ's will. Whereas a worldly revolutionary strikes out vengefully hoping to realize his own truth for all, a Christian revolutionary strikes out with the love of God to open the eyes of the oppressors to help them choose Truth for themselves.

Thus Christians become true revolutionaries when they realize there is only one Truth worth fighting for, and that Truth is the only thing able to truly set people free. They would rather die than deny that

Truth, but even more they are willing to forsake comfort for the privilege of living for that Truth and representing it to their world.

Thus a woman walks from the crowd of bystanders and is willing to risk embarrassment (in countries such as Pakistan, even imprisonment) by praying in the name of Jesus for the healing of an enemy. Thus a man riding down the street living only for his own desires becomes a revolutionary when he encounters the Truth. The pain of a broken leg as the result of a senseless accident is unbearable, but the pain of a broken leg at the hands of enemies who need to know the Truth is inconsequential. Somehow knowing the Truth makes nothing else seem to matter.

Our Lord Christ has surnamed himself Truth, not Custom.

Tertullian
Christian who wrote bravely in defense of Christianity
and the martyrs during the fourth and fifth
Roman persecutions
Some believe he died a martyr himself
c. A.D. 150–229

What is more, I consider everything a loss compared to the surpassing greatness of knowing Christ Jesus my Lord, for whose sake I have lost all things. I consider them rubbish, that I may gain Christ and be found in him, not having a righteousness of my own ... but that which is through faith in Christ—the righteousness that comes from God and is by faith. I want to know Christ and the power of his resurrection and the fellowship of sharing in his sufferings, becoming like him in his death, and so, somehow, to attain to the resurrection from the dead.

Paul
(Philippians 3:8–11 NIV)

33

"Put Down My Name"

Adrian and Natalia	Nicomedia	c. A.D. 303

During the tenth and last major Roman persecution under Emperors Diocletian and Maximian, a young military officer who loved honor and courage distinguished himself to his superiors by faithfully and efficiently carrying out the letter of their orders in trying to suppress the Christians. His skill and daring in both this and in battle had led to one promotion after another.

But Adrian's task of torturing Christians bothered him. In the face of pain and death, Christians were repeatedly peaceful and unrelenting in their commitment to their Lord. He saw in these men and women a courage greater than any he had ever seen in battle.

Adrian was so intrigued by this that one day as he was bringing a group of Christians before a judge for sentencing, he asked one of them, "What gives you such strength and joy in the midst of your sufferings?"

"Our Lord Jesus Christ, in whom we believe," the man replied.

Suddenly Adrian saw it as he never had before. The Roman gods he was defending could never give a person such courage! They were nothing compared to the God of these Christians.

He made his way to the front of the line of prisoners and stepped before the judge. "Put down my name with those to be tortured. I also have become a Christian." The emperor's son Galerius, who served as Diocletian's caesar (or junior emperor) and had been present at the trials with his father, tried to persuade Adrian to strike his name from the list of Christians and to beg for forgiveness. Adrian assured him that he had not lost his mind but had acted thus according to his own conviction.

What Adrian did not know at the time was that his wife, Natalia, had secretly become a Christian some time before and had been praying for him. When she heard that he was in prison, she

went to him and encouraged him by telling him of her conversion and more about the God who loved him.

The group of Christians Adrian had put his name down with were soon sentenced to die. Before this, because of his former status in the empire, Adrian was allowed to go home that he might make his peace with his wife before he was killed. When Natalia saw him coming down the road, she at first thought he had renounced Christ in order to be freed and wouldn't let him into the house!

Though this might have been an opportunity for Adrian to escape, he did not. He soon returned to the prison. When he did, he watched as others were subjected to terrible tortures: Their arms and legs were broken with heavy hammers until they died from the agony and internal bleeding. When Adrian's turn came, his wife feared most of all that her husband would become fainthearted and renounce Christ, but he finally knew the courage that could only belong to Christians and never backed away from his commitment. She strengthened Adrian and held on to his arms and legs while the executioner broke them with the hammer. Adrian died together with the rest.

When they began to burn the bodies of the Christians, a thunderstorm arose, the furnace was extinguished, and lightning killed several of the executioners. The attempt was abandoned and the rest of the bodies were released to their families. Sometime later, after Adrian's body had been moved to the city of Byzantium, Natalia's body was found lying on top of her husband's grave. She had died while attending it.

His sacrifice has stood as a shining example for the last eighteen centuries. During that time Adrian has been known as one of the patron saints of soldiers.

* * *

Love... rejoices with the truth; bears all things, believes all things, hopes all things, endures all things.

Paul

(1 Corinthians 13:4, 6–7 NAS)

35

36

O loving Christ, draw me, a weakling,
after Yourself; for if You do not draw me I cannot follow You. Give me a brave spirit that I
may be ready and alert. If the flesh is weak,
may Your grace go before me, come alongside
me, and follow me; for without You I cannot
do anything, and especially,
for Your sake I cannot go to a cruel death.
Grant me a ready spirit, a fearless heart, a
right faith, a firm hope, and a perfect love, that
for your sake I may lay down my life with
patience and joy.

JOHN HUSS
AS HE LAY IN CHAINS IN PRISON
BEFORE BEING BURNED AT THE STAKE
BOHEMIA (CZECHOSLOVAKIA)
1415

No Greater Honor

Twenty-six Christians	Japan	1596-1597

On August 15, 1549, Francis Xavier and two other priests from the Society of Jesus (the Jesuits) brought the Gospel to Japan. He called Japan "the delight of my heart ... the country in the Orient most suited to Christianity."

Though Christians and missionaries (mostly Jesuits from Portugal and Franciscans from Spain) had been allowed freedom in the nearly fifty years following this, the rulers of Japan had a growing concern that Christianity was a threat to local religion and culture, and therefore to the security of their rule. On July 24, 1587, an edict was issued stating that all Jesuit missionaries must leave Japan in twenty days. Though some churches were destroyed, no missionaries left Japan permanently.

The incident of the cargo ship *San Felipe* brought this to a head. When this ship ran aground on Japanese soil on August 26, 1596, the cargo was seized by the local shogun, or military leader. The captain, upset over the loss of his cargo, threatened Japan with a Spanish invasion (something he had no power to bring about) if his cargo was not returned. He said that Spain would easily overrun Japan with the information they had from the Franciscan monks. The Franciscans were immediately labeled as spies for this, and the tide of opinion that was already unfavorable for the Christians turned in favor of annihilating them.

So on November 23, 1596, Toyotomi Hideyoshi, the absolute ruler of Japan, better known by history as Taikosama, ordered the Christians of Kyoto arrested. This began a period of persecution called the Kirishtan Holocaust, which would see as many as one million believers executed for their faith. In fact, the Christian church of a nation has never been so thoroughly decimated as it

37

was during the persecution that began on this date and did not truly end until over 260 years later.

The twenty-six prisoners taken on that day were made up of Franciscan monks, Jesuit priests, and their converts, ranging in age from twelve to sixty-four, and were from various nations: twenty Japanese, four Spaniards, one Portuguese (born in India of a Portuguese father and an Indian mother), and a Mexican. Though they had committed no crime, it was soon decided that they would be crucified like the God they proclaimed near Nagasaki, roughly a thirty-day march away by foot. Just before the prisoners were sent on their journey under the guard of soldiers, each prisoner's left ear was cut off, though the original sentence had been that their noses and both ears would be amputated.

Nagasaki, Japan
1597

On the morning of February 5, the day appointed for the execution, Terazawa Hazaburo walked hesitantly through a wheat field outside the city gates as the men under his command prepared the crosses. It was around ten in the morning. A crowd was gathering in the morning mist, and there was a distant rumble of thunder coming from the direction of Mount Kompira, which towered over the village of Nagasaki.

Terazawa had been chosen for this task since he was the brother of the regional governor, but he did not look forward to it. One of the men he was to execute, Paul Miki, was a close friend, and Terazawa had often listened to his sermons. However, he so feared Taikosama that he dared not disobey his commands. In his sympathy for the prisoners, though, he allowed two Jesuit priests to remain close-by so they could minister to those men when they arrived.

About ten-thirty the long procession they had been awaiting finally reached the fields. The soldiers pushed their way through the crowd, and for the first time since he had seen them appear in the distance, Terazawa got a good look at the prisoners. Their hands were tightly bound and their feet were raw from the forced march. Each footstep colored the snow with blood. Most were pale and emaciated. They had divided into three groups, each led by a Franciscan who was praying as they made their way forward. Though physically they showed the toil of the journey and the rough treatment they had received along the way, their faces glowed with an anticipation Terazawa could make no sense of.

When Gonzalo Garcia arrived, he stepped forward to greet Francis Rodriguez Pinto, one of the two Jesuits there to minister to the prisoners. "My good friend, God be with you. I am going to heaven today. Please give a hearty hug to Friar Gonzalez on my behalf next time you see him." Then Brother Garcia turned to the cross nearest him. "Is this one mine?" he asked a soldier. It was not. So the soldier led him to another a short distance away. When he arrived there, he knelt and embraced it.

Partway back, Brother Philip of Jesus, a twenty-four-year-old Mexican who had struggled as a Christian most of his life, made a joke to comfort one of his friends. "The galleon *San Felipe* was lost so that Brother Philip could be saved." He also embraced his cross with great emotion and relief. His struggles were over. In the end, he would not fall away.

No nails were used to fix the Christians to the crosses, but their hands, feet, and necks were held in position with iron rings, and a rope was tied around their waists to hold them in place. Peter Baustista stretched out his hands on the cross and requested of his executioner, "Nail them down, brother."

Paul Miki, Terazawa's friend, was the son of a brave Japanese soldier but had given up a promising military career to preach the Gospel. Many considered him the most effective evangelist in Japan at the time. He was thirty years old. Since he was too short for his feet to reach the bottom rings, a soldier tied a piece of linen

around his chest to support him. When he stepped on Paul to tighten the knot, a priest from the crowd stepped forward to object, but Paul calmly said, "Let him do his job, Father. It doesn't hurt."

When they were all fixed to their crosses, they were lifted together, and all twenty-six crosses fell into place with an ominous thud that echoed through the hills. The jolt sent a shock of pain through each victim's body.

Anthony of Nagasaki had come home to be martyred. His parents were in the front row of the crowd not far from him. When his mother began weeping, he called out to comfort her. Then he joined a chorus that the others had started, not wanting his particular part to be left out. He was thirteen years old.

Martin of Ascension broke out into praise, crying out, "Blessed be the Lord God of Israel, for He has visited and redeemed His people." The younger ones among them (five were under the age of twenty) broke into a psalm learned in catechism: " 'Praise, O ye servants of the Lord, Praise the name of the Lord ... From the rising of the sun unto the going down of the same, the Lord's name is to be praised!' "

John of Goto, a nineteen-year-old, had just taken his vows as a Jesuit priest that morning. When one of the priests in the crowd came to comfort him, telling him that heaven was near, he responded gladly with a smile, "Don't worry, Father, I am quite aware of that."

Next to John was Louis Ibaki. At hearing the mention of heaven, he pressed against the ropes as if wanting to jump into his Savior's arms. He sang in his soprano voice, "Paradise! Paradise! Jesus! Mary!" He was only twelve years old. It was noted in the writings left behind by the others who died that day that young Louis was perhaps the greatest encourager of them all. He laughed and sang when his ear was cut off, and he sang along the entire route of the march from Kyoto. *"We have little Louis with us,"* Francis Blanco had written in his journal the night before. *"He is*

so full of courage and in such high spirits that it astonishes everybody."

Finally Terazawa Hazaburo, wishing for it all to be over, stepped forward to read the decree and sentence of Taikosama:

" 'As these men came from the Philippines under the guise of ambassadors and chose to stay in Miyako preaching the Christian Law, which I have severely forbidden all these years, I come to decree that they be put to death, together with the Japanese who have accepted that law.' "

Yet the martyrs weren't through. Suddenly a cry came out from among them that silenced Terazawa. "All of you who are here, please listen to me!"

It was the voice of Paul Miki. No one moved as all fell silent to listen.

"I did not come from the Philippines. I am Japanese by birth and a brother of the Society of Jesus. I have committed no crime, and the only reason why I am put to death is that I have been teaching the doctrine of our Lord Jesus Christ. I am happy to die for such a cause and see my death as the greatest blessing from the Lord. At this critical time, when you can rest assured that I will not try to deceive you, I want to stress and make it unmistakably clear that man can find no salvation other than the Christian way."

Some of the soldiers had stepped forward to listen more closely. Terazawa stood motionless as the executioners stood near him with the spears that would finally silence all of these men. Paul Miki smiled a moment, then looked deep into the eyes of his friend Terazawa. "The Christian law commands that we forgive our enemies and those who have wronged us. I must therefore say that I forgive Taikosama. I would rather have all the Japanese become Christians."

Then Paul fell silent. He had said what he wanted to say and was now ready for the end. He looked to the others who hung with him and spoke a few comforting words; then looking to heaven he proclaimed, "Lord, into your hands I commend my spirit. Come

meet me, you saints of God!"

At this the rest who could began singing again and shouting praises to God. Some prayed and shouted words of encouragement. Some of those standing by took up the choruses as well.

However, Philip of Jesus could not sing or shout. He was slipping and choking within the ring around his neck. Terazawa, though a veteran soldier, could take no more. He ordered the executioners to step forward and carry out the sentences. Usually the victims died instantly, but if not, then a quick flick of the sword blade severed their necks. One by one each of the twenty-six was dispatched.

In the end, Terazawa turned and walked away. Those who had died before him that day had greater honor in death than that of any samurai or soldier he had ever seen in battle. His steps were deliberate and heavy. Tears glistened in his eyes and made their way down his face.

• • •

Wherever Jesus is taken, He changes things. Those who love power always fear Him and seek to wipe His followers from their nations, but the seed that is planted by such a sacrifice remains. These, who would have turned Japan upside right with the Gospel of Jesus Christ, did not die in vain.

After persecuting Christians for over 260 years, Japan finally allowed a church to be built again in Nagasaki in the late 1800s to minister to the growing number of Westerners there. Soon after, priests were astonished to see Japanese citizens streaming down from the hills to attend services. Those people had been meeting in secret and passing along their faith for all of those years. They had survived all that time without the aid of a Bible or any other Christian direction, yet they all clung to the person of Jesus as Lord.

Though Christianity has enjoyed some freedom in Japan in the last one hundred years or so, it has always been viewed with suspicion by the Japanese as an invading Western religion. Only about one in a thousand claims to be a Christian there today. In 1995 when a religious cult attacked a subway station with a gas bomb, a number of laws were passed that were supposed to protect against such a thing happening again, many of which strongly opposed the further spread of Christianity in the country.

Pray for the spread of the Gospel in Japan that they will join with the faith of their brothers and sisters around the world and not be deceived by traditions.

You are from God, little children, and have overcome them; because greater is He who is in you than he who is in the world.

John
(1 John 4:4 NAS)

Suffering willingly endured is stronger than evil;
it spells death to evil....
The worse the evil, the readier must the
Christian be to suffer; he must let the evil
person fall into Jesus' hands.

DIETRICH BONHOEFFER
HUNG FOR RESISTING THE NAZIS
FLOSSENBURG, GERMANY
1945

I believe that unarmed truth and unconditional
love will have the final word in reality.
This is why right, temporarily defeated,
is stronger than evil triumphant.

MARTIN LUTHER KING JR.
ASSASSINATED FOR HIS STAND ON CIVIL RIGHTS
MEMPHIS, TENNESSEE
1968

The Thundering Legion— Part One

A Legion of Roman Soldiers	Northern Roman Empire	C. A.D. 174

Emperor Marcus Aurelius Antoninus led his legions to subdue the Quadi and Marcomanni in Germany, who had mounted an open military defense against the progression of northern Roman provinces. Antoninus, who had made his fame as a military leader, decided to handle the situation personally.

However, he greatly underestimated the cunning of these northern kings and found himself and his army trapped by an ambush in the mountains without water. They pleaded to their gods for deliverance as the soldiers neared dying of thirst, but they received no response.

Overall, Antoninus had little tolerance for Christians. He was a stern and impatient general who would not stand for inefficiency or failure in his troops, and he ruled Rome the same way. He had grown up well trained in philosophy and civil government and felt that the worship of the Roman gods was part of the very fabric of the empire. Therefore, Christianity was equivalent to treason, and the fourth major Roman persecution (c. A.D. 163–180) took place under his rule.

Yet in the desperation of this situation, when a legion made up entirely of Christians stepped forward and offered to pray for their rescue, Antoninus gave them his permission.

Shortly after they prayed, a huge storm broke out, and they were caught in a downpour. Soldiers rushed to collect water any way they could, even building dikes to store it as a future supply. The tempest rumbled so powerfully in the faces of their enemies that many left their ranks and defected to join the Romans. The rest were easily routed and the army was saved.

This group of soldiers came to be known as "The Thundering Legion."

After this incident, Antoninus stopped the persecution of Christians for a time, though he made no official edict legalizing their worship. However, he eventually forgot what God had done for his army and again outlawed Christianity, threatening those who would not sacrifice to the Roman gods with torture and death.

• • •

Many may remember the story from the first Jesus Freaks (pg. 96) of the forty soldiers of "The Thundering Legion" some 150 years later who refused to come in off the ice of a lake in winter to maintain their testimonies, but few know this story of how they received their name. Like Elijah before the prophets of Baal, they were not afraid to put their God to the test. They believed that God would answer their prayers because He had done it before. They believed He would answer them because they knew His nature. Faith says, "If Jesus said it, I can count on it."

Faith uses as much wisdom as it has to accomplish the task at hand and then lets God step in as He wills. It is unafraid to obey God even when that obedience would seem foolhardy. It is something that comes from a real relationship with God where we listen to Him more than we ask Him for things. It is the adventure of doing whatever God tells us to do without fear.

Is there really any other way to live?

How much longer will it take you to make up your minds? If the Lord is God, worship him; but if Baal is God, worship him!

Elijah
(1 Kings 18:21 TEV)

46

Profitable for the Ministry

| John Mark | Alexandria, Egypt | A.D. 64 |

Though John Mark must have been hurt deeply by Paul's rejection and must have felt responsible for the division between his uncle Barnabas and Paul, the rest of his life shows little sign of discouragement or the lack of resolve that had led to his earlier desertion of Paul and Barnabas in Phaphos, Cyprus. In fact, Mark preached boldly in Cyprus when his uncle and he returned there after they split with Paul before his second missionary journey.

It seems that God even gave John Mark the opportunity to redeem himself in the eyes of Paul. It is believed by most historians that Paul was in prison twice in Rome: the first time being freer, during which he continued to preach; the second being more severe and ending in his execution. John Mark was present with Paul during his first imprisonment and so distinguished himself that Paul sent John Mark to the church at Colossae with his commendation. Later, when Paul was in prison for the last time, he wrote to Timothy, "When you come, bring Mark, for he is profitable to me for the ministry."

John Mark eventually traveled with Peter and, at the request of the church in Rome, wrote the gospel of Mark from Peter's teachings. Peter endorsed the writings and had them distributed to the churches for the encouragement and education of their growing congregations.

Peter later sent John Mark into Egypt and Africa as a missionary. He traveled throughout Lybia, Marmorica, Ammonica, and Pentapolis (northern African prefectures above the Sahara), preaching and teaching wherever he could. Finally he established and shepherded a church in Alexandria, Egypt, where he stayed for several years. Mark's teaching that all people are free in Christ by accepting Jesus as their Lord and Savior had begun to transform the community there. The local heathen priests began to lose business and were so pricked in their hearts by his preaching that they began to loathe him. It was not long before they were plotting to kill him.

It is recorded that on the twenty-first day of April, A.D. 64, in the eighth year of Nero's reign as emperor, Mark preached a sermon remembering Jesus' suffering on the cross and resurrection from the dead as his Easter Sunday sermon. The local heathen priests chose this day to rouse as many as possible against Mark and see that he never preached again.

With a large crowd, they stormed the church with huge hooks and ropes, overpowering those in the congregation, and seized John Mark. Tying him with the rope and snagging and jabbing him with the hooks, they dragged him through the congregation, through the streets of the town, and out of the city, leaving a trail of blood and flesh in the gospel writer's wake. By the time he was outside of town, there was not one place on Mark's body from which blood did not flow.

48

John Mark commended his spirit into the hands of his Lord and died.

Yet his death was not enough for the enraged crowd. The priests wanted to desecrate his body so badly that it could not be buried. They called for a fire to be built to burn the body, but a sudden and mysterious storm arose that scattered the crowd. John Mark's body was deserted on the spot where he had died.

In the excitement of the storm, members of his congregation came and reclaimed Mark's corpse. When things had calmed down some time later, they gave his body a proper and respectful burial.

• • •

What may be a failure in our eyes is seldom one in God's eyes. John Mark could have easily been discouraged at his own giving in to fear on Cyprus and determined that he was not fit for the ministry. However, God was not willing to take His call off of John Mark's life. By returning to face his fears and obey God again, John Mark was restored and went on to greater things than he probably thought possible.

Be not afraid, only believe.
The words of Jesus as recorded by John Mark
(Mark 5:36 KJV)

*God didn't call us to be successful,
just faithful.*

MOTHER TERESA
GAVE HER LIFE TO THE POOR IN INDIA
1910–1997

*It is not my ability, but my response to God's
ability that counts.*

CORRIE TEN BOOM
HID JEWS IN HER HOME TO PROTECT THEM FROM THE
NAZIS DURING WORLD WAR II
HOLLAND
1892–1983

Placing Targets on Their Backs		
Zhang Rongliang, Shen Xianfeng, and Zhen Xianqi	Mainland China	1999

Zhang Rongliang, Shen Xianfeng, Zhen Xianqi, and other house church leaders, representing roughly fifteen million underground believers, signed and published the "House Church Confession of Faith" that called on the Communist government to stop treating the members of house churches in China as criminals. Officially, to give the appearance of freedom of religion in China, the government there recognizes its state-controlled church, the Three-Self Patriotic Church, as a freely worshiping assembly but allows no other Christian gatherings this protection. At the same time, the state makes sure that little within the meetings of the sanctioned Three-Self Patriotic Church is Christian or free. According to official state documents, house churches are identified with the Chinese word that means "evil religion," a word that has occult connotations for the people of China. The "House Church Confession of Faith" called for changes to this reference as well as real religious freedoms within the nation.

Only months after making the document public, several of the signers, including Zhang, were arrested and placed in prison. In December of 1999, Zhang was sentenced to three years but was released on a seven-year probation providing that he "behaved" himself.

Shen Xianfeng, who was arrested around the same time as Zhang, suffers from rheumatoid arthritis. This condition has forced him to walk with the aid of crutches. During his arrest, the officers used his own crutches to beat him. Zhen Xianqi also suffered arrest and harassment.

By signing the document and meeting with Western journalists, Zhang and the others knew that they were placing targets on their backs, yet this didn't concern them. They felt called of God to make a statement of faith to the world and to use any means at their disposal to proclaim Jesus Christ to their fellow countrymen and women.

Pastor Zhang still travels by car and train to minister to his various flocks, but he never sleeps in the same bed more than four nights in a row to avoid arrest.

• • •

China continues its "hard strike" policy, which is supposed to be a crackdown on organized crime and petty criminals, but it has put more Christians behind bars than are presently in prison in any other nation on the earth today. Any Bible found by a Public Security Bureau (PSB) Officer is immediately confiscated, even if it is a version authorized and printed by the Chinese government.

Recent statistics have revealed that from 1983 to 2001 there have been at least 23,686 Christian arrests in China for religious reasons, and of these, 208 have been beaten to the point of being crippled for life. Because of such things, world leaders are starting to speak up.

Despite this, an estimated 1,200 Chinese come to Christ every hour.

Political pressure, though it is constantly needed in such cases, has had little effect on countries such as China in recent decades. What is needed are equipped Christians to fight the same spiritual fight that brought down the Berlin Wall and crumbled the Soviet Union.

Pray for these believers in China. Pray for their protection and that God will sanctify the Word in their hearts for their encouragement and strength.

We don't obey people. We obey God.

Peter
(Acts 5:29 CEV)

51

Preaching in the Russian Army Barracks

Richard Wurmbrand	Romania	c. 1948

"The Russians were very fond of watches," wrote Pastor Wurmbrand of the forces that occupied his country in the late 1940s. "They took watches from everyone. They would stop people on the street and ask them to hand them over. You would see Russians with several watches on each arm. You would see Russian women officers with alarm clocks hanging around their necks. They had never had watches before and could not get enough of them. Romanians who wished to have a watch had to go to the barracks of the Soviet army to buy a stolen one, often buying back their own watch. So it was common for Romanians to enter the Russian barracks. The Underground also purchased watches from them, giving us entrance into their barracks.

"The first time I preached in a Russian barrack was on the day of St. Paul and St. Peter, an Orthodox feast. I went onto the military base pretending to buy a watch. I pretended that one was too expensive, another was too small, and another too big. Several soldiers crowded around me, everyone offering me something to buy. Jokingly I asked them, 'Is any of you named Paul or Peter?' Some were. Then I said, 'Do you know that today is the day when your Orthodox church honors St. Paul and St. Peter?' Some of the older Russians knew it. So I said, 'Do you know who Paul and Peter were?' Nobody knew. So I began to tell them about Paul and Peter.

"One of the older Russian soldiers interrupted me and said, 'You have not come to buy watches. You have come to tell us about the faith. Sit down here with us and speak to us! But be very careful! We know about whom to beware. Those around me are all good men. When I put my hand on your knee, you must talk only about watches. When I remove my hand, you may begin your message again.'

"Quite a great crowd of men was around me, and I told them about Paul and Peter and about the Christ for whom Paul and Peter died. From time to time someone would come near in whom they had no confidence. The soldier would put his hand on my knee and I would talk about watches. When that man went away, I resumed preaching about Christ. This visit was repeated many, many times with the help of Russian Christian soldiers. Many of their comrades found Christ. Thousands of Gospels were given out secretly."

Of one experience in the fourteen years he spent in prison after his arrest for activities such as the above, he wrote: "The political officer asked me harshly, 'How long will you continue to keep your stupid religion?'

"I said to him, 'I have seen innumerable atheists regretting on their deathbeds that they have been godless; they called on Christ. Can you imagine that a Christian could regret when death is near that he has been a Christian and call on Marx or Lenin to rescue him from his faith?'

"He began to laugh, 'A clever answer.'

"I continued, 'When an engineer has built a bridge, the fact that a cat can pass over the bridge is no proof that the bridge is good. A train must pass over it to prove its strength. The fact that you can be an atheist when everything goes well does not prove the truth of atheism. It does not hold up in moments of great crisis.'

"I used Lenin's books to prove to him that, even after becoming prime minister of the Soviet Union, Lenin himself prayed when things went wrong."

• • •

Not just anyone would try to save those oppressing their country or reach out to those torturing them. Only someone who truly understands the love of God and the true weight of things in eternity can do such things. Only someone who has that love in his heart can turn right around after being delivered from that oppression and start an organization focused exclusively on trying to touch these oppressors with the Truth.

Richard and Sabina Wurmbrand were people who knew this love. They were Jews who reached out to Nazis who were fugitives behind the lines after the fall of Berlin ending World War II, even though they had lost most of their families to the concentration camps. They met the tanks with Bibles as the Russians marched in to take over at the end of the war. After Richard spent fourteen years and Sabina spent three being tortured in Communist prisons, they were ransomed to the West, where, though they had been threatened with assassination if they spoke out, they started a ministry called Jesus to the Communist World, specifically designed to reach Communists. That organization has grown up into what today is The Voice of the Martyrs. And the countries of the Soviet Union and the Eastern Block that the Wurmbrands focused so much prayer and ministry on are now free.

54

Who can truly measure the impact of a single revolutionary armed with the love of God?

This is how we know what real love is: Jesus gave his life for us. So we should give our lives for our brothers and sisters. Suppose someone has enough to live and sees a brother or sister in need, but does not help. Then God's love is not living in that person. My children, we should love people not only with words and talk, but by our actions and true caring.

John
(1 John 3:16–18 NCV)

Love never fails.

Paul
(1 Corinthians 13:8 NIV)

I am prepared to die in the army of Jesus.
While the opportunity is there, I preach the Gospel
with all my might, and my conscience is clear before
God that I have not sided with the present govern-
ment, which is utterly self-seeking. I have been
threatened many times. Whenever I have the oppor-
tunity I have told the president the things the church
disapproves of. God is my witness.

JANANI LUWUM
ARRESTED FOR DEFYING THE CRUELTIES UNDER
IDI AMIN AND SHOT TO DEATH
UGANDA
1977

An End to Cruelty

| Stanislas | Krakow, Poland | 1079 |

Boleslaw II's actions were becoming more and more of a concern to everyone. Men had begun to give him the title "Boleslaw the Cruel" behind his back, because of his harsh judgments and viciousness in battle and against those who displeased him. No one, however, had the courage to confront the king, who was given to fits of rage, with the excesses of his actions.

No one, that is, except Stanislas. As bishop of Krakow, the seat of the Polish kingdom, Stanislas felt it his God-given duty to confront the king and turn him toward repentance. He felt the king had many good qualities that would take over if he would turn from his anger. So, when given the opportunity to speak with the king privately, Stanislas confronted him.

The king listened quietly to Stanislas's rebuke. It is unsure whether the king felt any sincere repentance at the bishop's words or merely let him speak, as he had always been a loyal and trusted advisor. In the end, however, he decided that Stanislas had spoken out of place, and that as king he could do as he willed. Because of this, he assigned soldiers to murder Stanislas when he heard that he was alone nearby in the chapel of St. Michael.

The soldiers descended on the chapel and rushed in to slay Stanislas. Yet as they approached him, he did not stir from prayer at their pounding footsteps. As one of the soldiers approached and raised his sword, Stanislas still remained kneeling in prayer, unaffected. Convicted in his heart against his murderous orders, the soldier lowered his sword and left. The other soldiers soon followed.

When they returned to the king and reported their refusal, Boleslaw flew into a fit of rage. He charged one of the men, pulled the man's dagger from its sheath, and threw him to the floor, racing from the room. He ran straight to the chapel and, finding Stanislas still kneeling in prayer, thrust the dagger into his heart. Stanislas died on the spot.

This proved to be one of the last official acts of King Boleslaw II. The death of the bishop united the rest of Boleslaw's court against him, so he fled for his life to Hungary, where he died two years later.

• • •

Standing up for what is right is a key to freedom. God's revolutionaries on the earth have always been marked by their refusal to kneel to injustice or silence the truth for the sake of convenience, being accepted by the crowd, or personal gain. A chain of bondage is placed upon a person link by link each time she turns away from the Truth or refuses to voice what is right.

On a personal level, over time this can enmesh us in a lifestyle of self-justification and lies. Then the Truth becomes so obscured that we hardly notice when we violate it ourselves until something tragic happens. This is what Paul called the searing of our consciences with a hot iron in 1 Timothy 4:2: Little by little, just as skin can be deadened and hardened into a callus by frequent friction or heat, our consciences can be silenced by persistent disregard. We become bound in a world of delusion that only God and His Word can deliver us from. This is why James wrote of God's Word as a mirror: Just as we look into a physical mirror each day before we go out to make sure that our appearance is right, we look into His Word each day to make sure our heart and actions are right.

On a community or societal level, power is accumulated by those who love it above all else when righteous people are silent. Freedom is not always taken away by military force. Often it is whittled away by the controlling bodies when no opposition is voiced to immoral or gradually more entrapping legislation. Liberty evaporates without the refreshing wind of Truth.

In a modern society where the media thrives by dumping the problems of the world onto our doorsteps, speaking up for righteousness can seem an overwhelming task. Of the thousands of problems in the world today, how can I make them all mine to help solve? We can't, of course. But through prayer and following our consciences, we can make a difference in our personal worlds. This is the revolution and world-changing God has called each of us to. Whether or not our obedience to Him takes on international importance is not of concern to God. What is important is that we seek Him, live for Him, and obey Him daily, and He will do the rest. There is no higher calling than this, and there is no calling more dangerous to ignore.

Do not deceive yourselves by just listening to his word; instead, put it into practice. If you listen to the word, but do not put it into practice you are like people who look in a mirror and see themselves as they are. They take a good look at themselves and then go away and at once forget what they look like. But if you look closely into the perfect law that sets people free, and keep on paying attention to it and do not simply listen and then forget it, but put it into practice—you will be blessed by God in what you do.

James
(James 1:22–25 TEV)

I have lost all of my friends at school. Now that I've begun to "walk my talk," they make fun of me....
I am not going to apologize for speaking the name of Jesus. I will take it. If my friends have to become my enemies for me to be with my best friend, Jesus, then that's fine with me....
I am not going to hide the light that God has put into me. If I have to sacrifice everything, I will.

Rachel Scott
Murdered at Columbine High School
April 20, 1999

58

Valuing His Soul Above All Else

| Anthony Ricetti | Venice | c. 1542 |

Anthony Ricetti had been sentenced to death by drowning for his adherence to the teachings of Christ. A few days before the sentence was to be carried out, his son came to him, pleading with him to recant that he might not be left fatherless.

Anthony replied, "A good Christian is bound to give up not only goods and children, but life itself, for the glory of his Redeemer; therefore I am resolved to sacrifice everything in this transitory world for the sake of salvation in a world that will last for eternity."

The lords of Venice also sent him word that if he would recant, he would not only be freed but would receive a considerable estate that had just been reclaimed.

Anthony's response was again direct and to the point. He sent them word that he refused their offer absolutely, because he valued his soul beyond all other considerations.

Again they urged him to reconsider, telling him that a fellow prisoner, Francis Sega, had just recanted and was set free.

"If he has forsaken God, I pity him," Anthony answered, "but I shall continue steadfast in my duty."

Finding that Anthony would not turn from his confession, the lords executed him as sentenced. He died cheerfully commending his soul to his Redeemer.

Francis Sega, whom he had been told of, had in fact not recanted and was executed only a few days later in the same manner.

• • •

If you love your father or mother more than you love me, you are not worthy of being mine; or if you love your son or daughter more than me, you are not worthy of being mine. If you refuse to take up your cross and follow me, you are not worthy of being mine. If you cling to your life, you will lose it; but if you give it up for me, you will find it.

Jesus
(Matthew 10:37–39 NLT)

The life, the self-sacrifice, the blood, which they are ready to shed for their faith, is the greatest argument for Christianity presented by the underground church. It forms what the renowned missionary in Africa, Albert Schweitzer, called "the sacred fellowship of those who have the mark of pain," the fellowship to which Jesus, the Man of sorrows, belonged. The underground church is united by a bond of love toward its Savior. The same bond unites the members of the church with each other.
Nobody in the world can defeat them.

RICHARD WURMBRAND
FOUNDER OF THE VOICE OF THE MARTYRS
SPENT FOURTEEN YEARS IN A COMMUNIST PRISON
ROMANIA
1940s, '50s, AND '60s

"I Would Rather Die Than Leave the Church"

Juan and Maria	Colombia	2000

Juan and his wife, Maria, knew the risks when they felt God leading them to become missionaries to the indigenous tribes north of Cali, Colombia. The area was controlled by guerilla forces of the Revolutionary Armed Forces of Colombia (known better by their acronym in Spanish, FARC), a leftist military group. Many of the pastors and Christian workers had fled because of the constant threat the guerillas posed to their lives and property. Regardless of this, Juan and Maria began ministering in the region in the mid-1990s.

Roughly three years ago, while traveling between villages, Juan met with a group of about fifty FARC guerillas. Juan took the opportunity to share the Gospel with them, and twenty of them received Christ. As he says, they exchanged "pistols for epistles."

Though Juan and Maria continue to work in the area without opposition from FARC members, these are still dangerous times for them. Another military organization, The National Liberation Army (ELN), has been attacking Christian churches in the region. During late 1999 and early 2000, at least twenty churches were closed with the pastors fleeing the area, concerned for their lives and the lives of their families. It was not uncommon for members of the ELN to come into services and demand all the money from the church's tithes and offerings while holding the pastors at gunpoint. Juan is now the only pastor left in the area. He receives no aid from any outside organizations.

Juan and Maria don't look down on any who have left, nor do they want to talk about the danger they face by staying or the other difficulties they have faced in recent months. Their burden is for reaching the people in this area with the Gospel and ministering in any way they can. Juan and Maria would rather think of new ways to reach and help these people than spend one minute in fear for their lives.

Juan says, "If I am to die because I preach the Word of God, then I would rather die than leave the church."

• • •

It has often been said that fear is the opposite of faith. As faith motivates us toward something, fear makes us cower away from it. Faith in ourselves is key to all endeavors; fear of failure often leads to not trying something in the first place. Faith in God frees us to talk about Him; fear of man keeps our mouths shut worrying about what others will think.

Faith liberates. Fear incapacitates.

However, there is one type of fear that does free us: the fear of God. In this modern era where we want to call Jesus our friend and think of God as our helper, the concept of the fear of the Lord gets explained away in a lot of different ways as a healthy respect for God or an awe and reverence for who He is. But the fear of God is more than that. It is not a fear like the fear of heights or the fear of getting mugged along a dark street. It is a revelation of who God really is in all of His power as the creator of the universe. It is a revelation of the God to whom the devil and all of his forces are an insignificant bother. It is the fear that Jesus talked about in Matthew 10:28 when He told us not to fear those who can kill the body and not the soul, but fear Him who can destroy both soul and body in hell.

If we have this fear of God, who is on our side, then how can we ever fear what people might think? How can we ever disobey Him for fear of what others might do? How can we really fear anything on this earth ever again? Strange as it may sound, the fear of God sets us free from fear itself.

Jesus is the Liberator. Faith in Him, and holy fear of Him, enables us to try what others have called impossible.

63

In the fear of the Lord there is strong confidence,
And His children will have a place of refuge.
The fear of the Lord is a fountain of life,
To turn one away from the snares of death.

Solomon
(Proverbs 14:26–27 NKJV)

God doesn't want us to be shy with his gifts, but bold
and loving and sensible.
So don't be embarrassed to speak up for our Master or
for me, his prisoner. Take your share of suffering for the
Message along with the rest of us. We can only keep on
going, after all, by the power of God, who first saved us
and then called us to this holy work.

Paul
(2 Timothy 1:8–9 THE MESSAGE)

The First Roman Persecution

Under Nero	Roman Empire	c. A.D. 64-68

Nero was only seventeen years old when he became emperor in A.D. 54 and was a tenderhearted and just young man. With his teacher, Seneca, and the commander of his household guard, Burrus, as his advisers, it seemed assured that Rome would experience peace and prosperity under his rule. Seneca held that "compassion is the chief virtue of a ruler," and Burrus had a great understanding of politics and dealing with the military. Once, when asked to sign the death warrant for a highwayman, Nero was so distraught at the idea of putting a man to death that he exclaimed, "Oh, that I could not write!" According to Emperor Trajan, there had never been a better emperor than Nero had been his first five years on the throne, nor a better period for the Roman Empire.

Yet jealousies within the court began to turn his heart. His mother's thirst for control over him, and thus over the empire, made her begin to plant suspicions in his mind about those whom she saw as a threat to her influence. These suspicions led to the death of Nero's half brother, Britannicus. This decision to kill on the whim of rumor turned Nero to his basest instincts. He became so full of hatred, murder, and the thrill of shedding blood that soon the only things that could entertain him were torture, violent killings, and mass destruction. It is said that he eventually poisoned his own son, had his mother cut open so that he could see the place he had lain in her womb, had his faithful wife killed with a sword because she was barren, and found his teacher, Seneca, guilty of an assassination attempt on his life but allowed him to poison himself rather than be executed.

One night in July of A.D. 64, in a fit of boredom, he desired to see something greater than the burning of Troy as recorded in

The Iliad. He thus had Rome set on fire and ascended to an exterior tower to watch, singing, "Troy is on fire! Troy is on fire!" The fires burned for nine days, and thousands were left homeless, having lost everything but their lives.

In answer to the public backlash from the event, Nero blamed the Christians for setting the fire. Soon a decree went throughout the Roman Empire that stated in part, "If anyone confesses that he is a Christian, he shall be put to death, without further trial, as a convicted enemy of mankind." He must have hoped to wipe Christianity from the face of the Roman Empire.

This began the first government-endorsed period of Christian persecution in world history, and the first of ten periods of persecution in the Roman Empire that took place sporadically over roughly the next 250 years. Everything from jealousies between neighbors to overheard conversations in the streets led to the accusation that someone was a Christian, and though many of these were false, the decision to call yourself a Christian had to be accompanied by the conviction of the truth of the Gospel as eternal and more significant than a torturous death. It was under Nero that the practice of dressing Christians in the skins of beasts and letting them be torn to pieces by dogs, lions, or other wild animals began, as well as the practice of burning them on crosses as lamps and torches to light evening activities.

• • •

It has been said that the lives of the early Christians consisted of "persecution above ground and prayer below ground"—their existence being defined by the coliseum and the catacombs. It was about this time that they began to create the nearly six hundred miles of mole-like catacombs to pray and have their services. The earliest of the approximately four thousand inscriptions found in the catacombs is marked at A.D. 71. It is also believed that as many as four million Christians may have been buried there over time. As the Christian graves have been opened, the skeletons tell their own terrible stories of what happened during the Roman persecutions: heads found severed from the bodies, ribs and shoulder blades broken, and other bones showing signs of exposure to fire.

The walls of the catacombs are still covered with the symbols of their faith. Among the most common were the Good Shepherd with the lamb on His shoulder, a ship under full sail, harps, anchors, crowns, vines, and above all the ichthus, or fish. Many statues found in the catacombs show figures with their hands above their heads praying or singing, their hands open toward heaven. They are also covered with faith-filled sayings and inscriptions such as

Victorious in peace and Christ.
LIVE in God.
The Word of God is NOT BOUND.

However, the full force of these epitaphs is better seen when they are contrasted with the selfishness and hopelessness of other epitaphs of their time:

Live for the present hour,
since we are sure of nothing else.
I lift my hands against the gods
who took me away at the age of twenty
though I had done no harm.

Once I was not. Now I am not.
I know nothing about it, and it is no concern of mine.

Traveler, curse me not as you pass,
for I am in darkness and cannot answer.

Unnumbered tens of thousands of Christians were executed for their profession of faith during these persecutions, unnamed and unrecorded in any histories. Unrecorded in history, yes, but not unrecorded in the Lamb's Book of Life.

Do you see what this means—all these pioneers who blazed the way, all these veterans cheering us on? It means we'd better get on with it. Strip down, start running—and never quit! No extra spiritual fat, no parasitic sins. Keep your eyes on Jesus, who both began and finished this race we're in. Study how he did it. Because he never lost sight of where he was headed— that exhilarating finish in and with God—he could put up with anything along the way: cross, shame, whatever. And now he's there, in the place of honor, right alongside God.

Hebrews 12:1–2 THE MESSAGE

The early Christians were revolutionaries of the Spirit,
heralds of the last judgment and the coming transformation;
they had to be ready for martyrdom at any moment.
Their witness meant they had to reckon with being sentenced
to death by state and society. Therefore, "martyrs" were those
witnesses ready to die for their faith, those who bore this
testimony before kings and judges with the
steadfastness of soldiers of God.
They were martyrs, that is "confessors," even if they
did not have to die. To give witness is the essence of
martyrdom. Martyrs uphold the truth of their testimony as
eyewitnesses of the Lord and his resurrection.
They see Christ and become his prophetic spirit-bearers.
Through the Spirit, the blood-witness of the martyrs becomes
part of the decisive battle waged by Jesus, the
battle in which he himself died as champion and leader of the
future. By dying, he finally judged and routed the hostile
powers of the present age. Put to death by the most devout
Jewish people and the Roman state, Christ fettered and
disarmed the demons and their darkness through his cross.
Since then, each new martyrdom—each new dying with
Christ—becomes a celebration of victory over the
forces of Satan.

FROM EBERHARD ARNOLD'S
THE EARLY CHRISTIANS: IN THEIR OWN WORDS

69

A Heavenly Toast

| Anthony Parsons and Others | England | c. 1540 |

Having refused to turn from their beliefs, Anthony Parsons and those with him approached the stakes on which they were to be burned. Arriving there, Parsons requested some drink. With it, he turned and toasted his fellow sufferers: "Be merry, my brethren, and lift up your hearts to God; for after this sharp breakfast I trust we shall have a good dinner in the Kingdom of Christ, our Lord and Redeemer."

At this toast, Eastwood, one of the fellow sufferers, lifted his eyes and hands to heaven and commended his spirit to his Lord.

Parsons walked to his stake and pulled some straw near to it before he allowed himself to be tied to it. Holding the straw, he looked to the spectators and said, "This is God's armor, and now I am a Christian soldier prepared for battle. I look for no mercy but through the merits of Christ; He is my only Savior, in Him do I trust for salvation."

Soon after this the fires were lit, and these men exchanged their mortal lives for ones immortal through Christ Jesus.

• • •

Then I heard a loud voice in heaven say: "Now have come the salvation and the power and the kingdom of our God, and the authority of his Christ.
For the accuser of our brothers, who accuses them before our God day and night, has been hurled down. They overcame him by the blood of the Lamb and by the word of their testimony; they did not love their lives so much as to shrink from death."

John
(Revelation 12:10–11 NIV)

Not Ashamed of His Chains

Onesiphorus	Rome	C. A.D. 65

The soldier watched the man suspiciously from where he was sitting with his friends. The man approached looking somewhat harried, but determined. As he looked around, his eyes locked on the soldier, and he made his way toward their table. The soldier looked away, hoping the man would move on.

"Excuse me, sirs," the man began. "I am looking for a friend. He is in prison. I wonder if you might help me find him."

Saturus, a burly guard to the soldier's left, stood up. "Riff-raff! If he is in prison, then he is a criminal. If you are his friend, then you are probably one too. Leave us before we arrest you and throw you in with your friend."

Saturus could be intimidating, even to the other soldiers, but the man stood his ground. "My friend is no criminal, sir. And if you must arrest me before you will take me to him, then so be it. I am ready to go."

Saturus stared at the man. "If he is not a criminal, then why is he in jail?"

"He is a Christian," the man replied. "As am I."

The whole table of soldiers stood except the one who had first seen the man. "Do you know we could kill you for that?" another soldier said. "How dare you—"

The soldier still seated put his hand on the other's arm. "We don't want any trouble," he said. "Tell me; what is your friend's name?"

"Paul of Tarsus."

"Boy," he said to a youth sitting nearby. The boy jumped to attention. "Take this man to the prison near the barracks." He looked back to the man. "And your name, sir?"

"Onesiphorus."

"Well, Onesiphorus, if I ever see you again, I will arrest you myself. Now leave us!"

Hellespontus
C. A.D. 68

After comforting Paul in jail and probably being present for his execution, Onesiphorus went on to be a pastor, becoming bishop of either the church in Colophon or Coronia. (There is some confusion about this. These may have been two names for the same place, or he may have been bishop of two different churches at the same time.)

From there he went on to take the Gospel to Hellespontus, being accompanied by Porphyrius, who was probably a faithful member of his congregation. Nero's edict to kill Christians was in full effect by this time, and the governor of the province—a man by the name of Adrianus—had them beaten and whipped. When they still would not deny their Christianity, he had them tied to wild horses, then released the horses to run. They were dragged and torn until they died.

• • •

One can only begin to imagine what it must have been like for Onesiphorus to walk into Rome, a Rome at the dawn of Nero's rage against Christians, and start looking for a friend who was in prison not only because he was a Christian but because he engaged every person he met in a conversation about Jesus. Paul was being held for execution, and Onesiphorus must have known that his finding Paul might very well mean that he would be executed alongside him. Still, he sought out his brother to comfort him in one of his greatest times of need. What kind of friend is it that is not ashamed of the other's chains, especially at the risk of torture and death?

How much, then, can we truly love our friends if we are not even willing to risk our reputations, let alone our lives, to tell them about Jesus?

72

May the Lord show mercy to the household of Onesiphorus, because he often refreshed me and was not ashamed of my chains. On the contrary, when he was in Rome, he searched hard for me until he found me. May the Lord grant that he will find mercy from the Lord on that day! You know very well in how many ways he helped me in Ephesus.

Paul
(2 Timothy 1:16–18 NIV)

"This is my command: Love one another the way I loved you. This is the very best way to love. Put your life on the line for your friends.... I've named you friends because I've let you in on everything I've heard from the Father.
"You didn't choose me, remember; I chose you, and put you in the world to bear fruit, fruit that won't spoil."

Jesus
(John 15:12–13, 15–16 THE MESSAGE)

73

"It Is Not Time"

Dominggus Kenjam	Indonesia	1999

"Allah-u-Ahkar!" (Allah is Almighty!) *"Allah-u-Ahkar!"*

Dominggus awoke with a start out of his bed as someone grabbed him and dragged him to the ground. His screams were muffled as they continued to shout and rain blows down on his body. He couldn't see any one of them, and he could see no means of escape. "We will allow the women to live, but the men must die!" someone shouted.

As Dominggus struggled to escape, a sickle came down on the back of his neck, cutting deeply. He went nearly unconscious but sensed that his assailants had left the room, leaving him for dead. He felt ill as the growing pool of his own blood began soaking through his T-shirt.

Rather than lapsing all the way into unconsciousness, though, Dominggus reported that his spirit left his body and was escorted up by two angels. As he rose, he could look back down on where his body lay huddled on the floor in the dark room. He was sure that he had died.

Every feeling of fear and pain left him immediately as an indescribable peace flooded his being. *I am going to be with Jesus,* he thought.

Then Dominggus heard the words, "It is not time for you to serve me here." Then he felt himself floating back toward his body.

Suddenly Dominggus could feel that someone else was in the room with him. They were discussing which morgue to take his body to, because they didn't know if he was a Muslim or a Christian.

"I am a Christian," he was able to say weakly. The two emergency medical workers must have had quite a start when the

74

"corpse" they were discussing answered their question for itself!

Dominggus was back. His work on the earth was not through.

• • •

Today, Dominggus has fully recovered. He still bears the scar of the attack on his flesh, but not in his spirit. He has forgiven his attackers and has a deeper commitment to pray for Muslims in Indonesia than ever before. Not only that, but he now knows he has a purpose to fulfill on the earth or Jesus would not have sent him back. His faith is now stronger than ever, and he is eager to follow God's will daily as it is revealed to him.

And Indonesia gravely needs people with hearts like that of Dominggus. The government has promoted a belief called Pancasila— meaning that all may freely choose to follow Christianity, Islam, Buddhism, or Hinduism—but in reality Muslims receive preferential treatment. The political strength of Islam has been used to limit evangelism and reduce Christian influence on public life. Islamists' stated aim is the complete elimination of Christianity in the country. In recent years there has been an orchestrated jihad, or "holy war," against Christians—with over six hundred churches destroyed by mobs. Some areas where Christians are the majority, such as Timor Lorosae (East Timor) and Ambon, have been subjected to outright military attacks and killings.

Over the last forty years, evangelicals have grown from 1.3 million to 11.5 million. The increase of Christian persecution has brought about a greater unity among the Body, the growth of a national prayer movement, and a commitment to outreach in Indonesia and beyond. The vision for the evangelization of Indonesia has grown despite the tremendous persecution.

So be truly glad! There is wonderful joy ahead, even though it is necessary for you to endure many trials for a while.

These trials are only to test your faith, to show that it

75

is strong and pure. It is being tested as fire tests and purifies gold—and your faith is far more precious to God than mere gold. So if your faith remains strong after being tried by fiery trials, it will bring you much praise and glory and honor on the day when Jesus Christ is revealed to the whole world.

Peter
(1 Peter 1:6–7 NLT)

"For I know the plans I have for you," declares the Lord, "plans to prosper you and not to harm you, plans to give you hope and a future."

God the Father
(Jeremiah 29:11 NIV)

Not-So-Blind Chang

Chang Shen	Mainland China	c. 1890

Chang Shen was known to those villages in the surrounding areas as *Wu so pu wei te*, meaning "one without a particle of good in him." He was a gambler and thief, a womanizer who had driven his wife and daughter from their home. The townspeople said it was the judgment of the gods for his evildoings when he was stricken with blindness.

As always, though, Chang cared little for what the villagers said. When he heard there was a hospital run by missionaries in another province and that these missionary doctors could operate on a person and their sight would be restored, he had to go and find out. Though he was completely blind at the time, he traveled the hundreds of miles to the hospital in the hope of regaining his sight. Yet when he arrived, he was turned away, being told every bed in the hospital was full.

However, the hospital evangelist was so moved by Chang's determination to get to the hospital that he gave Chang his own bed. After treatment Chang's natural eyesight was partially restored, but what he heard while staying in the hospital opened eyes that Chang didn't know he had—spiritual eyes. This man who had not "a particle of good in him" heard the Gospel and accepted Jesus as his Lord and Savior. One doctor reported, "Never had we a patient who received the Gospel with such joy."

Chang asked missionary James Webster to baptize him, but Webster, who had seen some fall away after such an emotional conversion, told him, "Go home and tell your neighbors that you have changed. I will visit you later and if you are still following Jesus, then I will baptize you." Webster was not able to visit Chang's village until five months later. When he arrived, there was more than

77

just one seeking baptism—there were more than four hundred! Chang had obviously not only told everyone he could that he had changed, he had also told everyone he could that they could change too!

Eventually Chang lost his physical sight again at the hands of an unskilled native doctor, but he did not care so much since he still had his spiritual sight. He could quote practically the entire New Testament by heart, and many chapters from the Old Testament as well. This was enough "sight" for him. Thus he took to the road again, much as he had when he first sought to be healed, but now he was going out to do the healing himself. He won hundreds to the Lord and only rejoiced when he was cursed and spit on by those who rejected his message. Missionaries had more than a full-time job following after him to baptize the new believers and organize churches to teach and nurture their new faith.

When the Boxer Rebellion broke out, many felt Chang would be among the first of their targets. Believers took him and hid him in a cave in the mountains.

The first village the Boxers reached in the area was Ch'oay nagshan. They immediately rounded up fifty Christians to execute. But a resident told them, "You are fools to kill all these. For every one you kill, ten will spring up while that man Chang Shen lives. The only way to crush the foreign religion is to kill him."

So the Boxers said they would let these go if someone would lead them to Chang Shen.

Chang's response? "I'll gladly die for them." Again, through his supernatural sight, Chang saw salvation when everyone else saw only death.

When Chang arrived, local authorities took him to the temple of the god of war and demanded that he worship.

"I can only worship the One Living and True God," Chang replied.

"Then repent."

"I repented years ago."

"Then believe in Buddha," they responded.

"I already believe in the one true Buddha, even Jesus Christ."

"You must at least bow to the gods."

"No. Turn my face toward the sun." He knew that at that time of day he would be standing between the sun and the temple, so when he was turned, his back was toward their gods. He knelt and lifted up a praise song to Jesus. Three days later Chang was beheaded.

The Boxers then heard a rumor that Chang would rise from the dead because of the power of his God, so they had his body burned. Still they feared what Chang's spirit would do to them if they stayed in the area, so in the end they left peacefully and quickly.

Because of this, all the other Christians in the local churches were spared.

. . .

JESUS loves me!
He who died
Heaven's gate to open w i d e ;
He will WASH away my sin,
Let His little child come in.

JESUS loves me!
He will stay
Close beside me all the way;
If I love Him when I die
He will take me home on high.

THE SONG CHANG SHEN SANG
ON THE WAY TO BE BEHEADED

I came into the world to bring everything into the clear light of day, making all the distinctions clear, so that those who have never seen will see, and those who have made a great pretense of seeing will be exposed as blind.

Jesus

(John 9:39 THE MESSAGE)

79

The Slave of Ireland and the Gospel

Patrick	Ireland	C. A.D. 432

As Patrick's boat pushed west, he felt a strange chill from the memory of the same journey he had made years earlier under very different circumstances. The smells of the sea and the fog clinging to the waves and the cliffs took him back to when he was a lad of sixteen, traveling to Ireland in bonds with the raiding party that had burned his home and taken him as a slave.

Despite the hardships of having been a slave for six years, tending the herds of a Druidic high priest named Milchu, Patrick had come to have a supernatural love for Ireland. It was in Ireland that Patrick had come to know God personally as he walked the woods and mountains alone with the animals. He had grown up in a Christian home in a British Roman settlement but had never embraced the faith while he lived with his family. He had been a lax student during that time, something he now greatly regretted, and was too independently minded to walk so easily in his family's faith. Alone and seemingly forsaken in Ireland, Patrick sought out God and found Him. Then, through a dream, God led him to escape and eventually return to his family, who welcomed him warmly. Upon his return to Britain, Patrick resumed his studies with more vigor, intending to join the ministry as his father and grandfather had.

Now, as the oars pulled against the dark waves, Patrick began to see God's hand in it all. Shortly after his return to Britain, Patrick had a dream about Ireland in which he heard "the voice of the Irish" calling to him: "We beg you, holy youth, come and walk among us again." Patrick felt this was God's call to return to Ireland with the Gospel.

Yet he felt unfit for the task, so he journeyed to a monastery in Britain, again leaving his family, and poured himself into being ordained. Roughly twenty years had passed since then. At his first opportunity to return, Patrick was passed up by his church elders to be a missionary to Ireland, and another, a man by the name of Palladius, was chosen. When Palladius was killed a short time later, Patrick was elected to go.

Upon landing, Patrick returned to the village where he had been a slave. His intent was that his first convert would be the man who had been his master, Milchu. But when he arrived there, he found Milchu's home in ashes. At word of his coming, Milchu had gathered all of his possessions into his home and lit it on fire, killing himself in the flames. Patrick was horror-struck at the madness of this act and determined to act dramatically to release these people from the fear of false gods that would drive a man to do such a thing.

Patrick spent some time preaching to the locals there and finding out what had happened since his departure and who was in power. His years as a slave had served him well, as he still spoke their language fluently and with little accent, making it easy to communicate. In his conversations he learned that the high king of Ireland, King Laeghaire, would be celebrating the Druidic feast of Beltine, which coincided with Easter that year, at his courts in Tara. Patrick headed there immediately, intent on making a statement for the power of God over the idols and occult practices that bound these people.

It was tradition that on the eve of the festival, it would be the high king who lighted the first bonfire of the festival. Any who defied this would be put to death. Yet as the king emerged that night to start the festival, Patrick's bonfire was already glowing brightly for all to see on the hilltop of Slane (pronounced *slay-ne*) not far away. As had Elijah before the prophets of Baal, Patrick had uttered a formal challenge to the Druids and their king.

As Laeghaire gave the order for the perpetrators to be found and killed, his two Druidic high priests offered him a word of caution and prophecy: "O king, live forever. This fire, which has been lit in defiance to the royal edict, will blaze forever unless it is put out this night on which it has been lit. The man who lit the fire and the coming kingdom by which it was lit will overcome us all!" But the king would hear none of it. He had twenty-seven chariots prepared, and he, his guests, and his court rode to subdue Patrick.

When the chariots arrived, Patrick was summoned before the king. The king ordered Patrick's bonfire extinguished, but no matter what his soldiers did, the fire refused to be put out. Patrick gave a bold testimony for Jesus before them and refused to be silent. When Laeghaire commanded his soldiers to execute Patrick to quiet him, confusion descended on them, and they attacked one another. When the two Druid priests then turned their vehemence on Patrick and Jesus' name, one fell and cracked his head on a rock, while the other somehow fell into the fire and perished. One version even records that when the king himself pulled his sword to slay Patrick, his arm froze in the air as stiff as a statue and stayed that way until he knelt in surrender to Patrick. Though it is unclear how many of the details of this encounter are legend and how many actually happened, Patrick's victory over Laeghaire and his Druids opened the political doors of Ireland to the Gospel.

Patrick thus had a captive and royal audience to be among the first to be converted during his ministry. Though the king did not become a Christian on this day, his chief bard, his two daughters, and one of his brothers did. Less than two weeks later they were baptized. The brother gave Patrick land and a barn that became the first church, and wealth to use to spread Christianity throughout Ireland. Laeghaire also gave Patrick legal sanction to preach throughout the island.

For the next thirty years Patrick established Christianity throughout Ireland, and though he had other miracles attributed to his ministry, he was not often far from trouble. Ireland was not neatly organized in kingdoms under Laeghaire, so whenever he went into a new area, it was likely that Laeghaire's sanction would mean very little. Patrick and his followers were imprisoned on several occasions—Patrick once spent two months in prison wondering if his ministry was over—and he saw many of his converts die, as well as being sentenced to death himself more than once. Through it all, though, Patrick remained humble and counted only on God's protection to free him from any situation. He wrote the following in a chant or prayer, which he titled "The Breastplate," that he taught others to remind them of their purpose and Protector:

CHRIST shield me today
against poison,
against burning,
against drowning,
against wounding,

So that there may come to me
ABUNDANCE of reward,

Christ with me,
Christ before me,
Christ behind me,
Christ in me,
Christ beneath me,
Christ above me,
Christ on my right,
Christ on my left,
Christ when I lie down,
Christ when I sit down,
Christ when I arise,
Christ in quiet,
Christ in danger,
Christ in the heart of every man
who thinks of me,
Christ in the mouth of everyone
who speaks of me,

Christ in every eye that sees me,
Christ in every ear
that hears me.

Having successfully planted churches and established pastors and priests in every district in Ireland, Patrick died around the age of seventy-two on March 17, A.D. 461.

• • •

Though more people today probably associate Patrick with green beer than the Gospel, he has left us an important heritage as a revolutionary for Christ. It is important for us to remember such men as Patrick and Nicholas (who most call Santa Claus today) for who they were and not who the world has transformed them into in order to nullify their testimonies.

The life of Patrick is another example of the love of God that can make no sense to the world. How can a slave love his master so much as to return for the master's good once he has escaped? How can he love the people who enslaved him and took him away from his family as a youth so much as to dedicate his life to their good? How can the persecuted love their persecutors?

Is there any greater proof of God than the existence of such a love in the hearts of those who call Him Savior and Lord? Is there any greater evidence of His existence than what can be accomplished through a heart submitted and obedient to His will?

I, Patrick, a sinner, am the most ignorant and of least account among the faithful, despised by many....
It was not any grace in me, but God who is victorious in me and resisted them all, so that I came to the Irish people to preach the gospel and to bear insults from unbelievers, to hear the scandal of my travels, and to endure many persecutions even to the extent of prison; so that I might surrender my liberty as a man of free condition for the profit of others, and if I should be found worthy, I am ready to give even my life for His name's sake unfalteringly, gladly, and without hesitation; and there (in Ireland) I desire to spend it until I

die, if our Lord should grant it to me. I owe it to God's grace that so many people should through me be born again in God....

But I implore those who believe in and fear God, whoever consents to examine or receive this document composed by the obviously unlearned sinner Patrick in Ireland, that no one shall ever credit to me even the smallest of things that I achieved or may have told of that was pleasing to God, but accept and truly believe that it was the gift of God. And this is my confession before I die.

Patrick
Confession

But by God's grace I am what I am, and the grace that he gave me was not without effect. On the contrary, I have worked harder than any of the other apostles, although it was not really my own doing, but God's grace working with me.

Paul
(1 Corinthians 15:10 TEV)

If we Christians don't continue to share the gospel and push the envelope, the envelope will close in on us. If we maintain a "silent witness," there will be no witness, and Christianity will die in America.

RAY THORNE
A MISSIONARY TO THE PERSECUTED CHURCH

Sowing God's Word		
Rosa	Cuba	1999

"I was born into a Communist home where no one could even mention the word God. I remember being a little girl looking at a huge picture of Fidel Castro (the leader of the Cuban Revolution) in my living room.

"My parents are atheists. My father used to be a representative of a very important organization called the Communist Youth Union. Now he is in the Cuban Communist Party leadership. My mother is secretary of the Revolution Defense Committee. In summary, my home is a Communist 'nest.' However, my great-grandmother loves God and she has been faithful to God through all these years. She used to talk to me about the Lord and she sowed the seeds of the Lord's Word. On several occasions I tried to go to church with her, but my parents did not allow me to go.

"Years later my parents divorced, and then my mother allowed me to go to church, without my father's permission. Anyway, when I was twelve my mother tried to get me away from the Lord, organizing and inviting me to parties. I went away from the Lord living that way. But my great-grandmother persevered in praying for me.

"One day I went to church and received the Lord Jesus Christ as my Savior. My life started to change; even my way of dress changed totally. My mother did not accept it. She never beat me before, but now she does often. When my father learned that I was a Christian, he told me to choose God or him. I chose the Lord because I have understood that He is the only thing really worthy for me. I know that God is faithful and He cares for me and He is going to do wonderful things for my family.

"My mother got married again to another Communist man. He had a five-year-old son. They don't allow me to talk to him

87

about the Lord or to go to church, but I talk to him about the love of God anyway. Sometimes I listen to him praising the Lord.

"Now, even though I am only fourteen, I study far away from my home. When I first came to this place I was the only Christian, but I have sown God's Word and now we are four. We meet under a tree, hidden, to share God's Word. We feel the presence of the Lord in such a special way. We keep sowing and waiting that soon we will be many.

"God is faithful. He never forsakes His children. Please, pray for me. It is not easy to follow the Lord in a country so hostile to Him where opposition comes not only from the system but from our homes. Our parents are blind in this atheistic system and do not understand that we grow and make our own personal decisions. Mine is Jesus Christ. I will be faithful even at the price of death!"

• • •

People may call themselves revolutionaries, but they don't realize that without God they change nothing. All they do is perpetuate a world of hatred and strife. One dictator replaces another; one system of corruption and exploitation replaces another system; one set of devils is replaced by another set of devils. Things can go on this way for hundreds of years at a time.

They go on, that is, until someone is willing to stand up and get God involved. Then things really begin to change: Hatred is replaced by forgiveness; strife is replaced by brotherly love and a helping hand; oppression is replaced by freedom; and evil men to fear are replaced by God-fearing men to follow. In the wake of a godly revolution, the world is set upside right again.

"If you stick with this, living out what I tell you, you are my disciples for sure. Then you will experience for yourselves the truth, and the truth will free you....
"I tell you most solemnly that anyone who chooses a life of sin is trapped in a dead-end life and is, in fact, a

slave. A slave is a transient, who can't come and go at will. The Son, though, has an established position, the run of the house. So if the Son sets you free, you are free through and through."

Jesus
(John 8:31–32, 34–36 THE MESSAGE)

A Time to Speak Out

| Timothy | Ephesus | A.D. 98 |

"Great is Diana of the Ephesians!"

The masked revelers screamed and shouted as they made their way through the streets of Ephesus, banging their sticks on the ground, a wall, or a passing cart to make noise, and dancing before the statue of the god they were celebrating. The feast of Catagogion was a major money-maker for the craftsmen and pagan priests of the area, so there was always great support in the community of the festivities surrounding that day. Great support, that is, among all but the growing Christian church in Ephesus.

Timothy, now the elderly pastor of that church, hardly paid attention to the event. In fact, he had forgotten that it would be taking place on that day as he walked down the street. He was more concerned with the growing pressure on the church because of Emperor Diocletian's recent exile of the apostle John to the island of Patmos that was not far to the southwest, and the growing tension in the community between the pagans and Christians as a result. Timothy remembered what the church had gone through under Nero—he had in fact been present at Paul's imprisonment and execution in Rome—and it looked like the church would be going through much of the same under Diocletian.

So when Timothy turned the corner and walked right into the procession of revelers, he was more appalled then ever at the foolishness of it.

"Brothers, sisters, why do you worship and sacrifice to a statue made with human hands that is no god, when the true God of all sent His own Son that you could know Him and the joy of His righteousness? This partying is foolish and self-destructive! Why celebrate a dead statue and give place to your lusts when you can know the God of heaven and the real joy of walking in His ways?"

One of the priests at the lead came forward and roughly pushed Timothy out of the way. "Leave us alone, old man! We will do as we please!" Yet the procession had stopped, and it was obvious some in the crowd were wondering at what Timothy had said.

So Timothy continued, "Do as you please? And what if what pleases you is a trap? What if it is a bond that will take your life from you before you have even lived and chain you to regret and dissatisfaction? Jesus came that you might have life and life abundantly! Why accept the chains of sin when you can live free in His Spirit!"

"Enough, I said!" screamed the priest, bringing his stick down upon Timothy as hard as he could. The others stood and stared. The priest was not caught for a minute by their wonder. "Blasphemy! Blasphemy! Did you not hear what he said? He called Diana a false god and a curse! He does not deserve to live! Great is Diana of the Ephesians! Kill him! Kill him!" And he brought his stick down upon Timothy again.

"Great is Diana of the Ephesians!" another called behind him, raising his stick along with the priest. The others soon joined in, pounding Timothy with sticks or rocks and then kicking him to the side of the road out of the way to continue their parade.

A group of Christians soon collected the bishop and took him to his home to be cared for. Timothy died of the bruises and injuries two days later.

• • •

There is a time to be quiet, but there is also a time to speak out. If a friend is not looking and about to trip over something in her path, isn't it only natural for us to shout out and warn her before she hurts herself? How much more should we yell if she is casually on her way to hell and has no idea that there is something better?

Have I then become your enemy by telling you the truth?

Paul

(Galatians 4:16 ESV)

Timothy, my child, I am giving you a command that agrees with the prophecies that were given about you in the past. I tell you this so you can follow them and fight the good fight. Continue to have faith and do what you know is right.

Paul

(1 Timothy 1:18–19 NCV)

O friends, what about these heroic spirits?
What about those faces that look at you today
through that blinding smoke and those devouring flames?
Are there then two standards of service, one high and
Christlike for them, and one much lower, made to meet
the case of little, lean, and cowardly souls? Nay, are
there three ways for the feet of those who travel toward
eternity? One wide and broad for the wicked, another
straight and narrow for martyrs and martyr spirits, and
the other a middle middling, sort of silver-slipper path,
for those who would have the pearl without the price,
the crown without the cross.
No! No! No! Look again at those martyr-men.
They stood up there before heaven and earth, and said in
the loudest language that can be spoken in this or in any
other world, that they gladly gave up, not only friends
and kindred, lands and money, and every other earthly
treasure, but life itself, which to them, as to everybody
else, is far dearer than all else put together, for the truth
and love and cause of Jesus Christ.

WILLIAM BOOTH
FOUNDER OF THE SALVATION ARMY
1829–1912

Continuing to Preach

Li De Xian and Zhao Xia	Mainland China	2002

"Christ was the first to suffer," Pastor Li De Xian said. "We just follow Him. There are many thorns, but we are just injured a little on our feet. This suffering is very little."

As any know who remember his story from pages 170–175 of *Jesus Freaks*, Pastor Li speaks about suffering from experience. The man who said "I will preach until I die" has stuck to his word. Despite continued pressure from the Public Security Bureau (PSB), Pastor Li refuses to miss a service unless he is in prison or change his message of salvation through Jesus Christ. During the period from October 2000 to May 2001, he was arrested fifteen times for preaching in his unregistered house church in Guangzhou. He has been arrested so many times during the past two years that he has lost count. During one recent detention, jailers tied his arms and legs together and chained his arms and legs to a bedpost for three days. When they finally released him from this torture, he was forced to work on an assembly line in the prison factory putting bulbs into strings of Christmas lights to send to America! He and the others had a quota of between four and five thousand bulbs a day. "They suffered this inhumane treatment simply because they failed to meet their daily production quotas in the Chinese labor camp." Li has seen imprisoned Christians tortured so badly that their buttocks bled through their clothing. He spent fifteen days in prison on this particular occasion.

Yet rather than this experience teaching him to be afraid, it has taught him to be prepared. He travels at all times with a small black duffel bag that he keeps packed with a blanket and a change of clothes—the things he will need for prison whenever he is arrested next. "Arrests will come at any time, but we are not afraid, as we have prepared ourselves, and we have not done any crimes." Whenever possible he will spend his time in prison reading the Bible, something he manages to smuggle in with amazing regularity.

His wife, Zhao Xia, strongly supports him in this and refuses to worry. "God will take care of him," she says, "so there is no need to worry."

In 2000, PSB officials also confiscated Li's church and welded the doors shut. In early November 2000, in the city of Wenzhou, Zhejiang Province, they reportedly blew up and demolished at least 450 churches, temples, and shrines. Government officials said religious leaders had built the churches and temples illegally.

"Don't feel sorry for us," Zhao Xia says of their lifestyle. "At least we are constantly reminded that we are in a spiritual war. We know for whom we are fighting. We know who the enemy is. And we are fighting. Perhaps we should pray for you Christians outside of China. In your leisure, in your affluence, in your freedom, sometimes you no longer realize that you are in spiritual warfare."

• • •

The Chinese character for "crisis" is actually a combination of two other characters. One is "danger," but the other is "opportunity." We usually view a crisis as something to totally avoid. We see or experience the danger, never dreaming or desiring that it may involve an opportunity.

If we are truly dedicated to serving God with our lives, the circumstances of life will be springboards for opportunities to further God's kingdom. Paul acted much this way in his life: Being locked up in prison was an opportunity to save the jailer and his family; having a Jewish hit squad out to kill him was an opportunity to appeal to Rome and take the Gospel there. Perhaps Joseph said it best: "God turned into good what you meant for evil. He brought me to the high position I have today so I could save the lives of many people" (Genesis 50:20 NLT).

Because of this, people like Pastor Li and his wife never have the time to feel sorry for themselves as they are too busy looking for the door God will open next. When Pastor Li enters prison, he reaches people for Christ he might not have otherwise met. He has become so well known that whenever he is arrested again, it makes headlines worldwide and China's policies toward Christians are again under scrutiny. They know they are in spiritual warfare and believe that is just where they need to be to serve God properly. And they wouldn't miss that opportunity for the world.

> **Pray also for me, that whenever I open my mouth, words may be given me so that I will fearlessly make known the mystery of the gospel, for which I am an ambassador in chains.**

Paul
(Ephesians 6:19–20 NIV)

"The Gospel Is Sufficient"

| John Wycliffe | England | c. 1330-1384 |

John Wycliffe began his studies aimed at being a minister in the state church in England. He was sent to Oxford by his parents and soon distinguished himself at Merton College as a sharp mind and a clever debater.

He eventually became the master at Baliol College and found himself rising in the favor of the church. Archbishop Islip appointed him to a position at the newly founded Canterbury Hall, where he was quickly in line for promotion. Yet when the time came, he was passed up for political reasons and in such an unjust manner that he appealed to Rome. However, what he got was not justice but rhetoric. Edward III, then king of England, had stopped the tribute paid to Rome by his predecessor, King John, and was supported by Parliament in his decision. Until this channel of money began to flow again, any matters in England would be ignored.

Wycliffe bristled at the injustice of this and the greed of the church in Rome. He also felt that the king was right in his actions and should be recognized to have legitimate jurisdiction over the church in England. He began to skillfully argue these points where he had the opportunity. Rome soon turned its back on him, and no one had any doubts that it was because he had opposed them.

Wycliffe saw that the regulation of the established church at this time was thus not built on the righteousness, justice, and grace of God—not built on the precepts of the Bible—but upon the love of money and political power mongering. He set himself to expose this for the sake of truth and called for reformation to the church's corruption, abuses, and selfish uses of money.

Around 1376, Wycliffe enunciated the doctrine of "dominion as founded in grace," which stated, among other things, that "the Gospel alone is sufficient to rule the lives of Christians every-where," that "any additional rules made to govern men's conduct added nothing to the perfection already found in the Gospel of Jesus Christ," and that "no high-ranking clergy should have prisons to punish transgressors."

Wycliffe was soon commanded to be silent by local church authorities and eventually condemned by the state church hierarchy. Yet this only strengthened his convictions, and he grew bolder in preaching that truth was found in the Scriptures and did not come from the edicts of men.

Repeated attempts to capture him failed, often through the intervention of local nobles. Around 1378, after an illness nearly cost him his life, he set himself to release the truths he had been preaching and began translating the Latin Vulgate, the only Bible allowed at the time, into English for all to read. It was distributed in secret through pamphlets and books. Followers of his teachings grew in number despite aggressive efforts to suppress them. John Wycliffe continued this work until his death in 1384.

In 1415, the Council of Constance reviewed Wycliffe's teachings and found him guilty of heresy. As he had already died roughly thirty years earlier, they ordered that his body be dug up, burned, and the ashes scattered in the river. This was finally carried out in 1428. They had hoped that this action would put an end to Wycliffe's teachings and influence, but it did not. It was as if every bit of ash from John's burnt corpse carried a new thirst for Truth with it down the river, out to sea, and across Europe.

• • •

John Wycliffe has been called "The Morning Star of the Reformation" because he was the first to fight for the right of every man, woman, and child to have access to the Scriptures for themselves and to know God through His Word. In a time when the controlling church began to grow fat on political power and wealth rather than the true knowledge of God, John Wycliffe began a revolution of freedom that would rage for the next two hundred years. He did not shy away from the Truth, though it would have profited him greatly to look the other way and rise in the hierarchy to a place of power and wealth. Wouldn't he have been a greater man of influence if he had? Probably not, because by the time he would have arrived in that position, he would have made so many compromises in what he believed that he would not have been a man of the same convictions.

John Wycliffe fought with words and knowledge, not political authority, so that all would have the freedom of Truth. It is interesting to consider what our freedoms might be like today if John had not set the fire that would blaze into King James finally authorizing an English version of the Bible in 1611. Some believe that the greatest evangelical outpourings of missionary work happened because of the King James Bible, and great reform in England took place because people started to recognize the Scriptures as the basis for law and conduct. Would the Pilgrims have ever set out for America had they not had a Bible in their own language that made them believe there was more of God to be gained by moving to a new land free of the constraints of belief they were experiencing in Europe? It's hard to say.

But what can be said is that without people such as John Wycliffe who stood up for the Truth, it could easily have been lost, locked away in a language few understood and even fewer studied for themselves. It is important to comprehend the price that was paid so that we can have our own Bibles to read every day. Almost as important is remembering to take advantage of that freedom every day.

> That's why the prophet said,
> "The old life is a grass life,
> its beauty as short-lived as wildflowers;
> Grass dries up, flowers droop,
> God's Word goes on and on forever."
> This is the Word that conceived the new life in you.
>
> Peter
> (1 Peter 1:24–25 THE MESSAGE)

The Conqueror's Heart

| Russian Captain | Hungary | 1950 |

The Russian army captain walked haughtily down the aisle of the church and up to the pastor. "I will have a word with you alone. Take me someplace where we can speak privately!"

The officer was very young and brash and seemed very conscious of his role as a conqueror.

When the pastor had led him to a small conference room, the officer shut and locked the door. He nodded toward the cross that hung on the wall. "You know that thing is a lie," he said to the minister. "It's just a piece of trickery you ministers use to delude the poor people to make it easier for the rich to keep them ignorant. Come now, we are alone. Admit to me that you never really believed that Jesus Christ was the Son of God!"

The minister smiled. "But, my poor young man, of course I believe it. It is true."

"I won't have you play these tricks on me!" cried the captain. "This is serious. Don't laugh at me!"

He drew out his revolver and held it close to the body of the minister.

"Unless you admit to me that it is a lie, I'll fire!"

"I cannot admit that, for it is not true. Our Lord is really and truly the Son of God," said the minister. For a painful instant his muscles tightened as he awaited the bullet.

Instead, the captain suddenly flung his revolver on the floor and embraced the pastor. Tears sprang to the captain's eyes.

"It is true!" he cried. "It is true. I believe so too, but I could not be sure men would die for this belief until I found for myself one who would. Oh, thank you! You have strengthened my faith. Now I too can die for Christ. You have shown me how."

• • •

This is the kind of life you've been invited into, the kind of life Christ lived. He suffered everything that came his way so you would know that it could be done, and also know how to do it, step by step.
"He never did one thing wrong,
Not once said anything amiss."
They called him every name in the book and he said nothing back. He suffered in silence, content to let God set things right.

Peter
(1 Peter 2:21–23 THE MESSAGE)

102

God is "the Truth."
The Bible is the "truth about the Truth."
Theology is the "truth about the truth about the Truth."
Christian people live in these many truths about the
Truth, and, because of them,
have not "the Truth."
Hungry, beaten, and drugged, we had forgotten
theology and the Bible. We had forgotten the "truths
about the Truth," therefore we lived in "the Truth."
It is written, "The Son of man is coming at an hour
when you do not expect Him" (Matthew 24:44).
We could not think anymore. In our darkest hours
of torture, the Son of man came to us,
making the prison walls shine like diamonds and
filling the cells with light. Somewhere, far away, were
the torturers below us in the sphere of the body.
But the spirit rejoiced in the Lord. We would not
have given up this joy for that of kingly palaces.

RICHARD WURMBRAND
FOUNDER OF THE VOICE OF THE MARTYRS
SPENT FOURTEEN YEARS IN A COMMUNIST PRISON
ROMANIA
1940S, '50S, AND '60S

The Hiding Place

Corrie ten Boom	Holland and Germany	1942-1947

"This is a perfect house for a secret room," said Mr. Smit. The ten Boom home was very old and had lots of rooms with odd angles and nooks. One could easily add a wall and a hidden door, and there would be places for people to hide if the Nazis came. The ten Booms knew better than to be pleased by this information, but they also knew as Christians that they could not look the other way when God's chosen people, the Jews, were being so openly persecuted. Their consciences gave them no choice but to help. "This is where the false wall will come," Mr. Smit told them later, standing in Corrie's room on an upper floor. "I cannot make the room any bigger, but several people will be able to get in."

Over the next week or so several new "customers" came to the ten Booms' little watch shop carrying lunch sacks or what looked like packages. In these were the tools and materials needed to make the secret room. When it was finished, even the family, who knew the house well, could not tell that the wall was new. The workers had even matched the wallpaper that looked as if it had been a hundred years old.

During the following weeks they practiced getting their "guests" into the room quickly if someone came to call. They had to make sure that there was no trace that anyone had been there. If they were eating, everything from the table must disappear so that there was no sign; if they were sleeping, the mattresses must be turned over so that there wasn't a warm spot for the Gestapo to find. Soon they had four regular guests, and it only took about a minute for any trace of them to disappear from the house.

Soon all the ten Booms created their own code words that

they used with others in the underground to funnel people through their hiding place and on to freedom in an Allied country. "We have an old watch, with an unusual face. Do you know someone who would like to buy it?" or, in other words, "We have an old Jewish man who needs to be hidden who has a face that would immediately give him away. Where can we hide him?"

As time passed, their continual cooperation in this underground people-smuggling operation became more and more risky. But their consciences would not let them turn anyone away who needed help. They knew sooner or later something would give them away. And by this time their number of regular guests had grown to nine.

Then in early 1944 the inevitable happened. The Gestapo took prisoner one of the couriers who helped them relay messages. They knew he was very young and would not do well under their torturous questioning. Some days later a Dutchman asked Corrie for some money. She did not know him, but he said it was needed urgently to help some Jews. Corrie did not really trust him but gave him the money anyway—how could she refuse if there was even a chance he was telling the truth? It turned out he was a Nazi spy.

The knock on the door came suddenly that afternoon when Corrie had just lain down because she was feeling like she was coming down with the flu. The house was a mad scramble for a bit and then silent. All of the practicing had paid off, as there was no sign of their guests to be found anywhere in the house.

The Gestapo officers and the two Dutch Nazi officials burst through the door and ran about the house, gathering everyone into the front room. They had some guests with them who knew nothing of the Jews upstairs, and Corrie's brother Willem was in town. The officers began questioning them by taking them one by one into another room. Corrie's turn came first.

"Where have you hidden the Jews?" the officer demanded.

Corrie was flushed, but she hid it well behind her slight fever.

She looked straight into the officer's face. Growing up, she had been told Christians never lied, but what choice had she? If she told the truth, they would kill all of them. Finally Corrie answered, "Jews? There are no Jews here."

The officer struck her across the face. "Where are the Jews?!"

This time Corrie said nothing.

"All right, then, where is the secret room?" He would ask, then hit her, then ask again and then hit her again. It was not long before Corrie had completely lost track of how many times this had happened.

Corrie could taste blood in her mouth and feel it running down her cheek. Still she said nothing. Suddenly she felt even more sick than before and thought she would faint. "Lord Jesus, help me," she sobbed.

This time the officer hit her with even more vehemence. "If you use that name again, I'll kill you!" Instead, he had her taken back to the living room, and Corrie's sister, Betsie, was taken into the room.

As Betsie was questioned in the same manner, soldiers who had followed the officers were searching the house, smashing whatever was breakable, throwing anything loose across the room, and smashing cupboards and breaking down doors. But they never found what they were looking for, the room was so well hidden.

"Fine, then," the commanding officer said at last, "take them to the police station and set a guard on the house. If there is anyone hiding in here, they will starve to death."

For hours the family was left on the floor in a room of the police station. At nine o'clock, Father ten Boom gathered the family together for the devotions that always took place at this time at home. They had no Bible, so he quoted from Psalm 119 from memory, "You are my hiding place and my shield: I hope in your word.... Hold me up, and I shall be safe." Ten days after this, Father ten Boom died in a hospital, but because of their imprisonment it was

105

some time before Corrie and Betsie learned of his death.

The family was soon separated, and Corrie, "the ringleader," and Betsie were imprisoned to await their hearings. Corrie was taken to the hospital because she was sick, and when she returned to the police station she was put in a cell by herself. She had no idea what had happened to the rest of her family, but she soon received a hidden note in a tin of cookies that told her, "All the watches left in the cupboard are safe."

Before her hearing, Corrie was to be questioned by another Gestapo officer. After her previous questioning, she feared the worst. "Lord Jesus," she prayed, "you were once questioned too. Please show me what to do."

"Miss ten Boom, I would really like to help you. But you must tell me everything," the officer began in an understanding tone.

Corrie had been trained with the other underground members how to answer questions in a flowing line of conversation that seemed to be of interest, but in the end revealed nothing. For many of the questions, Corrie was grateful that she honestly didn't know the answers.

Slowly the officer saw this was leading nowhere and decided to change the subject. "And now tell me about your other activities, Miss ten Boom."

"Other activities? Oh yes, there's the girls' clubs and my work for the mentally handicapped...." This was not what he had wanted to hear, but her enthusiasm in talking about these things caught him off guard. For a short time he listened in astonishment. In the end he said, "But really, all of this is such a waste of time."

"Oh no," Corrie defended, "God loves everyone, even the weak and feeble. You see, the Bible tells us that God looks at things very differently from us."

"All right, all right," the officer interrupted, "that will be enough for today."

In the end, Corrie shared the entire Gospel message with the officer, who soon became as much of a friend as he could. He hated his work and listened attentively when she told him about praying for forgiveness. He arranged for Corrie and Betsie to see their family again. Unfortunately he did not have the power to see that they were released. Corrie spent the next four months in this cell alone, except when she was permitted out for questioning. She spent the time reading and rereading the gospel stories about Jesus.

Though no verdict was ever pronounced, eventually both Corrie and Betsie were sent to Ravensbruck concentration camp. In all, they spent ten months in prison. At Ravensbruck they spent hours in the cold as the thirty-five thousand women prisoners were counted and recounted if there was a mistake. In the following months the hard labor took Betsie to the point of death more than once. In the end she went to the infirmary and didn't come back. Through it all, though, it seemed that it was Betsie's faith that had helped the rest of them survive.

Three days after her sister's death, Corrie was called out at the morning head count. "Prisoner ten Boom, report after roll call."

She was terrified. Was it her turn to be executed? "Father in heaven, please help me now," she prayed.

But when she reported to the camp administrative offices as ordered, she was handed a card that said "Released" in German. She was given her original clothes back and a railway ticket for Holland. She left immediately. Eventually she learned that her release had been a clerical error. The week after her release, all of the women her age at Ravensbruck were put to death.

After the war ended, Corrie started a life of traveling and telling her story to encourage other Christians. Going back into Germany to minister was the most difficult of all for her, but she felt that she must go wherever God sent her.

In 1947, at a church in Munich, a man walked up to her who looked strangely familiar. As he shook her hand she realized where she knew him from: He had been one of the crueler guards at

Ravensbruck! As he realized that she recognized him, he looked at her with watery eyes. "Miss ten Boom, I have become a Christian since the war. I know now in my heart that God has forgiven me, but I must also ask for your forgiveness. Can you forgive me for all of the evil I did to you, your sister, and the others?"

It took some time for Corrie to respond. As she struggled over what she would say, she found that she had many more things than she had realized to release to God about what had happened to her during the war. In the end, though, her response was simple and straightforward: "I forgive you, brother, with all my heart."

• • •

Corrie went on to write a book about her experiences during the Second World War called The Hiding Place. *Eventually the book was turned into a movie. She returned to Germany several times after the war and took part in a ministry that specifically helped Germans who had been made bitter under Hitler's reign. Corrie spent the rest of her life preaching about the healing power of God's forgiveness and about His comfort and presence even in the worst of circumstances. She died in 1983.*

> *You are my hiding place!*
> *You protect me from trouble,*
> *and you put songs in my heart*
> *because you have saved me.*

Psalm 32:7 CEV

Lord Jesus, I offer myself for Your people. In any way. Any place. Any time.

Corrie ten Boom

If we do not radiate the light of Christ around us, the sense of the darkness that prevails in the world will increase.

MOTHER TERESA
GAVE HER LIFE TO THE POOR IN INDIA
1910–1997

Lord, I am your messenger. Throw me like a blazing torch into the night.

MARY SKOBTSOVA
DIED IN A NAZI GAS CHAMBER
MANY BELIEVE SHE DIED IN THE PLACE OF ANOTHER WOMAN
PICKED TO GO TO RAVENSBRUCK CONCENTRATION CAMP.
GERMANY, EASTER EVE, 1945.
THE CAMP WAS LIBERATED BY THE RED CROSS THE NEXT DAY.

Standing Firm for the Truth of the Word

George Wishart	Scotland	1546

"Sir!" The man stood in the middle of Mr. Wishart's message on the book of Romans to the congregation before him, cutting the teacher off in mid-sentence. "I would that you would stop and trouble this town no more. For I, for one, have determined to suffer no more of your lies."

George Wishart was shocked by the interruption and the accusation against his teachings from the Word of God. He had preached a similar message at Montrose and in this same church the night before in Dundee, and the exposition was a great blessing in both instances. It was not often assemblies were actually taught about the Word of God and not simply read in a language few if any of them knew. The crowd was silent as he collected himself and meekly addressed the speaker and the rest of the congregation. "God is my witness, I didn't have your trouble in mind but your comfort; in fact, your trouble is more grievous to me than it is to yourselves. In contrast I am sure that refusing to hear God's Word, and to chase away His messenger, shall not preserve you from trouble but shall bring you into it. God shall send you ministers who fear neither burning nor banishment. I have offered you the Word of salvation. In hazard of my life I have remained among you. If you now yourselves refuse me, I must leave any innocence I may have to be declared by my God, not by myself. If you can walk contrary to the Word I have preached to you and things be long prosperous with you, I am not led by the Spirit of truth; but if unlooked-for troubles come upon you because you have rejected His Word, acknowledge the cause and turn to God, who is gracious and merciful. But if you turn not at the first warning, He will visit you with fire and sword." Mr. Wishart then left the pulpit and walked out of the chapel.

At this, Robert Miln, the man who had been put up to disrupting the meeting, returned to the chambers of David Beaton and informed him that Wishart had been silenced. Beaton, who was the local head of the state church, was greatly pleased. Wishart's teachings clashed violently with the doctrine of the state church, which did more to enrich its leadership and keep control than to reach the common people with the truth of God's Word. As Jesus was to the Pharisees, to these leaders the likes of men such as George Wishart were a threat to their carefully laid web of power and wealth in their society.

After the disrupted meeting, Mr. Wishart did leave Dundee and took the Word of God to western Scotland, where it was warmly received. He was not far into his travels before he found out that a plague had broken out in Dundee just four days after he had left. An incredible number had died in the first twenty-four hours. Though his friends he traveled with tried to talk him out of it and forbid him from going, he made plans immediately to return to Dundee. "They are now in trouble," he told them, "and need comfort. Perhaps this hand of God will make them now to magnify and reverence the Word of God, which before they lightly esteemed."

He was received warmly by some on his return, and the town being shut up against the plague—no one allowed in or out from where the sick were quarantined—he chose to preach at the east gate of the city, the healthy on his side of the gate and the sick on the other. "Today I will be speaking from Psalm 107:20," he began. " 'He sent His word and healed them.' " He went on to expound upon the comfort of God's Word, the discomfort for those who had contempt for or rejected it, and the happiness of those whom He takes to himself out of the misery of the world. After his sermon the plague began to die down quickly.

When Beaton learned of Wishart's return and how circumstances had increased his popularity and seemed to support his message instead of that of the state church, he decided to seek a more permanent solution. He appointed a priest of the church,

111

John Weighton, to assassinate Mr. Wishart.

So it was that Weighton, with a dagger in hand hidden beneath his robes, stood waiting to meet Wishart after he had finished a later sermon at the gate, hoping to end his preaching of the Word then and there. Yet Wishart was a sharp-eyed man and saw the gleam of the dagger as he descended from the podium. Cordially he walked up to the priest and said, "My friend, what have you here?" and quickly placed his hand on Weighton's and disarmed him of the dagger.

Weighton fell terrified on his knees before Wishart, confessed his intentions, and pleaded for forgiveness. At the same time, those in the crowd saw what had happened and began to throng forward to push through the gate to apprehend the priest. "Deliver the traitor to us; we will take him by force!"

At this, Wishart took Weighton in his arms and turned to the crowd, protecting him. "Whatsoever hurts him shall hurt me; for he hath done me no mischief, but much good, by teaching me to be more heedful in the time to come." Wishart's defense of the man settled the growing mob, and they left agreeing not to harm Wishart's assailant.

In addition to continuing to preach, Mr. Wishart kept himself busy visiting the houses of those still afflicted and comforting and encouraging them from God's Word. Finally he took his leave to return to Montrose when the plague had all but ended. He preached at times there, but mostly he refreshed himself in private meditation and prayer.

Again Beaton conspired to have Wishart murdered. He sent a child to Wishart in Montrose with a forged letter claiming to be from a close friend of Mr. Wishart. The letter reported that the friend, the laird of Kennier, asked him to come as quickly as possible, as he had taken suddenly sick and wanted his friend at his side. The boy was also supplied with a horse for Mr. Wishart to take so that he could leave right away. Meanwhile Beaton had hired sixty men to lie in wait for Mr. Wishart on the road to Kennier to ambush and kill him. The boy met Mr. Wishart standing with some friends in town and delivered the note and the horse. After reading the note, Wishart took the horse, as some of his friends collected theirs, and they set out together for Kennier.

Yet not far down the road, Wishart reigned in his horse and drew to a stop. The others with him turned to ask the cause. "I will not go," he told them. "I am forbidden of God; I am assured there is treason. Let some of you go to yonder place, and tell me what you find."

Some of his friends rode on and discovered the ambush, the sixty men ignoring them because Wishart was not with them, and returned to tell what they found.

Mr. Wishart had discovered earlier from the priest who had tried to kill him that David Beaton was behind the plot, and he knew that Beaton was likely behind this one as well. He told his friends, "I know I shall end my life by that bloodthirsty man's hands, but it will not be in this manner."

Some time later Mr. Wishart left Montrose and went to Edinburgh in order to preach the Word of God. On the way he stayed in the home of a faithful brother. While there, in the middle of the night, he arose and went into the yard. His friend and another in the house, having heard him go out, got up and followed him out of the house to see what was happening. When they saw him in the yard kneeling in fervent prayer, they did not disturb him but followed and quietly watched. Then seeing him turn to go back to the house, they made their way back to the house before him. When he arrived they came down the stairs and asked him if all was okay, feigning to have never left the house. Wishart gave them no answer.

The next morning they again pressed him for an explanation and even told him that they had followed him and seen him praying. At their continual insistence, he eventually complied. "I will tell you. I am assured that my warfare is near at an end, and therefore pray to God with me, that I shrink not when the battle grows most hot."

When Mr. Wishart arrived near Edinburgh and Beaton discovered where he was lodged, Beaton sent men to arrest him

113

and brought Wishart to trial on no less than eighteen articles of heresy. The trial worked much to Beaton's embarrassment, as Wishart answered the charges with such composure, intellect, and clear reason that all there were astonished at the man. In the end, however, Beaton refused to acknowledge any of his arguments and asked Wishart to recant. Wishart refused, being too enlightened by the truth of the Gospel and fixed in its principles to be the least moved to turn from what he believed and preached. Beaton was greatly pleased by Wishart's response and sentenced him to die in the flames at the stake.

On the morning of his execution, Wishart was dressed in a black linen coat beneath which were tied several bags of gunpowder. He was then led to the stake and bound to it with a rope around his neck and a chain around his middle. Despite this, however, Wishart still managed to fall to his knees and pray:

"O thou Savior of the world, have mercy upon me! Father of heaven, I commend my spirit into Thy holy hands.

"I beseech thee, Father of heaven, forgive them that have, from ignorance or an evil mind, forged lies of me. I forgive them with all my heart. I beseech Christ to forgive them that have ignorantly condemned me."

He was then fastened more firmly to the stake, and the fire lit. It soon caught the powder beneath the coat and blew into flame and smoke. However, Wishart remained alive.

Standing so nearby that the flames singed him at the explosions of the powder, the governor of the castle, an unwilling accomplice in this execution, asked for forgiveness for his offenses. Wishart heartily replied, "This flame occasions to trouble my body, indeed, but it has in no wise broken my spirit. But he who now so proudly looks down upon me from yonder lofty place" [here he indicated Beaton] "shall, before long, be ignominiously thrown down, as now he proudly lounges at his ease."

Wishart's bravery and steadfastness also moved his executioner, the hangman, who, before the sight of Wishart's suffering in the flames and steadfast confession of love, fell before him on his knees and implored, "Sir, I pray you to forgive me, for I am not guilty of your death."

Wishart asked him to come closer and bent to kiss the man on the cheek. "Lo, here is a token that I forgive thee. My heart, do your duty."

After this, the flames subsiding, the trapdoor of the gallows was sprung and Wishart died hanging. His body was then burned to powder.

Those who left the scene that day were all the more convinced of his innocence because of his courage and words of forgiveness. They left sorrowful and complaining of the injustice of the act.

Less than three months later, David Beaton was assassinated in his bed by a group of men opposed to his cruelties. He died crying out, "Alas! Alas! Don't slay me! I am a priest!" calling out for the mercy he showed no other man. His body lay seven or more months unburied and then was thrown in the garbage dump.

• • •

For when we brought you the Good News, it was not only with words but also with power, for the Holy Spirit gave you full assurance that what we said was true.

Paul

(1 Thessalonians 1:5 NLT)

But you followed my teaching, conduct, purpose, faith, patience, love, perseverance, persecutions, and sufferings, such as happened to me at Antioch, at Iconium and at Lystra; what persecutions I endured, and out of them all the Lord delivered me! And indeed, all who desire to live godly in Christ Jesus will be persecuted. But evil men and impostors will proceed from bad to worse, deceiving and being deceived. You, however, continue in the things you have learned and become convinced of.

Paul

(2 Timothy 3:10–14 NAS)

"I Am the Grain of God"

| Ignatius | Antioch | c. A.D. 111 |

Emperor Trajan, having finally settled political matters of the empire by defeating the Scythians, Dacians, and other nations that had threatened the borders of Rome, made the decision to conquer in the area of religion as well, thus decreeing the third major period of Roman persecution. According to his edict, all those subject to Roman law were required to sacrifice to the Roman gods. This policy had been quite successful except for among the sect called the Christians. Deciding to make an example for the others, when he arrived at Antioch in his travels, he tried Ignatius himself before an assembly of Ignatius's peers and disciples in that city. Ignatius was the leader of the church in Antioch (only the third leader of the church after the apostle Peter) and one of the foremost Christians alive after John's passing.

When Ignatius was brought before him, Trajan just scowled. "Who are you, wicked wretch, who defies and ignores our commands, persuading others to do the same, even though you know that doing so will bring you to a most miserable death?"

"No one ought to call Theophoros wicked, for there are no evil spirits in the servants of God," Ignatius replied. "But if you are calling me an enemy of these spirits you worship, that I am wicked in respect to them, then I quite agree. For inasmuch as I have Christ the King of heaven in me, I will do everything within my power to turn men's hearts from their devices."

"Who is this 'Theophorus'?" Trajan demanded.

"Theophorus—'God bearer.' It is the person who has Christ living within his heart."

Trajan smiled at this, seeing it as a play with words and philosophy, something that he enjoyed. He decided to reply in kind.

"You claim God in your heart, but do you not see then that we have the gods in our minds, whose help we have enjoyed in defeating our enemies?"

"You are mistaken if you would call the demons of the nations 'gods.' There is only one God, the maker of heaven and earth, and the seas, and all that is in them. He is the one, Jesus Christ, the only begotten Son of God, whose kingdom I desire to enjoy."

"You mean the one who was crucified under Pontius Pilate?"

"I mean the one who was crucified for my sin, and defeated him who was the inventor of it, and who has condemned and emasculated all the deceit and malice of the devil under the feet of those who carry Him in their hearts."

Trajan wondered at this for a moment. "Then do you say that you carry this man who was crucified inside you?"

"Truly," Ignatius responded, "for it is written: 'I will dwell in them and walk in them.' "

Trajan had now tired of this game and, seeing the man resolute and unreasonable in his stand, pronounced the sentence: "We find this man incurable overrun with the superstitions of the Christians, therefore we command that Ignatius, who affirms that he carries within himself Him who was crucified, be bound by soldiers and carried to the great Rome, where he will be devoured by wild beast, for the gratification of the people of Rome."

Yet to Trajan's surprise, this condemnation to a painful death did not faze the man. Instead, Ignatius looked to heaven and said, "O Lord, I thank you that you have guaranteed to honor me with a perfect love toward You, and have made me to be bound with chains as the apostle Paul was."

In the following months, Ignatius was escorted to Rome by ten soldiers, whom he called "leopards" for the harsh way they treated him. Yet through this, he took what time he could to encourage the Christians he met on the journey and write to those he could not meet to strengthen their faith. Of these letters, seven have been preserved: five to congregations in Asia (modern Turkey) and Macedonia (Greece), one to the church in Rome that he would greet upon his arrival, and one to his friend Polycarp, who had been a disciple of the apostle John. It was said that the name of Jesus was constantly on his lips during this time, and he carried with him a rich and joyful expectation that he would soon see his Lord and Savior, a desire he put above all others in his writings. Of his journey and his desires to see Jesus, he wrote:

118

Through the cruelties and tortures which are daily inflicted upon me, I am more and more exercised and instructed; though I do not hold to this for my salvation. O that I had already been devoured by the beasts that await me! I hope that before long I find them as I have hoped, cruel enough to destroy me quickly. But if they should hold back as they have already spared several Christians, I will allure them so that they will quickly come to tear me to pieces and devour me. Forgive me for speaking like this, but I know what I need.

Only now do I begin to be a disciple of Christ. I care for nothing, of visible or invisible things, that the world is amazed by. I care only that I may but win Christ. Let fire and the cross, let the companies of wild beasts, let breaking of bones and tearing of limbs, let the grinding of the whole body, and all the malice of the devil, come upon me; be it so, only may I win Christ Jesus!

[Don't pray that I be delivered,] only pray for me, that inward and outward strength be given to me, not only to speak and write this, but also to perform and endure it, so that I may not only be called a Christian, but also be found one in truth.

Upon arrival in Rome, Ignatius was brought before the governor there and imprisoned. Over the next few weeks he was subjected to several tortures and trials to try to induce him to blaspheme the name of Jesus and sacrifice to the Roman gods. Yet Ignatius's faith did not weaken but grew bolder. In the end he was brought before the Roman Senate, who condemned him to be immediately cast to the lions.

As Ignatius stood in the center of the arena, ready to meet his sentence, he looked up to the audience and proclaimed,

> O you Romans, all of you who have come to witness with your own eyes this combat; I want you to know that this punishment is not because of any misdeed or crime, but that I may come to God, for whom I long, and for whom to enjoy this is my insatiable desire. For I am the grain of God. I am ground by the teeth of the beasts, that I may be found a pure bread for Christ, who is to me the bread of life.

As soon as he had spoken these words, two lions were released from their pits and charged this bishop of Antioch, and so tore and devoured him in a matter of minutes that very little of him was left, even of his bones.

Ignatius held the rare triple honor of being an apostle, a bishop, and a martyr. He had an utter fearlessness in the defense of Christian truth and a passionate devotion to duty. He is still known for his writings, which are included in all collections of material from the early church fathers. The light of his example has shown throughout the centuries.

• • •

Sometimes as Christians we forget how revolutionary what we believe truly is. That Jesus was crucified and rose from the dead on the third day? No other religion in the world has a founder that doesn't have a tomb somewhere that is kept in honor of his memory. In the

Holy Land there are a few places where it is believed Jesus may have been buried, but no one can be sure, as they are all empty.

The idea that the God who created the universe can live within a person's heart is simply incredible. That we can be strengthened from within by His Spirit and walk in the light of His advice through our consciences is equally amazing. And to say that we have yet to understand even one-millionth of what that means is an amazing understatement.

The adventure of being a Christian, however, is not so remarkable if it is not consciously lived. Walking daily with Jesus shows. It creates a confidence and boldness in a person that is simply supernatural. But, strangely enough, it is easy enough to survive without that in our modern world. Our bubble of cultural values protects us—for now. Surely we can live without His presence every day because of that. But how long will those around us "survive" if we don't live Jesus out every day in front of them?

Do not be afraid of what you are about to suffer. I tell you, the devil will put some of you in prison to test you, and you will suffer persecution for ten days. Be faithful, even to the point of death, and I will give you the crown of life. He who has an ear, let him hear what the Spirit says to the churches. He who overcomes will not be hurt at all by the second death.

Jesus as recorded by John
(Revelation 2:10–11 NIV)

Martyrdom is fullness, not because it finishes a human life, but because it brings love to the fullest point.

CLEMENT OF ALEXANDRIA
CHRISTIAN FATHER AND APOLOGIST
DIED C. A.D. 215

"I Forgive You"

| Abbot Iscu | Romania | c. 1951 |

Abbot Iscu lay quietly awaiting death in the Tirgul-Ocna prison as a result of the tortures he had endured at the hands of his Communist captors. He spoke very little and looked serene as he felt heaven draw closer. If he did speak, his words carried the weight of eternity, and all attention in the cellblock suddenly focused to listen to him. Yet each breath he took revealed the pain that wracked his body.

Across from him, horrified at the sight of the abbot, lay another prisoner near death. He was once a Communist officer, and it was at his hands that the abbot had been tortured to the point of death. He had been a faithful Communist, and for this he now shared the cell of those he had been told to make "recant the Christian superstition" for the sake of the party. As a result of something none of the other prisoners ever learned, he had been imprisoned as well and tortured by his own comrades.

Though he, too, was at the point of death, he could find no peace in death. He awoke in the middle of the night in a heavy sweat and grabbed the arm of the person nearest him. He knew most in that cellblock were Christians, so he begged prayer. "I have committed horrible crimes. I can find no rest. Help me, please."

Because of the damp cold and never really knowing when it was day or night, many in the cell were still awake. At the Communist torturer's words, Abbott Iscu motioned for two other believers to come and help him. With their help, he was lifted from his bed and brought over to the officer, where he was set down on his bedside. The abbot reached out and laid a comforting hand on his torturer's head. "You were young and did not know what you were doing. I forgive you and love you, as do all the other

Christians you mistreated. And if we sinners who have been saved by Jesus can love like this, how much more is He himself ready to erase all the evil you have done, to cleanse you fully. Only repent."

So in that common cell, others heard the confession of a murderer to one of the men he had murdered. They also heard the murdered absolving his murderer. They embraced at the end of their prayers and gave each other a holy kiss, as was the custom of Christians in Jesus' time as well as behind the Iron Curtain.

They both died that night and must have entered heaven together. It was Christmas Eve.

• • •

There is truly no more revolutionary action than to love those who have persecuted you and forgive them.

123

But I tell you who hear me: Love your enemies, do good to those who hate you, bless those who curse you, and pray for those who mistreat you. If anyone hits you on one cheek, let him hit the other one too; if someone takes your coat, let him have your shirt as well. Give to everyone who asks you for something, and when someone takes what is yours, do not ask for it back. Do for others just what you want them to do for you....

Love your enemies and do good to them; lend and expect nothing back. You will then have a great reward, and you will be children of the Most High God. For he is good to the ungrateful and the wicked. Be merciful just as your Father is merciful.

Do not judge others, and God will not judge you; do not condemn others, and God will not condemn you; forgive others, and God will forgive you.

Jesus
(Luke 6:27–31, 35–37 TEV)

"Now I Will Be Free"

Ptolemaeus and Lucius	Rome	c. A.D. 150

"This is the man!"

The guards brought Ptolemaeus before the city prefect, Urbicus. He had been accused of being a Christian by a man whose wife was trying to divorce him. He had earlier reported that his wife had become a Christian, and when he tried to force her to continue in the wild and decadent life they had been living together before her conversion, she served him a bill of divorce, as was legal in the Roman Empire. She would not live that lifestyle with him anymore and was afraid he would hurt her if she stayed with him. However, his accusation had come to nothing, as Emperor Pius had granted her protection from a trial until she put her household affairs in order.

So, since he could not see his wife tortured and killed, he would see her teacher suffer.

Urbicus looked at the old man. "Sir, I have but one question for you: Are you a Christian?"

Ptolemaeus, whose reputation was as a man who loved truth above all else, answered simply, "Yes."

"Guards! Take him away and execute him!"

"Your honor!" Another man stepped forward from those present at the trial. His name was Lucius. "What are the charges? This man is not a criminal! He is not an adulterer or a fornicator, nor is he a murderer, thief, or robber. He has broken no other civil laws either. All he has said is that he is a Christian. Such a sentence of death for such an honorable thing will not bring honor to yourself, Prefect Urbicus, nor to Emperor Pius, nor to the emperor's son, the philosopher, nor to the sacred senate."

Urbicus looked at Lucius questioningly. "It seems to me that you must be a Christian as well."

Again the answer was simply, "Yes."

"Good! Then the old man will not die alone. Guards! Take this one too!"

Urbicus expected Lucius to try to flee, but he simply bowed his head in respect and said, "My lord, I am grateful. No longer will I have to live among such unjust and evil rulers. I will happily go live with the Father and King of heaven."

At Lucius's proclamation, another stepped forward and declared himself a Christian, that he might share their punishment—but more important, their reward.

• • •

Being "eternity minded" is one thing that those who are so willing to give their lives for Jesus have that others seem to lack. Their perspective looks something like this: "So, ten thousand years from now, when I am just settling into heaven, will I remember the things I do today with satisfaction or shame?"

Though they are heavenly minded, they are not so wrapped up in thinking about heaven that they are content to just wait life out on earth in their impatience to get there, nor are they so excited about the Rapture coming that all they do is study end-times prophecies to the exclusion of almost all else. They want to do things in this life that will make a difference for heaven, and they want to make that difference every day.

What is life on earth really worth compared to an eternity in heaven? Isn't it worth living in a little discomfort or inconvenience here to make a difference for our eternity there?

Our lives are at constant risk for Jesus' sake, which makes Jesus' life all the more evident in us. While we're going through the worst, you're getting in on the best! We're not keeping this quiet, not on your life. Just like the psalmist who wrote, "I believed it, so I said it," we

say what we believe. And what we believe is that the One who raised up the Master Jesus will just as certainly raise us up with you, alive. Every detail works to your advantage and to God's glory: more and more grace, more and more people, more and more praise!

So we're not giving up. How could we! Even though on the outside it often looks like things are falling apart on us, on the inside, where God is making new life, not a day goes by without his unfolding grace. These hard times are small potatoes compared to the coming good times, the lavish celebration prepared for us. There's far more here than meets the eye. The things we see now are here today, gone tomorrow. But the things we can't see now will last forever.

Paul
(2 Corinthians 4:11–18 THE MESSAGE)

God, I pray Thee, light these idle sticks of my life, that I may burn for Thee. Consume my life, my God, for it is Thine. I seek not a long life, but a full one, like You, Lord Jesus.

Jim Elliot
Speared by headhunters in Ecuador
while serving as a missionary
1956

"Confession Is Made Unto Salvation"

| Wendelinuta | Netherlands | c. 1540 |

Wendelinuta, a pious widow, had already been through several trials in which she had refused to recant her beliefs. As a result, she was confined to a dungeon where one last attempt was made. A friend of hers was asked to go to her in her cell and convince her to turn from what she believed.

After a great amount of discussion, Wendelinuta was no closer to recanting than when they had begun. At this, the friend struck on an idea: Perhaps if she was unwilling to change her convictions, at least she might be quiet about them! "Dear Wendelinuta, if you will not embrace our faith, at least keep the things which you profess secret within your own bosom, and strive to prolong your life."

But Wendelinuta could no more be quiet about her Lord than she could turn on Him. "Madam, you don't know what you are asking; for with the heart we believe to righteousness, but with the tongue confession is made unto salvation."

Thus her friend left defeated. Wendelinuta's home and goods were confiscated, and she was sentenced to die at the stake.

At her execution, her friend stepped forward and asked for the mercy that Wendelinuta might be strangled rather than subjected to the flames. Those in charge agreed, and Wendelinuta was executed in this manner instead.

• • •

Wendelinuta believed that the proof of her salvation was what came out of her mouth every day. What do you see as the proof of your salvation?

If you confess that Jesus is Lord and believe that God raised him from death, you will be saved. For it is by our faith that we are put right with God; it is by our confession that we are saved.

Paul
(Romans 10:9–10 TEV)

Every one therefore who shall confess Me before men, I will also confess him before My Father who is in heaven. But whoever shall deny Me before men, I will also deny him before My Father who is in heaven.

Jesus
(Matthew 10:32–33 NAS)

What encourages us to preach the gospel in captive nations
is that there those who become Christians are full of love
and zeal. I have never met one single lukewarm Russian
Christian. Former young Communists and Muslims
become exceptional disciples of Christ....
Whoever has known the spiritual beauty of the
underground church cannot be satisfied anymore with the
emptiness of some Western churches....
One out of every five people in the world live in
Communist China, where thousands of lay Christians
evangelize without "permission."
Persecution has always produced a better Christian—
a witnessing Christian, a soul-winning Christian.
Communist persecution has backfired and produced serious,
dedicated Christians such as are rarely seen in free lands.
These people cannot understand how anyone can be a
Christian and not want to win every soul they meet....
These millions of dedicated, true and fervent believers in the
lay church have been purified by the very fires of persecution which the Communists hoped would destroy them....
In a letter smuggled out secretly, the underground church
said, "We don't pray to be better Christians, but that we
may be the only kind of Christians God means us to be:
Christlike Christians, that is, Christians who bear willingly
the cross for God's glory."

RICHARD WURMBRAND
FOUNDER OF THE VOICE OF THE MARTYRS
SPENT FOURTEEN YEARS IN A COMMUNIST PRISON
ROMANIA
1940s, '50s, AND '60s

A Hopeless Cause

| Sharbil | Edessa, Parthia (Urfa, Turkey) | c. A.D. 113 |

When word reached Edessa that Emperor Trajan had commanded that all Roman citizens should sacrifice to the gods or face cruel torture and possibly death if they continued to disobey, a great feast was organized to all the gods. All of them were thus brought together at the great altar in the center of town and lavishly decorated. Their priests came forward and offered incense and animal sacrifices before their gods. Among these priests, none was given more respect or held in higher regard than Sharbil, the chief and ruler of all the priests. Sharbil was dressed in magnificent robes that day and wore a headpiece embossed with figures of gold. He was the one to go before the gods for the king, or whomever's price was right, to receive word from these gods and return the answer to everyone who asked of him. For this he was given a great place of honor and power in Edessa.

As these festivities were taking place, Barsamya, the pastor of the church in Edessa, along with Tiridath, an elder, and Shalula, a deacon of the church, found a private place to confront Sharbil with the evil of what was being done before them.

The King of heaven and earth, Jesus Christ, will one day demand an account of your part in all of these activities that lead people to the sin of idols that are made by men. You have used these carved stones to deceive and control them and pull them away from the God of Truth. Neither do you have any pity on your own soul which is destitute of the true life of God. You lie to everyone telling them that these dumb statues speak to you!

You must stop this damning foolishness and come to the Truth! Abandon these idols made by men and worship the

God who is the Maker of all things and His Son
Jesus Christ.

Though many would have turned away at this, Sharbil listened without making a sound. Barsamya could tell that his words
were penetrating the priest's own emptiness and shame and reveal-
ing a heart that was hungry for God. Encouraged by this, Barsamya
plunged into the Gospel story and told Sharbil of all the things
Christ had done for him and the salvation that was available
through no other name than that of Jesus. When he had finished,
Sharbil lowered his head and replied,

Oh, that I could so easily accept your words! But look at
what I am! I am an outcast from all of these things you have
said—there is no salvation for the likes of someone like me.
Why do you waste your time on one for whom there is no
hope, a man that is already dead and buried, whose life has
long passed and cannot be resuscitated? Throughout my life
I have given myself to these gods, and they have slain me
as sure as any sacrifice to them. I am the property of the evil
one. What is left for me but sacrificing to and existing by
the lie of these fake gods?

When Barsamya heard these words, he fell down at Sharbil's
feet. He looked up to him and said,

In Jesus Christ there is hope for any who will turn and healing for those that are wounded. Look at me! I will make
myself the guarantee of the abundant mercies of the Son
Christ. He will forgive all the sin that you have committed
against Him, just as he forgave all my sin. He will not withhold His grace from any who will truly turn to His ways and
take refuge in His love that He displayed by dying on the

cross for all of us. As he did with the thief who was cruci-
fied next to Him, so he will do to you or any like you, if
only you truly turn to Him.

Sharbil then reached down and lifted Barsamya back to his feet.

You are like one of those skillful doctors who feel the pain
of their patients and know they are in need of treatment. I
would go with you to the church today, except for this festival. I must see it to its end. Go now, but tomorrow night
I will come to you and turn away from these gods made
with hands and confess that the Christ is my Lord and
Savior, the Maker of all.

And the next night Sharbil and his sister, Babai, came to
Barsamya and were received by the whole church as fellow heirs in
Christ.

The next day, Sharbil left his rich robes and put on the
clothes of a commoner, such as the other Christians wore. He
determined that he would spend the rest of his life undoing the evil
he had done for the false gods by repenting of his former life before
all and turning their hearts toward the One True God. He went
through the streets greeting everyone:

May the Son, Jesus Christ, forgive me of all the sins I have
committed against you. I made you think the gods could
talk to me and that they were real, but I am here to tell you
now that they did not talk to me. As I was a cause for
abomination and evil in your life before, now I want to be
a cause for good: Don't go to the pagan temples to worship
gods that were made with hands and men's lies anymore,
but turn instead and worship God the Maker of all things.

When the crowds had heard these things, many of the most powerful and influential people in the city, a crowd of nearly seven hundred, walked with him. They told Sharbil, "From now on, we will turn from these false gods as you have and we confess the King Christ, as you have done."

Because of the revival of the church in Edessa that sprang from this, it was not long before Sharbil was brought before the Roman authorities. They put the questions to him plainly, demanding that he sacrifice to the gods as he had done before, or suffer the consequences of Emperor Trajan's decree. Though questioned many times and put through many tortures, Sharbil refused to deny King Christ. Over the following weeks, Sharbil was scourged by ten men, hung from his wrist until it dislocated, torn with comblike instruments on his side and face, scourged again on his stomach instead of his back, his face and sides burned with flames from candles, nails driven in between his eyes, hung by his feet and whipped again, his fingers crushed between pieces of wood, cooked over a fire on a large piece of metal, his bones crushed between vices, and many other tortures until he was so torn and mutilated that there was not a place of his body left intact. Yet through all of this, he returned before the judge again and again and eloquently defended the Christian faith.

It had been the judge's intention to keep him alive and never kill him, but in the end Sharbil's endurance had outlasted the cruelty and determination of his judge. Seeing nothing left of Sharbil's body to torture, so disfigured was he, the judge ordered him beheaded with a sword.

• • •

What must have gone through Barsamya's mind when God told him to go and confront Sharbil with the Truth? Who in the city could have been considered a more hopeless cause for the Gospel? And yet, when Barsamya obeyed, the light of God's Word poured in and changed Sharbil's heart so that it could never go back, no matter what.

133

Barsamya must have gone to Sharbil almost certain that the outcome would be his own death, but in his obedience that did not love his own life more than doing God's will, this "hopeless cause" became the center of a revival.

> *When my mind was blinded by all these idols had to offer, I worshipped that which I didn't understand; but today, since the eyes of my mind are now clear, it is no longer possible that I should bow again to carved stones, or that I should any longer cause others to stumble before these dead statues. For how outrageous is it for someone who walks by the light of day with his eyes wide open to stumble into what is so obviously the pit of destruction?*

134

> Sharbil
> Before the judge

> *I ask—ask the God of our Master, Jesus Christ, the God of glory—to make you intelligent and discerning in knowing him personally, your eyes focused and clear, so that you can see exactly what it is he is calling you to do, grasp the immensity of this glorious way of life he has for Christians, oh, the utter extravagance of his work in us who trust him—endless energy, boundless strength!*

> Paul
> Another man who had been a "hopeless cause"
> (Ephesians 1:17–19 THE MESSAGE)

The true Christian is like sandalwood, which imparts its fragrance to the ax which cuts it, without doing any harm in return.

SUNDAR SINGH
DISAPPEARED TAKING THE GOSPEL TO TIBET
1929

135

A flower, if you bruise it under your feet, rewards you by giving you its perfume. Likewise Christians, tortured by the Communists, rewarded their torturers by love. We brought many of our jailers to Christ. And we are dominated by one desire: to give Communists who have made us suffer the best we have, the salvation which comes from our Lord Jesus Christ.

RICHARD WURMBRAND
FOUNDER OF THE VOICE OF THE MARTYRS
SPENT FOURTEEN YEARS IN A COMMUNIST PRISON
ROMANIA
1940s, '50s, AND '60s

"I Am Tied by the Scriptures"

Martin Luther	Germany	1483-1546

Around 1501 two bright law students were walking through a field in Germany, perhaps discussing the great careers and fortunes that lay ahead of them as lawyers. The dark clouds that had gathered overhead only made them hasten their pace a little, but they were not concerned about the gathering storm. The last thing they remembered of their walk was the white flash.

When one of them awoke, he was dazed for a moment and then realized what had happened. He had been struck by lightning! Amazed that he had survived, he turned to his friend to wonder at their luck, but his friend was not as fortunate—he was dead.

Devastated by this event, Martin Luther dropped out of law school without telling anyone why and joined the hermitage of St. Augustine, hoping he would find an answer there to why his life had been spared when he should have died with his friend.

As he was always a student, it was not long before Martin Luther had read the writings of St. Augustine and others who left their writings in the library of the hermitage. One day while looking for something else to read in the library, he happened upon a Latin Bible, which he had never seen before. He devoured the contents of the Bible quickly over the following weeks and was surprised at how little the church of his day had to do with what was written in it.

Thus he felt the call to the ministry and became a priest. His scholarship in the Bible and knowledge of the Christian fathers became so well known that he was invited to become a teacher at the newly forming University of Wittenberg sometime in 1508.

Though the university had wanted Luther for his reputation and standing to give credibility to their faculty, Luther was more interested in continuing to learn himself. He had lengthy discussions with another more experienced Augustine monk there, whom Luther greatly respected. They talked about various subjects in their time together, but again and again their discussions returned to the topic of the forgiveness of sins. At that time the established church taught that only through a priest could one's sins be forgiven, and often there were certain works or payments that had to accompany that. But Luther's friend pointed him to the writings of St. Bernard for a response to this: "This is the testimony that the Holy Ghost gives you in your heart, saying, your sins are forgiven. For this is the opinion of the apostle, that man is freely justified by faith."

We are justified by faith. The thought seemed to take possession of Luther's mind as he began to see it everywhere in things he read, especially in the letters of Paul to the church. This stayed with him for some time as he saw more and more that the practices of the state church seemed to have very little to do with faith in Jesus Christ and everything to do with obtaining more power and wealth. He especially saw this when he went to the Church in Rome to represent his university in debating an issue there before the church leadership.

Upon returning from this trip to Germany, Luther was made a doctor of divinity and started teaching directly from the Bible rather than from other texts, especially the books of Romans and Psalms. His words were so different from what any of the other teachers were teaching that "there seemed, after a long and dark night, a new day to arise, in the judgment of all pious and prudent men." He pointed to Jesus as the only remitter of sins and taught that people should gratefully embrace this free gift and not despise what it cost Jesus on the cross to win it. If people would truly come to Jesus and ask Him to forgive their sins, then there would be such a change that all around should notice.

The more he taught this, the more he felt his own heart

137

change and the hungrier he got for God's Word. He soon began studying Greek and Hebrew so that he could read the scriptures in their original forms.

In 1513 the church in Rome made a tremendous push to finish a new cathedral and needed money badly for the project. In order to raise the necessary funds, the churches throughout Europe began selling indulgences—documents absolving people of sin that were sold like lottery tickets. People began buying these for sins they were planning to commit later! Luther was outraged at this direct contradiction to the Word of God.

Thus on the eve of All Saints' Day in 1517, Martin Luther quietly nailed a notice to the chapel door of the church next to the castle in Wittenberg. In it he cited ninety-five statements of faith that he had taken directly from the Bible, all of which condemned the current hypocrisy of the church leadership and doctrines they were pushing.

Yet rather than seeing the reason in Luther's statements and accepting the correction of Scripture, the church leadership saw this as a threat to their lifestyles and authority. Fearing what others would think more than they feared God, they began to seek a way to silence Luther, even if it meant killing him.

Traps were set for Luther on several occasions, but somehow he walked into them to preach the Truth from the Scriptures and then out again without harm. On one such occasion in 1521, he was called to Worms in France to debate his teachings. Many warned him that it was a trap, but he responded, "Since they have asked me to come, I have decided to go in the name of our Lord Jesus Christ; even though I know there are as many devils to resist me as there are tiles to cover the houses in Worms."

Yet rather than a debate, he had come to a trial to find him guilty of heresy. All of his work was called into question. The ultimatum was set before him: "It is now time to answer the Holy Roman Emperor's demand. Will you stand by all you have written in your books, or admit and reject the parts of them that do not agree with the teachings of the state church?"

Luther answered without raising his voice, but he spoke with conviction and sincerity. "His honor the emperor and you judges here have asked for a plain answer, so I will say this as frankly as I can, without trying to be clever or insincere. If I were not already convinced that what I read in the Scriptures is truth—for no church leader, council, king, or emperor, all of whom are fallible men, can tell me otherwise—I would gladly renounce my writings. But my conscience is bound and held captive by these Scriptures and the Word of God, so I may not take back anything I have said before, especially considering that it is not godly or lawful to go against my conscience. I will stand by this, I cannot do otherwise. I have nothing else to say. God have mercy upon me!"

139

But the prince and the judges present were not satisfied with this answer. "You are required by the emperor to give a simple yes or no answer. Do you say that your works are truly Christian or not?"

"You have given me nothing to show that I am wrong; therefore, I am tied by the Scriptures."

Luther was dismissed and in the coming hours he was expelled from the established church and labeled a heretic. However, when they sought to imprison him, he was nowhere to be found.

Luther returned to Germany and went into hiding for some months. As always, though, he could never be idle in proclaiming the Truth, so he used the time to translate the Bible into German. He later returned to Wittenberg and began publishing books and essays against the false doctrines the church had been teaching and printed his translation of the Bible so that others could read and understand the Scriptures for themselves. Where the established church leaders probably would have had him executed or assassinated in better times, their own lusts had thrown them into a power struggle with the Holy Roman Empire, and many of them were imprisoned themselves. Because of this distraction, Luther's writings flourished and were widely distributed.

In 1527, Luther suffered from a heart attack that nearly killed him. In the coming years he spoke less and less in public as his health deteriorated. Yet his mark had been made and the question of final authority over Truth was out in the open for all to consider—would the Christian faith be governed by the Word of God or fallible men? Though the question still rages today in many ways, if it had not been for the stand of such people as Martin Luther, it would not be a question we would have the right to decide by the dictates of our own consciences and our own reading of God's Word.

In 1546 Martin Luther died peacefully at the age of sixty-three, with the final words on his lips being: "I commend my spirit into Your hands, because You have redeemed me, O God of Truth! 'God so loved the world, that He gave His only begotten Son, that whosoever believeth in Him should not perish, but have life everlasting.' "

• • •

True revolutionaries must have a love for the Truth that does not settle for what someone else says or believes. They will dig and question and read and study until they find the smallest vein of truth, and then they will mine that until they find more. They are not satisfied until they have something they can hold on to solidly, and then they will be open to the possibility that even that is probably incomplete, and keep looking. Meanwhile they do not preach their opinions and convictions as a reason to put others down, nor do they judge others because they fit a different mold. They stand, humbly, and say, "As far as I can tell, this is the truth. I am open to discussing it and being convinced otherwise, but if you've got nothing better to offer me, then I am going to hold to what I believe—I will stand by this, I cannot do otherwise." Then see if what is really important doesn't come to the forefront and begin to set people free from the constraints that are keeping them from God.

This is what Luther did at Worms. He didn't waste time bickering about meaningless opinions. He held to a crucial question about Truth, and that got a lot of people thinking. Once they started thinking and asking the right questions and sincerely looking for Truth, God was able to reveal himself to them.

Warn them before God against pious nitpicking, which chips away at the faith. It just wears everyone out. Concentrate on doing your best for God, work you won't be ashamed of, laying out the truth plain and simple. Stay clear of pious talk that is only talk. Words are not mere words, you know. If they're not backed by a godly life, they accumulate as poison in the soul.

Paul

(2 Timothy 2:14–16 THE MESSAGE)

141

Free From Fear of Suffering

| Faninus | Italy | 1100s |

Through careful study, Faninus became convinced of certain errors in the teachings of the established church. As he began to share these with others, hoping for a revival to the truth of God's laws, he was arrested and cast into prison.

He was urged by family and friends who visited to recant from his new beliefs and accept the authority of the established church. In the presence of his wife and children, he recanted what he had been teaching and was released.

Then, however, he found the chains of guilt far heavier than those of the prison. His conscience gave him no rest, and he repented of his rejection of the Truth and began again to win converts to the truths he had discovered in his studies, announcing to all that the church had adopted error as doctrine, and he would not live by or keep silent about such lies. His endeavors brought many to a closer walk with Jesus.

Again, when his evangelism was learned of, he was imprisoned and asked to recant his teachings or suffer the consequences. "I scorn living a life in denial of truth," he told his captors. "I will not renounce my beliefs again, no matter what you threaten."

Knowing what had caused his first surrender to them, his accuser then asked him, "Do you intend then to leave your wife and children in the distress of having no caretaker?"

"I shall not leave them in distress," he replied. "I have recommended them to the care of an excellent trustee."

"A trustee? What trustee?" the accuser asked with some surprise.

"Jesus Christ is the trustee I mean, and I don't think I could commit them to the care of a better one." After this response,

142

Faninus was sentenced to execution.

On the day his sentence was to be carried out, one of his jailers commented, "It is strange you should appear so merry upon such an occasion, when Jesus Christ himself, just before His death, was in such agonies that he sweated blood and water."

"Christ sustained all manner of pains and conflicts," Faninus replied, "facing hell and death for our sins. Through His suffering, He freed those who believe in Him from the fear of facing their sufferings ourselves."

After this, Faninus was strangled to death, his corpse burned to ashes and then scattered to the wind.

• • •

If we confess our sins, He is faithful and righteous to forgive us our sins and to cleanse us from all unrighteousness.

John
(1 John 1:9 NAS)

So, dear brothers and sisters, work hard to prove that you really are among those God has called and chosen. Doing this, you will never stumble or fall away. And God will open wide the gates of heaven for you to enter into the eternal Kingdom of our Lord and Savior Jesus Christ.

Peter
(2 Peter 1:10-11 NLT)

"Simon, son of Jonas,
do you love me more than these?"
Peter looked at Jesus.
"Yes, Lord," he answered. "You know I love you."
"Then feed my lambs." Then he looked at Peter
again. "Simon, son of Jonas, do you love me?"
Peter was perplexed.
"Yes, Lord, you know I love you."
"Feed my sheep." Then, with hardly a break, Christ
asked again, "Simon, son of Jonas, do you love me?"
Peter was grieved.
Three times he had denied Christ; now three times
Jesus questioned his love. He responded slowly this
time, as if weighing the significance of each word in
his heart, "Lord, you know all things.
You know that I love you."
"Feed my sheep," Jesus answered. Then He added,
"When you were young, you dressed yourself and
went wherever you wanted; but when you are old,
another will dress you and take you where you don't
want to go." Then Jesus said, "Follow me."

JESUS AND PETER
(JOHN 21:15–19, PARAPHRASED)

Footprints in the Snow		
Bible Smugglers	Romania/ Ukrainian Border	Late 1940s

In post–World War Two Eastern Europe, Bibles were considered as dangerous as guns for the countries controlled by the Soviet Union. Either was always immediately confiscated, and the bearer instantly imprisoned as a subversive. For this reason, the borders between the Soviet Socialist Republics were ardently guarded against any contraband that might come in from the freer—for the time being—Eastern Block countries that the Soviet Union had been awarded control over after helping to defeat the Nazis and to prevent any who might want to escape through the Eastern Block to Western Europe.

This cold winter night was no exception. Though the temperature was well below freezing, and several inches of new snow blanketed the hills, the Soviet guards were patrolling their usual routes. The sky was cloudy and there was no moon to be seen, so the soldiers traipsed through the snow with their flashlights shining in every direction.

Suddenly a whistle broke the silence of the night, and a flare shot into the sky. From all over, the sounds of dogs and shouting converged on the spot where the signal had been given. When the others arrived the guard merely pointed to the snow. Four sets of footprints were making their way toward Romania! The guards rushed down the path hoping to catch the fugitives before they crossed the border.

Some hours later the leader of the four Romanian Christians finished the story to the small congregation of the Ukrainian underground church with a laugh as they all held the Bibles he had given them in their hands. "Yes, comrades," he said affectionately, using the word with a deeper meaning than any Communist Party

145

member had ever used it, "we stood there like statues, frozen at the sound. Then slowly, the noises grew more and more distant. And with our backs to the Ukraine, we continued walking backward through the snow, leaving footprints as if they were headed for Romania!" They all laughed at this with tears in their eyes, hugging their new Bibles with both arms.

• • •

The power of God's Word and the price that has been paid that we might have it can never be underestimated. In some countries today owning an entire Bible of one's own seems a dream beyond possibility. It is not uncommon that even an entire fellowship would not have an entire Bible among them. They might just have a few books, or even a single page to share. This they trade off to take home and study for a time, until it is someone else's turn to have the Scriptures.

And for this short time that they have His Word, they are in more danger than ever. If they are caught with it, they could be imprisoned or killed. Yet they gladly risk everything to read the letters God has written to them. The price of persecution is not too much to pay for the sake of knowing Jesus better.

If you are not willing to die for what is in the Bible, you should not give money for Bibles. Because if you give, we will smuggle more Bibles. And if we smuggle more Bibles, there will be more martyrs.

Richard Wurmbrand
Founder of The Voice of the Martyrs
Spent fourteen years in a Communist prison
Romania
1940s, '50s, and '60s

"The Marriage of the Lamb Is Come!"

| James Renwick | Edinburgh, Scotland | 1688 |

As James Renwick sat at dinner with his mother, sisters, and some Christian friends, a drumbeat sounded in the distance. This was the first warning to the city that the executioners were ready and it was time to gather in the Grassmarket.

At this sound, James leaped to his feet. "Let us be glad and rejoice! For the marriage of the lamb is come!" James then took the opportunity to give a short message on the marriage supper of the lamb, which he would partake of that day. Then he invited them all to come to his wedding, meaning his execution that was to take place in a short time.

The drum had continued to beat all the while and continued as James made his way up the scaffold to the hangman. When he reached the top, he turned and lifted his voice so that all within earshot could hear:

> Spectators, I must tell you I am come here this day to lay down my life for adhering to the truths of Christ, for which I am neither afraid nor ashamed to suffer. No, I bless the Lord that ever He counted me worthy to suffer anything for Him; and I desire to praise His grace that He has not only kept me free from being polluted by sin in the time I have lived and in the time I was a child, and such that I was stained with, He washed me clean in His own blood....
>
> I think the truth is worth many lives, and if I had ten thousand I would think it little enough to lay them all down to preserve it....
>
> I join my testimony with all those that have been sealed by blood, shed either on the scaffolds, fields, or seas, for the cause of Christ.

147

One of the guards stepped forward to silence him, but James merely turned to him politely with a winning grin and said, "I am near done." Then he continued,

> You that are the people of God, do not grow weary in maintaining the testimony of the day, in your stations and places; and whatever you do, make certain you have a part in Christ, for the storm is coming that will shake the very foundations of your faith. Scotland must be rid of Scotland before delivery will come. And you that are strangers to God, break off from your sins by repenting, or else even I will be a witness against you on the day of the Lord.

At this, they stopped him and stepped him back to put the noose around his neck; all the while he sang a song from Psalm 103 and quoted from Revelation 19. Then he prayed,

> God, I die in faith that you will not leave Scotland, but that you will make the blood of my witness the seed of your church here, and return again, and be glorious in our land. And now, Lord, I am ready—"the bride, the lamb's wife, has made herself ready."

The executioner stepped forward and placed the hood over his face, but still he would not stop trying to encourage those around him. Though he could not see him, he turned to the friend who had attended him and said,

> Farewell. Be diligent in your duty. Make your peace with God, through Christ. There is a great trial coming. As to those remaining behind me, I have committed them to God. Tell them from me not to weary, nor to be discouraged in maintaining the testimony of the truth. Let them not

quit nor forgo one of these despised truths. Keep your ground, and the Lord will provide teachers and ministers, and when He comes, He will make these despised truths glorious upon the earth.

Then, as they dropped the ladder to make the rope go taut, he died with these words on his lips: "Lord, into your hands I commit my spirit, for you have redeemed me, Lord God of truth."

• • •

"Let us rejoice and be glad and give the glory to Him, for the marriage of the Lamb has come and His bride has made herself ready."

And it was given to her to clothe herself in fine linen, bright and clean; for the fine linen is the righteous acts of the saints.

And he said to me, "Write, 'Blessed are those who are invited to the marriage supper of the Lamb.' "

Recorded by John
(Revelation 19:7–9 NAS)

149

A Spectacle to the World

| Gasper Kaplitz | Bohemia | Mid-1400s |

As the eighty-six-year-old nobleman approached the platform where he was to be beheaded, he said, "Behold a miserable ancient man who has often begged God to take him out of this wicked world, but has not been able until now to receive his desire; for God reserved me till these latter years to be a spectacle to the world and a sacrifice to himself. Therefore God's will be done."

Considering his age, one of the officers overseeing the execution told him that he would be immediately released if he would ask for pardon.

"Ask pardon!" he answered. "I will ask pardon from God, whom I have often offended, but none of the emperor, whom I have never offended. No, I will die innocent with a clear conscience. I would not be separated from my noble companions in the faith."

Having said his piece, he cheerfully laid his neck upon the block.

• • •

If you belonged to the world, its people would love you. But you don't belong to the world. I have chosen you to leave the world behind, and that is why its people hate you.

Jesus
(John 15:19 CEV)

They did not receive the things God had promised, but from a long way off they saw them and welcomed them, and admitted openly that they were foreigners and refugees on earth. Those who say such things make it

*clear that they are looking for a country of their own....
Instead, it was a better country they longed for, the
heavenly country. And so God is not ashamed for them
to call him their God, because he has prepared a city
for them.*

(Hebrews 11:13–14, 16 TEV)

151

The times make demands on you in the same way a sailor requires wind and as one tossed by the sea requires a safe harbor. Be vigilant as God's athlete. Stand firm like an anvil under the blow of the hammer. It is the part of the great athlete to receive blows and to conquer. Be yet more diligent than you are. Learn to know the times.

152

IGNATIUS
IN A LETTER TO POLYCARP WRITTEN ON THE WAY TO
ROME, WHERE HE WAS TO BE EXECUTED
C. A.D. 111

"The Only Gold I Have to Offer"

Alphege	England	1012

Alphege was born into a wealthy family and at a young age gave himself to God. Fearing the entrapments of materialism he saw in the society of his parents, Alphege renounced the world and served in a monastery, to the great sorrow of his mother. However, he remained dutiful and respectful to his parents through this time until his desires for knowing God more perfectly pushed him to join the abbey of Bath, find a deserted cell there, and shut himself up determined to know all God had for him. As his dedication and humility became known, many of those in the abbey as well as outside came to him for instruction and guidance, and, at thirty-one years of age, Alphege was asked to take over the leadership of the abbey.

That same year, however, Alphege was asked to take over the leadership of the church in Winchester. Seeing that he could do more for the community as a bishop than as the leader of a monastery, Alphege went dutifully. During his twenty years there, the charity of the church he ran was so great that there were no beggars to be found anywhere in the district of Winchester.

These were still violent times for England, and they were subjected to frequent raids from the Danes. In his tenth year in Winchester, King Ethelred the Unready asked Alphege to mediate with the invaders. Yet instead of a political mission, Alphege saw it as a ministry task. Through his negotiations, the Danish chieftain Anlaf gave his life to Christ. A tribute was arranged to be paid to Anlaf and another chieftain, Swein, and Anlaf vowed to never lead his troops against Britain again.

In 1005, Alphege was asked to take over the leadership in the district of Canterbury. In his humility, Alphege thought the task of

the management of so large a responsibility beyond himself, but in the end was convinced to accept the post.

Though Anlaf kept his promise to never war on Britain again, other Danes were wreaking havoc in their raids. Alphege saw that the church did what it could to aid those devastated by these attacks.

In 1011, when Canterbury was threatened with invasion by the Danes, the nobles in the area urged Alphege to seek safety elsewhere, but he said he would not be a hireling that deserted his flock in times of danger. During the siege he made repeated appeals to the Danes to spare the innocent while preparing his congregation against the worst, both physically and spiritually. Constant prayer went up for divine protection.

When at last the Danes broke through the city gates, they massacred all in their path regardless of age or gender. Upon hearing of this, Alphege, who at the time was in the church with the monks, rushed out of the church, ignoring the monks' protests, and rushed to where the fighting was the heaviest, making it miraculously through the Danish troops toward their leaders.

"Spare these innocents!" he implored them as he went. "There is no glory in spilling their blood! If you must, turn your anger against me instead. I am the one who has rebuked you for your cruelties; it is I who has fed, clothed, and ransomed your captives."

Alphege was seized by the Danes and treated barbarously, being forced to helplessly watch his cathedral burn, the decimation of his monks and the citizens of Canterbury, as well as being beaten, kicked, and bound in irons and having his face torn. Eventually he was imprisoned in a filthy dungeon for several months. All the time, Alphege used the time to "negotiate" with the Danes as he had before—he preached the Gospel to all he could.

The Danes set a ransom of three thousand pounds for Alphege, counting on the riches of the church to pay it, yet while others were ransomed and freed, Alphege refused to pay. When some visiting friends came and suggested he impose a tax on those of Canterbury to pay for his release, Alphege responded, "What reward can I hope for if I spend upon myself what belongs to the poor? Better give to the poor what is ours than take from them what little they have."

As Alphege persisted in his refusal, he was beaten with blunt weapons and bruised with stones in vain attempts to make him give in. When an ultimatum was made by the commander of the Danish fleet, that he must now pay the ransom or suffer torture and death, Alphege responded, "The only gold I have to offer you is the true wisdom that comes from the knowledge and worship of the living God. If you will not accept that, then it will fare worse for you than Sodom, and your empire will not last long in Britain."

In response, Alphege was knocked to the ground with the backs of battle-axes, and those present began to stone him. In the midst of this, Alphege managed to raise himself a little and pray, "O good Shepherd! O unmatched Shepherd! Look with compassion on the children of your church, which I, dying, commend to your care."

A Dane whom Alphege had converted and baptized not long before was horror-stricken at this sight and, taking pity on him to end his suffering quickly, rushed into the midst of the beatings and beheaded Alphege with his battle-ax.

● ● ●

The Good Shepherd puts the sheep before himself, sacrifices himself if necessary. A hired man is not a real shepherd. The sheep mean nothing to him. He sees a wolf come and runs for it, leaving the sheep to be ravaged and scattered by the wolf. He's only in it for the money. The sheep don't matter to him.

Jesus

(John 10:11–13 THE MESSAGE)

155

When your enemies see that you are so determined that neither sickness, fancies, poverty, life, death, nor sins discourage you, but that you will continue to seek the love of Jesus and nothing else, by continuing your prayer and other spiritual works, they will grow enraged and will not spare you the most cruel abuse.

Walter Hilton
A Carthusian monk
England
Died 1396

"If You Only Knew Jesus"

Felicitas and Her Seven Sons	Rome	c. A.D. 161

"There are women who blaspheme the gods as well, Emperor," continued the priest in his plea to resume the persecution of Christians that had ended at Trajan's death roughly forty-five years earlier. "She and her brood of seven boys spread the Christian religion everywhere they go, right under your feet here in Rome! They pull people daily from the worship of the gods. It is a mockery and affront to your eminence!"

Emperor Antonius stirred uneasily at this. The priest saw that he had driven home his point. "Very well, then. I need not be mocked in my very own city. Have the prefect arrest her and threaten her. If she will not return to the worship of the gods, then he can deal with her."

Publius, the prefect of Rome, was not pleased with his task. Felicitas was well known in the city and well loved. For this reason, he first asked her and her sons to see him in his home secretly that he might question them and dismiss the case without being under the eye of the priests. Though this was in the prefect's home, it still had an official air as guards stood by them all and around Felicitas as Publius spoke to her. He made the initial plea with soft words and promises, but as she remained resolute in her refusal to denounce Jesus, his tone turned to shouts and threats of the severest tortures.

To both, Felicitas's words were frank and direct: "You do not move me with either your flattering words and promises nor am I intimidated by your threats; because I have experienced in my own heart the workings of the Holy Spirit who gives me a living power and prepares me for the struggles of torture so that I can endure anything that you might do to me and hold fast to the confession of my faith."

Seeing that he was wasting his time to push them further at this point, Publius then sent them away to think over their

decisions. The next morning he summoned them as he sat in the square before the temple of Mars.

From here he took a different tack. "Very well, then, Felicitas, if you are satisfied to die, then die alone, but have a mother's pity and compassion on your sons and instruct them at least to save their own lives by sacrificing to the gods."

Felicitas bristled at this. "Your 'compassion' is pure wickedness! And your advice is nothing but cruelty, for if my sons sacrifice to the gods, they will not save their lives but surrender them to the hellish fiends who are your gods! They would become their slaves and be chained in darkness for everlasting fire." Then she turned to her sons. "Remain steadfast in your faith and in your confession. Jesus and His saints are waiting for you in heaven. Therefore, fight bravely for your souls and show that you are faithful in the love of Christ, the love with which He loves you and you Him."

"Woman!" the prefect interrupted. "How dare you defiantly encourage your sons to defy the commands of the emperor under my very nose! Isn't it better that you instruct them to obedience rather than rebelliousness?"

But Felicitas knew what she was saying and what kind of death would probably result from her boldness. Yet she still persisted. Rather than condemning the prefect, though, she turned to him tenderly and bravely to try to bring him to the Truth. "Prefect, if you only knew our Lord and Savior Jesus Christ, and the power of His divinity and majesty, you would know better than to try to draw us away from Him, and you would stop this persecution. You would know that we cannot curse Him or turn away from Him, for anyone who curses Christ and His faithful ones curses God himself, who by faith lives in our hearts."

At this the guard that stood by her turned to her and struck her hard with his fist across her mouth, hoping to silence her, but even at this she continued to warn her sons against denying their faith and to fear neither torture nor painful death, as these were nothing compared to an eternity with Jesus in heaven.

Publius had Felicitas and her sons taken away, then brought each of the young men back one by one to question them privately. Yet whatever he promised or threatened, none of them would turn from Jesus.

Frustrated at his failure, he sent a note to the emperor that they all remained obstinate in their confession of Jesus. The emperor then sentenced them all to die at the hands of different executioners, and that Felicitas would die last of all, after she had watched each of her sons die first. Over the next four months these sentences were carried out.

Januarius, the eldest, went first while the others were forced to watch. He was scourged with a whip made up of cords that had a small ball of lead at the end of each strand. He was beaten with this on the back, neck, sides, and any other fleshy part of the body the torturer could reach with the scourge until he no longer moved.

159

Felix and Philippus, the next two oldest, followed. They were beaten to death with rods.

Sylvanus was tossed down from a great height.

The youngest three, Alexander, Vitalus, and Martialis, were each brought before their mother separately and beheaded.

Last of all, with tears glistening in her eyes at both the pain of watching her sons die and the anticipation of soon being with them again before Christ, Felicitas was beheaded with a sword.

• • •

It is one thing to believe in a cause so much that we are willing to die for it, but it is quite another to believe in it so much that we would let others suffer and die for it, especially if they are our own children and family.

For God so loved the world, that he gave his only begotten Son, that whosoever believeth in him should not perish, but have everlasting life.

Jesus
(John 3:16 KJV)

160

Was one of us ever accused on any other ground
[than that bearing the name "Christian"?]
The Christian never has to suffer for any other affairs
except those of his sect, which during all this long time
no one has ever proved guilty of incest or any cruel
act. It is for our singular innocence, our great honesty,
our justice, purity, and love of truth, yes, it is for the
living God that we are burned to death. Thus you
inflict a punishment on us which usually you do not
inflict on actual temple robbers
or enemies of the State or on the great number guilty
of high treason.

TERTULLIAN
IN A DEFENSE OF CHRISTIANITY TO SCAPULA VI
C. A.D. 150–229

"Let Me Take His Place"

| Maximilian Kolbe | Germany | 1941 |

The siren sounded and the prisoners of Maximilian Kolbe's bunker were led out into the summer morning. From the activities of the German guards it was obvious that something was wrong. Maximilian looked at the guard towers and watched the officers standing stiffly as he and the other prisoners were gathered before them.

The commandant of the prison camp stepped forward. "There has been an escape! As you know, for this ten of you will die. Let that be a lesson to the rest of you—your freedom will cost the lives of ten other men."

Ten men were selected from among the ranks and brought to the front. Maximilian watched as Sergeant Francis Gajoniczek was marched forward. "No, no, you can't! I don't want to die."

At this, Maximilian stepped forward. "Sir, I am a priest. Let me take his place. I am old. He has a wife and child."

The officer looked at him for an instant, then at the young man. He could certainly use the young man more for the daily labors that were required of the prisoners. "All right. You, back in line. Old man, you go with the others."

The ten men were taken to a cell, where they were left to starve. All the while there, Maximilian comforted the others with prayers, songs, and stories of Christ's sacrifice for all of them. At the end of two weeks only four of them were still alive and only Maximilian was fully coherent. These four were then executed with an injection of carbolic acid.

• • •

Greater love has no one than this, that one lay down his life for his friends.

Jesus

(John 15:13 NAS)

161

The Power of the Gospel and a Helping Hand

William and Catherine Booth	England	1829-1912 and 1829-1890

"Did you know that men slept out all night on the bridge?" William Booth bellowed gruffly as he entered the offices that morning.

His chief of staff, who was also his eldest son, Bramwell, replied, "Yes, I have heard of such things."

William looked back on him, shocked at the response. "How could you know about such a thing and not be doing something about it? I want a shelter provided for those poor wretches at once!"

So by January of 1888—the very next month—a building had been rented to house these people. It was the Salvation Army's first food and shelter depot. By the end of the first week more than two thousand people were being fed each day, over seven hundred of them children. A donation of six hundred pounds covered the initial cost of setting it up.

Such was a typical outreach for the Booths—seeing a need in their society and acting immediately to meet it with a helping hand, the love of God, and the message of salvation that gave people the hope they needed to escape the decay that was so prevalent in late-nineteenth-century England.

William and Catherine Booth grew up in the beginnings of the industrial revolution, when farmers and villagers were being turned into low-paid factory workers who could barely make enough to keep a roof over their families' heads. It was the England of *Oliver Twist* and *A Christmas Carol*, a place where the gap between the classes had grown so much that the poor were barely allowed in the churches, and one in ten people in England was

162

homeless and more were jobless. Of those who did have some money, much of it was absorbed by the bar owners. Prostitution rings also took advantage of these people's poverty to "buy" young girls from their parents; these girls were either employed in local brothels and kept like prisoners or shipped off to mainland Europe as white slaves.

Into this came a fiery young evangelist who was receiving little acceptance as a preacher among the denominations himself, and his quiet wife who had grown up largely housebound due to illnesses and had spent most of her youth reading the works of such ministers and revivalists as John Wesley and Charles Finney, among many others. Each individually may have accomplished little in their lifetimes, but when God brought them together, they so complemented each other's strengths that they became a powerful force for God. When they saw the needs among the poor, William decided he had finally found a congregation that could not turn him away, and Catherine supplied the organization and structure to their ministry that held everything together and ensured the proper training of their "Salvationists," soldiers who did not come from seminaries or Bible schools, but out of the pubs, off of the streets, or saved from prostitution.

It was in 1865, the same year that the Civil War ended in the United States, that the Booths declared their own revolutionary war against the social and spiritual ills of their day by opening the East London Christian Mission. In the following years their organization would become the Salvation Army and take on an air and a mission like no other Christian organization has before or since. Armed with the Gospel and a few musical instruments, these Salvationists would set themselves up in the worst parts of English cities, often right outside of pubs, and start drawing crowds to Jesus. They often took so much business away from the bars and local public houses and so challenged this way of living numbed continually by alcohol that a group of thugs and ruffians formed what they called the Skeleton Army to openly oppose them. With skull and crossbones emblazoned on their banners and armed with weapons of flour, red ochre, and deadly jagged brickbats, Skeleton Army units ferociously attacked the Salvationists. In the early days, local law enforcement would often look the other way as the Salvationists were attacked and beaten in the streets for their stands for righteousness. But the Salvationists wore their cuts and bruises like medals and returned to preach the Gospel regardless of how they were treated. It was not long before these outcasts won the support of the government, and the police dismantled the Skeleton Army and began providing regular protection for the Salvationists.

William never let anyone forget that their main purpose was to reach people with the Gospel. All the activities of the Army were focused on this. William and Catherine knew that real help and permanent change only came when the Spirit of God would touch these people's lives. Though William was a great preacher when he stood in the streets to address the crowd, he was quick to relinquish his position to others if it meant a better reception. Once when he gave up his soapbox for a Gypsy hawker to give his testimony of how God had saved him, he saw that this man drew a better response than he did. Rather than being offended, William made the presentation of testimonies a regular part of the Army's street preaching.

Catherine was also greatly on the move. Although her responsibilities in raising the Booths' nine children and overseeing the structure of the Army were certainly enough to keep her busy, she felt a call to preach as well. Though initially timid, she was soon in as much demand as a speaker, if not more, than William. In an era when women played a secondary role in society, Catherine became a strong proponent of women's leadership in the ministry and was key to seeing that there was no discrimination because of sex in the Salvation Army. Though initially opposed to this, William later admitted, "Some of my best men [officers] are women."

The Salvation Army was always quick and inventive to meet any need. William and Catherine refused to rob anyone they helped of their dignity, so there was always a small fee required to stay in any of their housing facilities. If the occupants could not pay, they were given work to cover the costs—people did everything from repairing furniture to sweeping floors in order to earn room and board. When they saw the horrid conditions in the local match factories, where the gases from the sulfuric mixtures used to make the matches rotted peoples' teeth and slowly poisoned them to death, the Salvation Amy started its own match works with open, bright, airy facilities and safer mixtures for making safer matches. Salvation Army personnel then canvassed the neighborhoods selling these matches and chastised shop owners who carried matches from the factories where workers were suffering. Financially the enterprise soon struggled and had to be closed, but by the time the factory was shut down, working conditions in the other factories had changed to match those of the Salvation Army's workshop. They had accomplished their goal.

Also, in what eventually ended up as the most publicized trial of the nineteenth century, the Booths, with the help of a local newspaperman named W. T. Stead, exposed the local white slavery trade that was being run by the prostitution rings. To do this, Stead "bought" a young girl from her mother, and with the help of a Salvationist who had been saved out of the prostitution rings, documented the girl's travels right up to the point she was to be shipped off to the European mainland. Stead printed this story and others in his newspaper, and the public outcry in reaction to his articles soon forced Parliament to raise the legal age of consent for young women from thirteen to sixteen (something that had previously allowed men to proposition teenage girls without legal repercussions) and brought the force of the law down on the brothels. In

165

reaction to this, those who profited from prostitution found the father of the young girl who had been used as the subject of the article (the girl was at this time saved and working at a Salvation Army post in France) and brought kidnapping charges against the Booths and Stead. In a trial that looked at first like it would be the end of the Salvation Army and all the Booths had accomplished, the true nature of their work came out, and instead of bringing condemnation, it won more public support for them than ever before. In the end, the Booths were absolved of all charges, and Stead spent a short three months in prison. Following that, he always wore his prison uniform on the anniversary of the verdict as if it were a badge of honor.

Then in 1890, shortly after Catherine's death, William published *The Darkest England and the Way Out*, a book exposing the ills of the impoverished and his solutions for these problems. The book was the combined efforts of William, Catherine, and Stead. It outlined the formation of employment offices, missing-persons services, and other institutions that seem the norm today but were nonexistent at the time.

By 1900 the work of the Army had spread to over twenty-five other nations around the world.

William continued to minister until his death in 1912. He often traveled by car, a novelty at the time, and was met by crowds of thousands. At his funeral, the Queen of England snuck into the back of the service unknown to anyone and sat down by a poor but neatly dressed woman. In her conversation with the woman, the queen discovered that the woman had been saved from prostitution through the Army's work. As the coffin came past them, the woman stretched out her hand to drop three faded carnations onto the lid. "What brought you here to the service?" the queen asked her as they were leaving. "Well," she replied, "he cared for the likes of us."

• • •

There are countries and entire denominations that have not existed for as long as the Salvation Army nor have accomplished as much in their entire existences. Though the Salvation Army is very different today than it was a hundred years ago, it was the strong foundation laid by the Booths that has enabled it to last as long as it has. William's uncompromising drive and thirst to spread the Gospel, and Catherine's tempering of that enthusiasm with structure and sound teaching, created a world-changing organization that still shows the importance of God's love and a helping hand today. Though few histories even mention them, they probably did more to save Victorian England from civil war and change the industrial revolution into a positive force than any political figure or statesman of the time.

167

"My father has blessed you! Come and receive the kingdom that was prepared for you before the world was created. When I was hungry, you gave me something to eat, and when I was thirsty, you gave me something to drink. When I was a stranger, you welcomed me, and when I was naked, you gave me clothes to wear. When I was sick, you took care of me, and when I was in jail, you visited me."

Then the ones who pleased the Lord will ask, "When did we give you something to eat or drink? When did we welcome you as a stranger or give you clothes to wear or visit you while you were sick or in jail?"

The king will answer, "Whenever you did it for any of my people, no matter how unimportant they seemed, you did it for me."

Jesus
(Matthew 25:34–40 CEV)

Jesus' presence always brought astonishing peace to me no matter how bad the situation I was in. Whenever I was in a prison, he was always there for me. He transformed the jail into a heaven and the burdens became blessings.

There are many Christians who do not feel His glorious presence as something real, because for them Jesus only occurs in their minds and not in their hearts. Only when someone surrenders his heart to Jesus can he find Him.

SUNDAR SINGH
DISAPPEARED TAKING THE GOSPEL TO TIBET
1929

The Seeds of Revival

| Peter Waldo | Lyons, France | c. 1160 |

"Mon Dieu, he is dead!"

Peter Waldo stared blankly at the face of his friend who now lay before them. The small group of shop owners and community leaders had been standing in the town square enjoying the long summer evening and discussing matters of local politics and interest. Suddenly their friend simply fell to the ground. When they checked him they found that he was dead. The effect upon all of them was sobering. Yet it affected Peter Waldo most of all.

This blatant example of human mortality and the brevity of life made Peter turn dramatically to God for answers. Being a wealthy merchant in Lyons with a good education, he was one of the few in town who could read the Scriptures for himself, so he turned to the texts of the Bible in his search. What he found there had a profound effect on his outlook on life.

Peter found that there was much in his own lifestyle that did not agree with the spirit of Jesus' teaching, so Peter immediately repented of his former ways and began to live a godlier lifestyle. He gave substantial amounts of money away to help the poor and needy. When a situation arose that called for decisions or correction, Peter admonished those in his household and others he came into contact with using the Word of God and a loving attitude. Those who heard him speak in this way were astonished by his wisdom and even more amazed to have the Scriptures explained to them in their own native tongue of French. Thus he encouraged them to live in true godliness and repent of anything in their lives that would displease Christ.

Over time his reputation and skillful explanations of the Scriptures caused many to seek him out for instruction. Whereas

169

many leaders and priests seemed to present and discuss right and wrong in terms of their own ideas, Peter backed up everything he said from the Scriptures. It was not long after this that he began distributing passages and chapters of the Bible that he had translated into French to any who asked. So loved was the Word of God among them that uneducated country people were able to recite entire books of the Bible by heart. Others even knew the entire New Testament. With this love for the Scriptures also went the teaching to worship Jesus and adhere to His Word above all other practices and traditions of the established church.

As Peter's wealth diminished because of his newfound generosity, his influence increased. Soon the leaders of the local church took issue with Peter's activities and demanded that he stop at once. But Peter and his growing flock, who were labeled Waldenses, knew they should obey God rather than man and continued to spread the truth of God's Word. Because the local church authorities saw this as a serious challenge to their authority and doctrines, they began seeking ways to quiet Waldo and his followers.

Almost from the start, people began to see discrepancies between what they were taught in the local church and what they read in the Bible. It was as if the teachings of the established church were there only for controlling and gaining money from the people of Lyon with little regard for what was in the Scriptures. Though the Waldenses continued to tithe to the local church, they began to more and more openly question church doctrines. Now when questions of truth came up, Peter Waldo defended their own views not only with the Scriptures but also the teachings of the early church fathers. In order to silence them, the established church excommunicated Peter and any who adhered to his teachings. When captured, if Peter's followers held to their Waldenses teachings, they were imprisoned, tortured, and executed with the sword or fire as heretics.

However, Peter followed Jesus' advice: "Whenever they persecute you in this city, flee to the next" (Matthew 10:23 NAS), and having given away almost everything he owned in Lyons, he used his network of friends and relatives to facilitate the escape of himself and his followers. Though few if any Waldenses remained in Lyons by 1170, those who dispersed settled throughout Europe, keeping Bibles in their native language and taking on new names from their new homes or whatever the local townspeople called them. When reform and return to the Scriptures as the authority of all truth erupted in these areas, it either erupted from the Waldenses or was strongly supported by them.

Just as the Word of God had spread to all corners of the world from Jerusalem when persecution arose during the time of the apostles, so the love for the Word of God also spread throughout Europe from Lyons with the persecution of the Waldenses. Though persecution followed these people wherever they went, the effect was like that of tossing water on a gasoline fire—instead of extinguishing their zeal, it only multiplied into numerous smaller fires in the surrounding areas. In this way the established church, with its foundations in the Roman Empire and its sights set on political power and control, helped spread the seeds of revival throughout Europe.

This persecution continued for nearly four hundred years, peaking between 1545 and 1560. Finally, around 1559, in a region called Piedmont in the Italian Alps, the duke of Savoy granted them protection and freedom to worship as they believed, forty-two years after Luther posted his Ninety-five Theses in Wittenberg.

• • •

Many look at church history and point their finger at one denomination or another, showing the evil that they committed or the false teachings they got into to show where that group of people was wrong and how they were right. But the truth of the matter is that the history of the body of Christ, the universal church, is only one history, and the mistakes and errors of the past belong to any who would call themselves Christian.

Infighting and political maneuvering are no less present today than they were hundreds of years ago. A key difference may be that today individual churches or denominations do not have the power to torture "heretics" or put them to death. Once hatred or bitterness rises in our hearts toward another group—whether they are part of a different denomination or part of our own congregation—we do not realize how close we are to committing the same atrocities if only we had the chance. As John said in his letter to the churches, "Anyone who hates his brother is a murderer" (1 John 3:14 NIV).

Thus Jesus Freaks constantly have before them the narrow road. Just as Jesus taught that the weeds grow up with the wheat, and we will not see them separated until the final harvest, we must realize that small seeds of bitterness, resentment, or condemnation will grow up alongside the good things of God's Word that are planted in our hearts if we do not either first stop them from entering our hearts or pluck them out while they are still small. We are not immune from the mistakes of the past unless we search our own hearts regularly to ensure that none of those things that have caused strife in the past are allowed to take root. We must constantly keep before us the example of Jesus and make sure we do not step off of the path of following His example.

The goal of our instruction is love from a pure heart and a good conscience and a sincere faith.

Paul
(1 Timothy 1:5 NAS)

172

A Bible for Sudan

Kayleen and James Jeda	U.S.A. and Sudan	2001

Kayleen sat in the service that night with her heart welling inside her with a desire to help—to do something—to make a difference for these people the minister was telling her about. But what could a thirteen-year-old girl do? What did she have to give that would make a difference? Kayleen felt helpless against this growing burden inside of her. She was used to praying with her family for those persecuted in other countries and had even prayed for one young man by name whom they had heard about from Sudan—a boy by the name of James Jeda who had been tortured with fire because he refused to convert to Islam after they had killed his parents and siblings. Still, the more the preacher spoke, the more Kayleen wanted to act. But what could she do?

The minister continued to talk about the plight of the families in Sudan and what life was like for them. There were fathers and mothers there in their late thirties who had never known a time when their country, even their own village, was not being torn apart because of the civil war (between Arab Muslims in the north and Black Christians in the south) that had been raging there since the early 1960s. Children have had to dig foxholes outside of their classrooms to hide in, as their schools are often targets of bombing raids, as are the hospitals and churches. Though approximately half of Sudan is in the Sahara, the temperatures there, especially in the Nuba mountains, where the fighting is the most intense, can get below freezing at night, and due to the lack of blankets, constant exposure to such conditions often means poor health and little sleep while shivering through the night. Though the land is rich for farming in the south, food is still scarce, as army raids often confiscate what is grown or bombs destroy fields of

crops. Thus starvation is also a problem.

Yet as always in times of war and persecution, what the Sudanese were the most hungry for was God. Because of the war, many missionary groups in other countries had stopped sending people to Sudan due to the danger, and Bibles and other Christian literature were in short supply.

Suddenly Kayleen felt a tug of hope in her heart. She looked suddenly at the youth Bible she held in her hands, with all of the doodles and notes she had made in it since she had received it as a Christmas present some three years earlier. She clutched it to her chest as the minister continued to speak.

When she heard that a family friend was going to Sudan with VOM workers, she sent the Bible with him. "Please give it to somebody special," she told her friend.

When this friend arrived in Sudan with Kayleen's Bible, among many other provisions the team had brought with them, his heart went out to all those he met. Yet as the days of their visit were coming to a close, he felt a special attachment to one young man who bore the scars of being thrown into a fire when a Muslim raiding party had killed his family. He was now living with his grandmother and was attending school, hoping to grow up to be a teacher. The missionary friend gave this young man Kayleen's Bible with some special words of encouragement. The young man's name was James Jeda.

* * *

No one can truly say they have nothing to give when God puts it into their hearts to help. What may seem little to us can mean so much to someone else. God does not measure the amount, but the willingness and obedience of the heart.

And He looked up and saw the rich putting their gifts into the treasury. And He saw a certain poor widow putting in two small copper coins. And He said, "Truly I say to you, this poor widow put in more than all of them; for

*they all out of their surplus put into the offering; but she
out of her poverty put in all that she had to live on."*

Jesus
(Luke 21:1-4 NAS)

*Two very dirty villagers came to my home one day to buy
a Bible. They had come from their village to take the job
of shoveling the frozen earth all winter long to earn
money in the slight hope they might be able to buy an old,
tattered Bible with it and take it back to their village.*

*Because I had received Bibles from America, I was able
to hand them a new Bible, not an old tattered one. They
could not believe their eyes! They tried to pay me with
the money they earned. I refused their money. They
rushed back to their village with the Bible.*

*A few days later I received a letter of unrestrained,
ecstatic joy thanking me for the Scriptures. It was signed
by thirty villagers! They had carefully cut the Bible into
thirty parts and exchanged the parts with one another!*

Richard Wurmbrand
Founder of The Voice of the Martyrs
Spent fourteen years in a Communist prison
Romania
1940s, '50s, and '60s

175

Tear me to pieces and rip my soul from my body, but you will never force that detestable word of denial from my mouth.

MICHAEL NAKASHIMA
TORTURED AND HAD BOILING WATER POURED
ON HIS HEAD AND BODY UNTIL HE DIED
JAPAN
CHRISTMAS DAY, 1628

Faithful to the End

| Luke | Greece | c. A.D. 93 |

"It seemed fitting for me as well, having investigated everything carefully from the beginning, to write it out for you in consecutive order, most excellent Theophilus; so that you may know the exact truth about the things you have been taught," wrote the physician Luke in the beginning of his gospel that was either meant for a close friend or all those who love God, as is the meaning of the name Theophilus.

As an educated man, Luke was a good companion for Paul on all of his journeys. While so many study and read to try to discover the truth of the matter, Luke chose instead to go to the source and find out for himself. Having learned of Paul during his ministry in Antioch, Luke went to hear the man speak on this new religion called Christianity. When it came time to take the message of that faith on the road, Luke volunteered to go along and record all of it for posterity. Thus Luke became the first Christian historian and contributed more to the New Testament than anyone who was not an apostle.

While other men passed in and out of Paul's ministry, Luke stuck close to the end. Not long before his execution in Rome, Paul wrote in 2 Timothy, "Do your best to come to me quickly, for Demas, because he loved this world, has deserted me and has gone to Thessalonica. Crescens has gone to Galatia, and Titus to Dalmatia. Only Luke is with me." Despite persecution and temptation, Luke had stayed faithful to the end.

After Paul's execution, Luke left Rome. He was so committed to the missionary life that he continued to travel and teach for the rest of his life. His ministry after the death of Paul lasted almost thirty years. Everywhere he traveled is not well recorded; the book

177

of Acts ends at Paul's second imprisonment, and no writings of Luke still exist beyond that. It is known, though, that he ended his days in Greece, where he preached the Gospel and opposed the worship of the Greek gods among the people of the Peloponnesian cities, probably proclaiming what he had earlier recorded in the book of Acts: "There is salvation in no one else but Jesus! There is no other name in all of heaven for people to call on to save them."

Luke so upset the world of the idolatrous priests with his teaching that they incited a mob against him and took him to an olive grove near the port city of Patras, where he was hanged to death in a green olive tree. He was eighty-four years old when he died.

• • •

Blessed are you when men hate you, and ostracize you, and heap insults upon you, and spurn your name as evil, for the sake of the Son of Man. Be glad in that day, and leap for joy, for behold, your reward is great in heaven, for in the same way their fathers used to treat the prophets....

But I say to you who hear, love your enemies, do good to those who hate you, bless those who curse you, pray for those who mistreat you. Whoever hits you on the cheek, offer him the other also; and whoever takes away your coat, do not withhold your shirt from him either. Give to everyone who asks of you, and whoever takes away what is yours, do not demand it back. And just as you want men to treat you, treat them in the same way. And if you love those who love you, what credit is that to you? For even sinners love those who love them. And if you do good to those who do good to you, what credit is that to you? For even sinners do the same thing. And if you lend to those from whom you expect to receive, what credit is that to you? Even sinners lend to sinners, in order to receive back the same amount. But love your enemies, and do good, and lend, expecting nothing in return; and your reward will be great, and you will be sons of the Most High; for He Himself is kind to ungrateful and evil men.

Jesus, as recorded by Luke
(Luke 6:22–23, 27–35 NAS)

The Apostle of Germany

Boniface	Germany and Northern Europe	c. A.D. 675-754

"He cannot do it! He will be struck down by the thunderbolt of Thor!"

"He is a madman!"

"Ha! He will do it no harm! It is too big. It would take a team of men all day to cut it down. He will tire and quit before the job is done!"

Yet despite the skepticism and fear, a crowd formed and followed the Englishman, who carried an ax, through the streets of town toward the sacred oak of Geismar. The enormous tree had stood and protected the village as long as anyone could remember. No one ever dared to go near it unless carrying a sacrifice for Thor, for fear that he would be offended and remove his blessing from their crops, his protection from their lands, or even strike them dead on the spot.

Boniface, who had now been in the village for some time, already had many converts to Jesus from his preaching. However, he was not satisfied with this. He found many more of the people stubborn and in bondage to their pagan beliefs, unable or unwilling to desert their ancient tribal deities for fear of what would happen. Boniface saw the sacred oak as a symbol of all that was holding them back from coming to the one true God. He felt called of God to remove this last barrier so that the rest of the people in the region would be free to come to Christ.

As Boniface and his parade approached the tree, there was already a large crowd waiting to see if the rumors were true about what the Englishman planned to do. As they saw him approach, someone said, "We should stop him and have done with this foolishness. This foreigner has no right to bring down the wrath of the gods upon us!"

"No," cried another, "let the gods defend themselves. If Thor does not have the power to stop one crazy Englishman, then perhaps the God he preaches is the one to follow."

A chorus of others agreed and it was decided to wait and see what happened.

Boniface walked straight up to the tree and took the ax in his hand, sizing up the job he had before him. He had never before been this close to the tree, and it seemed larger than he had remembered. However, without hesitation he took the ax in hand, bowed his head to say a short prayer, then raised up the ax and took the first swing.

The crowd gasped and took a step back, looking at the sky as the blade took its first bite out of the tree.

As Boniface raised his ax for a second swing, a strong wind kicked up behind him and bore down on them all. Boniface dropped his ax to cover his face from the debris that was kicking up from the ground with the gust. Suddenly the trunk of the tree groaned and a cracking sound filled the air. As Boniface and the townspeople now turned to look, the oak began to lean away from the wind and groan even louder. Suddenly with a few loud pops and snaps the entire tree tumbled over and shattered into four huge pieces as it struck the ground. As the people stared in unbelief at the fallen giant, they could see that the inside of the tree had rotted away from within.

Boniface used the wood to build a church on that very spot, and so many more came to Jesus afterward that it was as if his mission there had only just begun.

Frisia
A.D. 754

For the rest of his life, Boniface continued on as a missionary in Germany, France (to the Franks), and the areas that are today Belgium and the Netherlands. When he was seventy-four and his eyesight failing, he had pushed into Frisia, just beyond the protection of the Frankish princes, with a group of fifty-two missionaries taking the Gospel to the people there. Again they had great success and were rising early on the morning of Pentecost to finish the preparation for baptizing their latest group of converts in the River Boorn. Suddenly a harsh and violent ruckus shook the camp as a mob attacked.

"Do not fight back!" Boniface called to the other missionaries. "Follow the example of our Lord in Gethsemane!"

In a matter of minutes, the entire missionary team lay massacred, with Boniface left among the last to die. As he was finally attacked, he instinctively raised the book he had been holding to protect himself, but he died from the first blow to his head. The book fell beside him, twice hacked and now covered with Boniface's blood. It was a copy of the first volume of Ambrose's *On the Advantage of Death*.

• • •

Supernatural boldness is a gift anyone can tap into through prayer and knowing God personally. Though we sometimes go out on a limb to try to accomplish something and fail, the number of times we go out on that limb and accomplish something for God more than makes up for any failures. Besides, how many of us really test that limit? Sure, it would be foolish to walk into the front of a building and announce to the crowd that Jesus was going to blow it over to prove His power, but what about looking the fool to preach in the streets of your city, or go on a missions trip and share your testimony? Few if any will tell you that they were sorry they did such things. Most are glad and hungry for a chance to do it again.

Certainly boldness must be tempered with wisdom, but far too often we lack boldness more out of fear than wisdom.

Revivals happen when people are bold because they are hooked up to God's will for their lives, their communities, and their world. Obeying God's will with confidence makes all the difference. But that boldness does not come from determination; rather, it comes from knowing God will follow up when you go out on that limb.

> **Let us fight for the Lord in these days of bitterness and affliction. If this be the will of God, let us die for the holy laws of our fathers, that we may arrive with them at the eternal inheritance.**
>
> Boniface

> **Take care of their threats and give your servants fearless confidence in preaching your Message, as you stretch out your hand to us in healings and miracles and wonders done in the name of your holy servant Jesus.**
>
> A prayer of the early church
> (Acts 4:29–30 THE MESSAGE)

183

As the Communist atheists allowed no place
for Jesus in their hearts, I decided I would leave
not the smallest place for Satan in mine.

RICHARD WURMBRAND
FOUNDER OF THE VOICE OF THE MARTYRS
SPENT FOURTEEN YEARS IN A COMMUNIST PRISON
ROMANIA
1940S, '50S, AND '60S

"Our Father Foxe"

| John Foxe | England | 1516-1587 |

Young John Foxe had proven himself such a bright young man since his coming to Oxford at the age of sixteen that he was chosen as a fellow of Magdalen College there in 1539, an honor seldom bestowed except in cases of great distinction. He soon made a mark for himself as a poet and writer, but his thoughts turned to the more serious issues of religion and the questions that had erupted from the writings of a monk in Germany named Martin Luther and John's martyred friend, William Tyndale. "Is it necessary for priests to act as mediators between God and man? Shouldn't people be able to read the Scriptures for themselves and not have them interpreted for them by someone else?"

185

John made a thorough study of both ancient and modern church history to see how these controversies had developed. He studied the works of the Greek and Latin Fathers, the transactions and decrees of church councils, and acquired a very competent skill in the Hebrew language to study the Scriptures. It was not uncommon for him to work late into the night, often passing the entire night without any sleep.

He began going to a grove near the college that was frequented by the students in the evening on account of its isolation and quiet. On these solitary walks he would pour forth his prayers and questions to God with heavy sobs and tears. It was not long before he was overheard and reported to the college. These nightly retirements gave rise to the first suspicion of his alienation from the dictates of the state church.

Being pressed for an explanation of his conduct, he refused to deny his convictions and was, by the sentence of the college, convicted, condemned, and expelled as a heretic.

Upon leaving Magdalen College, John found employment as a tutor in the home of Sir Thomas Lucy of Warwickshire, which was within walking distance of Stratford on Avon, where William Shakespeare was born some years later in 1584. Here John married but soon fled for fear of the local church authorities. Though Henry VIII, king of England during this time, had broken with the Church of Rome for his own reasons, forming the Church of England with himself as its head, he had not broken with the traditions that empowered the Roman church. Persecution for "heresy" was still common, even though the accusation was used more to eliminate political opponents than for any heartfelt religious convictions. People who were labeled as "Reformers" were seen as a danger to the structure of the Church of England and the crown and could not be left to spread their questioning teachings wherever they would like. John soon came to learn that his name was being discussed in the local church hierarchy as someone who may have to be dealt with.

So John and his wife fled for a short time to the home of his in-laws but soon headed for London in the last years of Henry VIII's rule. Here, being unknown and finding no employment, he and his wife nearly starved to death.

Yet one day as he was sitting in St. Paul's Church, exhausted with hunger, a stranger took a seat beside him and courteously greeted him. John did not recognize the man, but before he could respond to the kind greeting, the stranger thrust a sum of money into his hand. "Cheer up," he said to John. "In a few days new prospects will present themselves to see you through." Then the man just walked away. John never discovered who he was.

Three days later he received an invitation from the duchess of Richmond to tutor the children of the earl of Surrey, who, together with his father, the duke of Norfolk, was imprisoned in the Tower by the jealousy and ingratitude of King Henry. This employment supported the Foxes for some time.

In 1547 Henry VIII died, and his ten-year-old son, Edward IV, took the throne. Edward's short reign was friendly to the Reformers, but he died six years later. After Edward's death, Henry's eldest daughter (and Edward's older sister), Mary I, became queen, and the tide of opinion and political power swung violently back to the doctrines that had originated in Rome. In the next five years, nearly three hundred people were executed for "heresy."

During Edward's reign, John's outspokenness on the truth of the Scriptures and every person's right to read them for themselves made enemies among those who still quietly supported the Church of Rome. Most notably among these was Dr. Gardiner, who became the bishop of Winchester when Mary I took power. Thomas, duke of Norfolk, who had been one of Master Foxe's pupils, convinced him to stay in England under his protection, but it soon became evident from the bishop's frequent visits and questions about John that it was not safe for him to remain.

John and his wife, who was pregnant at the time, attempted to sail for the mainland, but a vicious storm returned them to the port from which they left a day and a half before. During that time, an officer from the bishop of Winchester with a warrant for John's arrest had knocked down the door at the place they had been staying prior to their initial departure for the mainland. Upon finding this out, John rode out of town, then sneaked back. He entreated the ship's captain to set out again as soon as the wind shifted, and two days later they landed safely in Nieuport, Belgium.

They then made their way to Basle, where, set to expose the evil behind the current church system, he published his *History of the Acts and Monuments of the Church*, which eventually became known as *Foxe's Book of Martyrs*.

In 1558, Mary I, who had become known as "Bloody Mary" for the massacres during her reign, died and was succeeded by her younger half sister, Elizabeth I. John and his family returned to England, where he was ordained in the Anglican Church. He did not, however, take an active part in the new church, but set himself to correct and verify the stories in his *Book of Martyrs*.

In 1563, when the Black Plague hit England, he stayed at his post (unlike many of his peers who fled for safety), cared for those who had no one else to care for them, and distributed money to the poor.

He became a unifying force in England, reportedly looking past all doctrinal differences and backgrounds to help any who called on the name of Jesus. He exerted his influence with Queen Elizabeth to put an end to the practice of executing those of opposing religious viewpoints. She held him in such respect that she referred to him as "Our Father Foxe," and by her order copies of the *Book of Martyrs* were placed in common halls, colleges, and chapels throughout the kingdom. Though John died in 1587, his *Book of Martyrs* has continued to exercise a great influence upon the church ever since. In fact, until the last century, most Christians had a copy of the book, which was kept with the same respect as the family Bible.

• • •

We are troubled on every side, yet not distressed; we are perplexed, but not in despair; Persecuted, but not forsaken; cast down, but not destroyed; Always bearing about in the body the dying of the Lord Jesus, that the life also of Jesus might be made manifest in our body.

(2 Corinthians 4:8–10 KJV)

If the Communists are overthrown in our country, it will be the most holy duty of every Christian to go into the streets and at the risk of his own life defend the Communists from the righteous fury of the multitudes whom they have tyrannized.

IULIU MANIU
PRIME MINISTER OF ROMANIA
(1928–30, 1932–33)
DIED IN PRISON UNDER THE COMMUNISTS
C. 1953

"I Do Not Suppose It"

Justin Martyr and Others | Rome | c. A.D. 165

A group of Christians were arrested and brought before the prefect of their province, a man by the name of Rusticus. As they stood before the judgment seat, Rusticus called Justin forward from among the others and spoke directly to him. "Above all things, you must have faith in the gods and obey the emperors."

"We have done nothing wrong," Justin replied. "We cannot be accused or condemned for obeying the commands of our Savior, Jesus Christ."

Rusticus looked at him, puzzled. "What system of philosophy do you say is true?"

Justin answered, "I have tried to learn about every system, but I have accepted the true teachings of the Christians, though they are rejected by those who would prefer to love a lie."

"So you would tell me that these teachings are the truth then, even though you stand here a criminal?"

"Yes," Justin replied, "because I follow them with their correct teaching."

Rusticus sat forward in his chair. "What sort of teaching is that?"

"Worship the one true God, the God of the Christians. He has been the only God since He made the earth and all of creation, both the things that are seen and those that are unseen. And we worship Jesus, His son, as Lord and Savior."

"You are a Christian, then?"

"Yes," Justin said, "I am a Christian."

Rusticus paused to think for a moment. "You call yourself a wise and studied man," he said while looking over those who stood with him, then to the galleries of those who had come to witness this trial, then fixed his eyes again upon Justin. "You say you have insight into what is truth. If so, answer me this: If I have you flogged and executed, do you believe you will go to heaven?"

"I believe that if I bear these things I shall have what Jesus promised me," Justin replied. "I know that His divine gift of salvation will stay with all who hold to His name until the end of the world."

"I take it, then, that you think you will go to heaven and receive some appropriate reward there?"

"I do not suppose it; I know it. I am certain of it."

Rusticus sighed in exasperation. "Then there is only one thing left and your life rides on it. You must come forward and sacrifice to the Roman gods."

Justin did not move, nor did he delay in his response. "No one in his right mind would turn his back on his relationship with the one true God by showing even the slightest respect for these godless statues."

Rusticus's temper flared and his voice carried every ounce of threat he could muster. "You have no choice. You either obey, or I will have you punished and executed without mercy."

"You speak of punishment and death as if it is to be feared, but the truth of the matter is that it is our salvation," Justin responded. "When I go before the judgment seat of Christ, as the whole world will have to do—even you—this will be my confidence that I may enter into heaven—that I did not deny Jesus, even unto death."

At this, those who stood with Justin stepped forward and said, "You can do whatever you want to us. We are Christians, and Christians do not sacrifice to idols."

Rusticus stood as if to attack them himself, but then steadied himself and placed his hands on his sides. "Then it is decided. Your own testimony condemns you." He turned to the guards that surrounded them. "All of these here who have defied the command of the emperor by refusing to sacrifice to our gods shall be scourged with whips and beheaded according to the law."

• • •

The truth of the Gospel works on so many levels. Though some will argue that God does not exist and that man is the highest form in the universe, they will still strive for a moral code. Challenge them to find a better moral code than that which is outlined in the New Testament. Ask them to compare it to the other systems of morals in the world: those of atheists, other religions, or political systems. You will have to know it well to spell it out, but have them compare the law of love to all other philosophical systems and challenge them to show you a better one. Ask them to come up with a better moral law than the Golden Rule of "Treat others the same way you would want them to treat you." Ask them to show you a country where innovative breakthroughs emerge where Christians are not in the majority. Discuss the list of great scientists and achievers of all time and see how many of them were Christians or Jews or at least believed in God's existence. Do the study yourself. Look at the top ten people of the last millennium and look at their beliefs and accomplishments. Newton, Gutenberg, Michelangelo, Luther, Washington, Martin Luther King Jr., Mother Teresa, and others you will find on any list of important people of the last one thousand years. They all had tremendous faith in God. Look at nations that have tried to exist without God: the Soviet Union, China, Albania, Vietnam—which of these has been as successful as those that built their foundations on the laws of the Bible?

But then you will have to add that even though this is a great philosophy, it cannot work without its power source. Man has no motive to be "good" without gratitude to a Savior who granted they should not have to suffer for their own sins. Without the love of God in their hearts to motivate them to put the needs of others before themselves, they will ultimately act selfishly despite what philosophies they hold on to. The views of Marx and Lenin sound like they are a solid foundation for heaven on earth, but their applications have brought more hell than any other. What brought this about? When those in power saw that they could do whatever they liked and tried to force others into a mold of service to the state, selfishness took over and whenever convenient they began to reword their philosophies to justify their own selfish desires. To free ourselves from cultural restraints to rise to a higher and better system seems a great idea, but such cultural revolutions in the Orient have done little but bathe their countries in blood.

You may or may not convince them of the Truth, just as Justin did not convince Rusticus that the empire's edicts to worship their gods should be ignored, but if you don't stand up for what you believe, who will? If you don't tell those in your world about the Truth, why should God send someone else to do it?

For not only does sound reason direct us to refuse the guidance of those who do or teach anything wrong, but it is by all means vital for the lover of truth, regardless of the threat of death, to choose to do and say what is right even before saving his own life.

Justin Martyr

Jesus must increase, but I must decrease.

John the Baptist
(John 3:30, paraphrased)
Beheaded for his testimony
c. A.D. 29

The Apostle of the Bleeding Feet

| Sundar Singh | India and Tibet | 1889-1929 |

"Oh, all-pervading, impersonal, unknowable, incomprehensible universal spirit, if you do exist, show me the right way, or I will kill myself."

Fifteen-year-old Sundar Singh had come to the end of his despair and felt he could take no more. Having grown up a Sikh (the member of a sect of monotheistic Hindus) under the careful tutelage of his mother in a wealthy household, Sundar had been exposed to various religions to try to find the truth. In his studies his mother had not only guided him to master the Veda, the ancient sacred books of Hinduism, but he had also read the Koran, the sacred book of Islam, and attended a Christian missionary school. Though his religious path seemed carefully set before him to become a *Sadhu* (a Hindu who takes a vow of poverty and celibacy, forsaking all the worldly pleasures by devoting himself entirely to his religion), when Sundar's mother died when he was fourteen, all that held his world together died with her. It had been she who had made God seem real to him, and without her he could no longer find any peace in his life. He turned his anger on the Christians and began disrupting their meetings and forming mobs to throw stones at their ministers. The final straw came as he ripped up and burned a New Testament, page by page, in front of his father and friends to show his contempt for Christianity.

Following this incident, he shut himself up in his room praying to the "universal spirit" for it to reveal the truth to him. On the third day of this, he woke up at 3:00 A.M. and decided to end his life in front of the express train that passed through the village every morning at 5:00. Thus he prayed the desperate prayer to either know the truth or die. As a Hindu, he believed that if there was no answer to this prayer, at least he might be able to find peace in his next incarnation.

But the Truth did not leave him stranded. Shortly before 5:00 A.M., such a bright light filled his room that he thought it had caught on fire. For a moment he kept his eyes shut tightly hoping to die in the flames, but when nothing happened, he opened them to see what the source was. Before him stood Jesus.

"How much longer are you going to persecute me? I have come to save you. You were praying for the right path. Why have you not followed it? I am the way."

Sundar fell to his knees before Him and realized that what all the Christians had taught him about Jesus' resurrection was true. How could it not be?! Here He stood before him! Suddenly a peace beyond anything he had ever known flooded his spirit. *So this is what it is like to know the Truth!* When he looked up again, Jesus was gone, but the peace in his spirit was not.

The next morning he declared to his family, "I am now a Christian. I will no longer serve anyone else but Jesus." Thus began a struggle in his home to get him to return to Hinduism that ended with his expulsion from the house and one of his relatives trying to poison him.

So on September 3, 1905, his sixteenth birthday, Sundar was baptized as a Christian at a local church mission and went into the hills for a month to seek God's direction for what to do next. During this time he realized how uncomfortable he was with the Christianity that was practiced in the missions, as it was more Western culture than Christian truths in many ways. Indians who became Christians changed their dress to match that of the English missionaries, sat in pews in Anglican Church buildings, spoke mostly English, sang English hymns in English services, and relied on Western missionaries for leadership. He felt that there was no way Christianity could ever be relevant to India unless it was

195

present in an Indian way. So Sundar made the decision that he would return to the path that he had always been on, to become a Sadhu, only he would be a Sadhu dedicated to Jesus. At this decision, he put on the saffron robe of a Sadhu, gave away what few possessions he still had, and began wandering northern India with the gospel of Jesus Christ.

The traditions of India and Hinduism were that a Sadhu would never own a home or carry any food or money, but would go from village to village relying totally on the hospitality of others. For this reason, as Sundar entered a village, someone would take him in, thinking he was a Hindu holy man. Often when he would proceed to proclaim Jesus to them, they would become offended and throw him out. However, whenever this happened, Sundar showed them no malice and simply moved on again. This was strange to the villagers, as they were used to Sadhus throwing a fit and cursing those who rejected them. When Sundar simply walked away peacefully, many would often chase him down, ask for his forgiveness, and invite him back to their home. Through this, many of them came to know Jesus as Sundar did.

As he wandered, a growing passion to penetrate the barriers of the north, Hinduism, and Buddhism began to develop in Sundar's heart—he wanted to take the Gospel to Tibet. As he traveled in the foothills of the Himalayas, he began to realize the enormity of this task. However, roughly a year and a half after his baptism, Sundar made his first trip into Tibet after two missionaries had taught him some of the language and loaned him a young interpreter to travel with him. Though he found little success in his initial ventures, Sundar returned to Tibet every summer for the rest of his life. Some incredible miracles have been recorded about Sundar's visits to Tibet. He was imprisoned or beaten and left for dead on more than one occasion during these trips.

On one trip through Nepal, Sundar was attacked by four bandits in the middle of a jungle. Rather than putting up a struggle,

Sundar knelt and bowed his head, expecting the one thief with a sword to end his life then and there. The bandits were so surprised by this that they refused to kill him. Seeing the only thing he had of value was his blanket, they took that and told him to leave, yet his behavior still so perplexed them that one of the robbers called him back and asked him his name. Sundar turned back to the man, introduced himself, and opened his Bible and began reading him the story of the rich man and Lazarus from the book of Luke. When the robber saw how miserable the rich man was in the end, he asked Sundar what would happen to a man such as himself. Sundar took this open door to preach the Gospel to him and tell him of the forgiveness won for him by Jesus on the cross. The thief repented and took Sundar home to stay in his house.

During another instance, he was captured by a group of monks and sentenced to die by the local Grand Lama for spreading a foreign religion. He was thrown naked into a well used to discard the remains of murderers and criminals who had been killed and left to die. The well was then locked. The Lama had the only key. Sundar spent two days without food or water among the putrefying corpses but was miraculously rescued on the third day. A stranger had come, released him, and then simply relocked the well and walked away. When Sundar was later recaptured by the same monks, the Lama was perplexed to see him, knowing no one else could have released this man without the key he kept hidden. They became fearful of Sundar's God because of this and begged him to leave them.

As a wandering Sadhu, Sundar traveled all over India and Ceylon during 1918 and 1919, as well as China, Malaysia, and Japan. Between 1920 and 1922 he was invited to speak in Western Europe, Israel, and Australia. However, his heart was always for India and Tibet, so he always returned to continue his work there. Everywhere he went he dressed in the simple robes of a Sadhu and walked barefoot. Often he would arrive in villages with his feet

blistered and bloody from the journey. For this he became known as "the apostle of the bleeding feet."

Sundar always lived a literal Christianity, taking his actions directly from the Scriptures. One time while he was preaching in a marketplace, a man came up and struck him across the face. In response, Sundar turned to him his other cheek. The man left ashamed and later that evening sent Sundar a note asking for his forgiveness.

On another occasion, Sundar met some harvesters in a field and told them the parable of the wheat and the tares. They considered him a nuisance and told him to leave them alone, but he continued to preach to them. Finally one of them threw a rock and hit Sundar in the head. At this, the assailant was struck with a painful headache and lay down on the ground, unable to work. Sundar immediately took the man's place and helped them finish their harvesting. This action so turned their hearts that they invited him home to share their hospitality that evening. In return, he shared the Gospel with them and won a harvest of his own for Jesus.

Despite growing risks, poor health, and warnings from friends and other missionaries, Sundar left on his annual trek to Tibet in the summer of 1929. He was never seen or heard from again, and no one has ever learned what happened to him.

• • •

In our search to walk more closely with Jesus, it is an important exercise to distinguish between what we believe as part of our Christianity and what we believe as part of our culture. Few of us know how greatly we are affected by what those around us believe until we have taken some time to live in a different culture or share our faith with someone from a different part of the world. A church in an Arabic country will not look like a church in a Western nation or in an Oriental one. The interpretation of some scriptures may even be somewhat different. In exploring these differences, we can come to an understanding of what is more universally true.

In some countries, Christianity is so meshed with the culture that just by being born in that nation one is considered a Christian, and church attendance is thought to make up for a life of willful sin. Even different churches or denominations have cultures that constrain us to some extent or the other. It is important to ask ourselves if we believe things because they have been revealed to us through God's Word, or is it just a tradition of our church? Do we live a life of devotion to God through a personal walk, or do we just fulfill all the requirements of a "good" person according to the accepted behavior of our church friends and culture? Are we the same in front of them as we are in private? If we began to run with a totally different crowd, would their different morals change us more than our morals and beliefs would change them?

Sundar Singh wanted to discover a Christianity that was not Western, but Indian. Clothing styles, language, etc., were all being transferred over with belief in Jesus so that becoming a Christian seemed to also mean becoming British. What Sundar did to cut away the culture and preach only essential Christianity was a counter-cultural revolution that enabled Christianity's first firm foothold in India. People such as Watchman Nee did the same in China. When the church becomes indigenous and is preached by nationals rather than foreigners, it takes on an entirely new dimension.

Christianity is a counterculture that will change those things that are most essential without conforming all people to be the same. Yet this can only happen when the individuals in any culture prize meeting God through His Word above just being called a Christian so that they can fit in with their crowd.

Jesus Freaks have this value and are open to correction. They are willing to strip away what is cultural to live what is Christlike. Jesus Freaks are not those who flow with the crowd, but those who flow with the Holy Spirit. As Paul did, they can drop or accept cultural differences for the sake of sharing the essentials of Christ with whomever they come into contact. This is the life lived in the world but not of the world—the life lived in the Spirit as Jesus walked.

> Even though I am free of the demands and expectations of everyone, I have voluntarily become a servant to any and all in order to reach a wide range of people: religious, nonreligious, meticulous moralists, loose-living immoralists, the defeated, the demoralized—whoever. I didn't take on their way of life. I kept my bearings in Christ—but I entered their world and tried to experience things from their point of view. I've become just about every sort of servant there is in my attempts to lead those I meet into a God-saved life. I did all this because of the Message. I didn't just want to talk about it; I wanted to be in on it!

Paul

(1 Corinthians 9:19–23 THE MESSAGE)

200

*We are going to heaven…. A fountain fed
from many springs will never dry up. When we
are gone, others will rise in our place.*

BRUNO SERUNKUMA
BURNED TO DEATH
NAMUGONGO, UGANDA
1886

Responding to Evil With the Gospel

| Pelagius | Cordova, Spain | c. A.D. 925 |

When Pelagius was ten, he took the place of his uncle, Bishop Hermogius of Tuy, in the prison of the Muslim Caliph Abd ar-Rahman III so that the bishop could return to his flock. After his initial time in prison, Abd ar-Rahman set the boy's terms of release: that Pelagius convert to Islam and submit to the caliph's sexual advances. For this the caliph promised him wealth and freedom. In response, the young Pelagius preached about Jesus to the caliph and said he would die for the name of Christ before he gave in to any of the caliph's demands.

For three and a half years Pelagius remained in prison; all the while the caliph had his servants promise him all the pleasures and wealth that would be available to him in the royal house if he would convert. Pelagius continued to resolutely refuse. "I am a Christian, and will remain a Christian, and obey only God's commands all the days of my life."

Eventually the requests turned into threats, but still Pelagius remained firm in his confession of Christ. At this the caliph finally commanded his guards to "Take him and suspend him by iron tongs, pinch him with red-hot pincers, and haul him up and down in the river until he either dies or renounces this Jesus as his Lord!"

Thus the thirteen-year-old boy was taken to the river and tortured from seven o'clock in the morning until the evening. When the king questioned him again in the evening, Pelagius again refused to leave Christ. Suspended and bleeding before Abd ar-Rahman, Pelagius turned his eyes to heaven and prayed, "O Lord Jesus, deliver me out of the hands of my enemies." As he lifted up his hands toward heaven, the caliph had the guards pull the

tongs and chains tight, stretching his arms and legs in four direc-
tions. Then he had the soldiers cut off one arm, then the other,
then one leg, then the other, and lastly his head. When this was
done they threw the pieces into the river. Pelagius carried his faith
and his purity with him to heaven.

• • •

Do not let anyone treat you as if you are unimportant
because you are young. Instead, be an example to the
believers with your words, your actions, your love, your
faith, and your pure life.

Paul
(1 Timothy 4:12 NCV)

203

Standing Up for Jesus

| Athanasius | Roman Empire | c. A.D. 297-373 |

"No," Athanasius asserted, "Jesus was not *other* from the Father, but *of* the Father. Christ was of the same essence as the Father, eternal and divine. He was not created at a certain time, but was always one with the Father the Creator."

Thus, in summary, Athanasius answered Arius at the first church council before Emperor Constantine at Nicea in A.D. 325. Arius and his followers had declared that Jesus was created from nothing and was not of the same essence as the Father, nor was the Holy Spirit. Thus his arguments denied the divinity of Jesus and the existence of the Trinity. This early controversy had threatened to tear the church in two only twelve years after Christianity was legalized in the Roman Empire. It seemed that if the devil could not stop Christianity from without, he would try to divide it from within.

Thus, Athanasius, who was at the time the secretary to Alexander, the bishop of Alexandria, found himself the key opponent of Arius and his teachings, and the main proponent for Jesus' divinity. This struggle would mark the rest of his life.

In the end, the majority of the 318 church leaders Constantine had called to Nicea sided with Athanasius, and Arius was excommunicated and exiled to Illyria for his false teachings. The Nicene Creed was adopted by the assembly to state the essential tenets of the Christian faith. Though truth had won in Nicea, the conflict was far from over.

After the council, Athanasius retuned to Alexandria and a monastic lifestyle. When Alexander died, Athanasius was chosen as his successor and the bishop of Alexandria. During this time Arius, with the help of his friend Eusebius of Nicomedia (who was also a primary Christian historian of the period) who had some influence with Emperor Constantine, pleaded to return to

Alexandria. He claimed to have repented and wanted to be reinstated in the church. Constantine, hoping for a political reunion of the dissenting parties and a bartered peace, ordered Athanasius to take Arius back into the church. Anthanasius refused, stating that it was up to the church to initiate such a reunion, not the state. He could not call a spiritual brother any advocate of a doctrine "that was fighting against Christ."

Suddenly other charges were brought against Athanasius—of cruelty and even murder. When the charges were successfully refuted, charges were brought that Athanasius had opposed certain shipments of supplies to Constantinople. Though little proof was shown in these cases, Constantine's jealousy for his authority and his city were aroused enough that Athanasius was banished for the rest of Constantine's reign.

Though Athanasius won back his seat in the church leadership under Constantine's son, Constantine II, and Arius had died suddenly in A.D. 334, the battle was still not over. Due to continued Arian influences, Athanasius was exiled another four times and spent a total of seventeen of his forty-six years as bishop in exile. In one instance an Arian bishop was put in his place in Alexandria, and those who had favored Athanasius's view of Jesus were persecuted.

In A.D. 366 he returned to Alexandria after his fifth exile and remained free for the rest of his life. Through it all, he remained steadfast in his faith and defense of Jesus' divinity. He saw to the building of many churches and stood for the Truth in all that he did, whether it was in opposition of governors, emperors, or false brethren.

• • •

What are the essentials of the Christian faith? While it is clearly good that we are as open-minded as possible to be one in Christ and a unity of believers in His universal church, Christians are different from those in the rest of the world in many important ways. Paul seemed to acknowledge that while some things are essential, others are open to the dictates of conscience and personal convictions (see 1 Corinthians 7:6). What are those essential things?

This was the struggle Athanasius fought. What is it that truly separates the wheat from the chaff? What essentials must a Christian believe to be in Christ? To answer these questions, Athanasius helped create a creed or oath of basic beliefs to separate the true revelations of God from the fabricated. Though the Nicene Creed that was developed from this effort does not represent all the truth we need to live as Christians on the earth, it does express the essentials that can help us identify who is in the body of Christ and who is not. Questions of Jesus' divinity, His death and resurrection, the existence of the Trinity, the Virgin Birth, and others of the miracles surrounding Jesus' life are not optional for the true believer and revolutionary.

206

The Nicene Creed

We believe in one God,
        the Father, the Almighty,
maker of heaven and earth,
    of all that is, seen and unseen.
We believe in one Lord, Jesus Christ,
        the only Son of God,
    eternally begotten of the Father,
    God from God, light from light,
    true God from true God,
        begotten, not made,
of one Being with the Father;
    through him all things were made.
For us and for our salvation
he came down from heaven,
    was incarnate of the Holy Spirit and the
        Virgin Mary
and became truly human.
For our sake he was crucified under
        Pontius Pilate;
    he suffered death and was buried.
On the third day he rose again

in accordance with the Scriptures;
he ascended into heaven
and is seated at the right hand of the Father.
He will come again in glory
to judge the living and the dead,
and his kingdom will have no end.
We believe in the Holy Spirit, the Lord,
the giver of life,
who proceeds from the Father and the Son,
who with the Father and the Son
is worshiped and glorified,
who has spoken through the prophets.
We believe in one holy catholic and
apostolic Church.
We acknowledge one baptism for the
forgiveness of sins.
We look for the resurrection of the dead,
and the life of the world to come.
Amen.

For we did not follow cunningly devised fables when we made known to you the power and coming of our Lord Jesus Christ, but were eyewitnesses of His majesty. For He received from God the Father honor and glory when such a voice came to Him from the Excellent Glory: "This is My beloved Son, in whom I am well pleased." And we heard this voice which came from heaven when we were with Him on the holy mountain.

We also have the prophetic word made more sure, which you do well to heed as a light that shines in a dark place, until the day dawns and the morning star rises in your hearts; knowing this first, that no prophecy of Scripture is of any private interpretation, for prophecy never came by the will of man, but holy men of God spoke as they were moved by the Holy Spirit.

Peter
(2 Peter 1:16-21 NKJV)

208

While the troops of Mahomet II surrounded Constantinople in 1493 and it had to be decided if the Balkans would be under Christian or Mohammedan dominion for centuries, a local church council in the beseiged city discussed the following problems: What color had the eyes of the virgin Mary? What gender do the angels have? If a fly falls in sanctified water, is the fly sanctified or the water defiled? It may be only a legend, as concerns those times, but peruse Church periodicals of today and you will find that questions just like this are discussed. The menace of persecutors and the sufferings of the underground church are scarcely ever mentioned. Instead, there are endless discussions about theological matters, about rituals, about nonessentials.... In formerly Communist Russia, no one remembered the arguments for or against child or adult baptism, for or against papal infallibility. They are not pre- or postmillennialists. They cannot interpret prophecies and don't quarrel about them, but I have wondered very often at how well they could prove the existence of God to atheists.

RICHARD WURMBRAND
FOUNDER OF THE VOICE OF THE MARTYRS
SPENT FOURTEEN YEARS IN A COMMUNIST PRISON
ROMANIA
1940s, '50s, AND '60s

An Explosive Prayer

| Iranian Pastor | Iran | c. 1990 |

"Lord," the pastor prayed, "I cannot take any more of this questioning. Please, release me from this!"

Already the pastor had been in and out of prison, and now he was called every two weeks by the secret police for interrogations. The interrogations were the same questions over and over, accusing the pastor of being a spy from the West.

The next morning, the pastor was again to go to the secret police headquarters, and he asked his church members to pray that God would provide him a way out.

"I see you are here," said the officer, taking him into the questioning room. Before they could begin the questioning, however, the tape recorder sitting on the table exploded. Flames came out of it, and it was obvious it would never work again.

"What are you doing?" the guard asked angrily, seeing the slight smile in the pastor's eyes.

"I am praying for you," the pastor answered. "You are not fighting against me, you are fighting against God. You cannot win against Him."

"Go home," the officer yelled, and the pastor quickly left.

He ran into his house and asked his wife, "What happened?"

"Three older ladies from the church came here," she said. "We gathered around and joined hands and prayed for you, that God would protect you from the interrogation."

When they further discussed the two incidents, they found that the time the women had gathered for prayer was exactly the time the tape recorder had exploded.

• • •

It is essential that we never forget the power of prayer. "Ye have not, because ye ask not" (James 4:2 KJV) is the admonition of the Scriptures. Nothing is impossible for God! A revolutionary Jesus Freak is not afraid to ask great things from a great God. Let the example of these modern-day prayer warriors serve as a reminder to us.

This is the confidence we have in approaching God: that if we ask anything according to his will, he hears us. And if we know that he hears us—whatever we ask—we know that we have what we asked of him.

John
(1 John 5:14–15 NIV)

Loyal to **Their Bridegroom**

| Nunilo and Alodia | Osca, Spain | A.D. 851 |

Nunia and Alodia's father had been a Muslim man and when he died, their mother married another man who was a Muslim. With these two sisters desiring nothing more than to follow Jesus with all of their hearts, they were forced to leave their home and flee to their aunt's house, who was also a devoted Christian. Though they had hoped this relocation would solve their problems, it instead compounded them.

Being very devout Christians and having a Muslim father brought the mark of apostasy on them from those in the community, and they were soon called before a local Moorish judge. The judge began by offering them wealth and good marriages if they would recant Jesus and embrace the god of Muhammad, but as they persisted in their refusals, his offers turned to threats of torture and execution.

The sisters gave him the following testimony:

O judge! How is it that you command us to turn away from true godliness, since God has made it known to us that no one is richer or a better bridegroom than Jesus Christ, our Savior? No way of life is more blessed than the Christian faith by which we live and by which mere men have conquered kingdoms. To dwell with Him and to live in Him is our only true provision, but to depart from Him is eternal damnation. We will never be separated from communion with Him as long as we live in this life; for having given and entrusted our youth into His keeping, we hope to eventually become his bride.

The transient riches of this world, which you have offered

us, have no appeal; we count them as manure and loss that we might gain Christ, because we know that everything under the sun except Jesus and true faith in Him is emptiness.

Nor are we moved by your threats of punishment, for such things are even more temporary. As for death, the thing you have presented to us as the final terror is a thing not to be feared but desired, because we know that through it we go without delay to heaven, and to Christ our Bridegroom, and there to be embraced by Him and forevermore inseparable from Him through His love.

Seeing their determination at this point, he decided to wear them down slowly, separating them and putting them into homes with Muslim women who instructed them daily in the teachings of Islam.

After a time they were brought before the judge again and, rather than having succumbed to the indoctrination, spoke as strongly and as lovingly of Jesus as they had before. At this, the judge sentenced them to execution with the sword, which was carried out shortly afterward.

• • •

Without wavering, let us hold tightly to the hope we say we have, for God can be trusted to keep his promise.

Hebrews 10:23

We say we are Christians, we proclaim it to the whole world, even under the hands of the executioner, and in the midst of all the torments you inflict upon us to compel us to unsay it. Torn and mangled, and weltering in our blood, we cry out as loud as we are able to cry, "We are worshipers of God through Christ Jesus!"

TERTULLIAN
CHRISTIAN FATHER AND APOLOGIST
C. A.D. 150–229

Prepared for His Second Martyrdom

Sebastian	Rome	C. A.D. 304

Sebastian must have stood with tears in his eyes when, around A.D. 274, he watched his friends, the twin brothers Marcus and Marcellinus, die for their faith. "Don't despair," he told them, "you will soon be with the Lord." The twins had survived a day and a night tied to posts with their feet pierced through with nails before their suffering was put to an end as they were thrust through with lances. A year or so later, this period of persecution under Emperor Aurelian ended.

Around A.D. 283, young Sebastian joined the Roman army, perhaps to see that other Christians could have what protection he could provide them, and rose in favor with all his commanders because of his goodness and bravery. However, he kept his Christianity secret from many of his superiors.

Despite the uniform and his secrecy, Sebastian still saw himself as a minister of the Gospel and a representative of Christ. When he found the opportunity, he would share his faith with other soldiers, many of whom were converted. One officer became a Christian after Sebastian prayed for his wife, who was deaf. When Sebastian made the sign of the cross over her head, she was healed. When Sebastian shared the Gospel with her, she converted as well.

While serving under the prefect of Rome, a man by the name of Chromatius, Sebastian had the opportunity to pray for him as he suffered from gout. Chromatius was instantly healed and became a Christian, as did Chromatius's son, Tiburtius. After his conversion, Chromatius freed all of the Christian prisoners under his jurisdiction, freed his slaves, and resigned as prefect. The jailer, Claudius, was also saved as a result of Sebastian's witness.

Because of his excellent service record, Sebastian soon became a captain in Emperor Diocletian's guard, the emperor not knowing that he was a Christian. Sebastian served him faithfully and had great favor with the emperor, who gave him leeway to carry out his duties however he saw fit.

When Diocletian took the throne, the Roman Empire had been struggling. Through his leadership, though, it had found a renaissance of sorts. Part of his strategy in bringing about this rebirth was to share his authority with another so that the emperor could be in more than one place at a time. Thus he appointed Maximian as a co-emperor, or augustus, and named two junior emperors, or military leaders, under each of them given the title of caesar. Diocletian took his son-in-law, Galerius, who was a cruel and fanatical heathen, as his caesar while Maximian took Constantinius (the father of Constantine the Great) as caesar under him.

Galerius used his influence to push Diocletian to renew the persecution against the Christians. Diocletian resisted this at first, but as had other emperors before him, Diocletian saw the worship of the Roman gods as the bond that held the empire together. By refusing to sacrifice to and worship these gods, he believed Christians were thus a threat to the structure of the empire. As a result of this, he soon gave in, and the first of many edicts against the Christians started spreading throughout all of Rome.

At this Sebastian forsook his secrecy to visit brothers and sisters in prison, bring them supplies, and minister to them. It was not long before the Roman captain was found out, informed against, and betrayed to his superiors. However, because of his high rank, no one could have him put to death except the emperor.

His trial was like no other. After being summoned by Diocletian, instead of being brought under escort and in chains like a normal prisoner, Sebastian marched in before Emperor Diocletian in full uniform. He bowed, then stood at attention

before his emperor, giving him all the honor due to the highest official in Rome.

Diocletian was little impressed and came straight to the point. "I have been informed that you are an enemy to the gods of the empire because you refuse to sacrifice to them. Is this true? Are you not a faithful Roman?"

"The proof of my faithfulness is that I pray every day to the one true God for the well-being and prosperity of the emperor and the empire."

"What! Insolence!" Diocletian fumed. "There is no 'true god' other than those of Rome!" He turned to his guards and gave his command. "Have him taken to the Campus Martius and shot to death with arrows!"

Sebastian was removed from the emperor's presence and taken to Campus Martius as ordered, but not without his sentence being discovered by fellow believers. They followed him to this field of execution to take his body and give it a proper burial after his death. Once the soldiers had carried out the sentence, they left Sebastian's body in the field to rot.

However, when the group of Christians picked up his body, he began to move. Realizing that he was still alive, they took him to one of their homes and nursed him back to health. When he had recovered, however, he didn't see his deliverance as an opportunity to live out the rest of his life in peace, but as a second opportunity to be a witness for Christ before the emperor.

As soon as he was able to walk, Sebastian dressed and went back into Rome. He found a procession leading the emperor to the temple, and just as the emperor approached, Sebastian jumped out into the road in front of him, proclaiming, "Diocletian, what you are doing is an abomination before the true God! You must stop this unlawful persecution of the Christians!"

The emperor was of course quite shocked to have a dead man appear before him and rebuke him for his crimes. But when he realized that he was not seeing a ghost, he ordered Sebastian taken into custody again and sentenced him to be beaten to death with clubs and his body tossed into the sewer, where it would not so easily be recovered. The sentence was carried out immediately.

Once his body was abandoned, fellow believers recovered it from the sewers and gave Sebastian's corpse a proper burial in the catacombs.

• • •

God's calling on each of our lives is important to our entire family in Christ. Sebastian's position as a soldier in a persecuting army gave him a unique place from which to minister to those who needed God the most and protect his Christian brothers and sisters. To have laid down his life by putting on the uniform of an enemy is indeed a strange calling, but one that God honored when Sebastian obeyed.

217

We know what love is because Jesus gave his life for us. That's why we must give our lives for each other.

John
(1 John 3:16 CEV)

Underground and Undercover

Romanian Believers	Romania	c. 1945-present

"We instructed Christians to join the secret police and put on the most hated and despised uniform in our country," Pastor Wurmbrand wrote, "so they could report the activities of the secret police to the underground church. Several brethren of the underground church did this, keeping their faith hidden. It was difficult for them to be despised by their own family and friends for wearing the Communist uniform and not reveal their true mission. Yet they did. So great was their love for Christ.

"When I was kidnapped by the police and kept for years in strictest secrecy, a Christian doctor actually became a member of the secret police to find out my whereabouts! As a secret police doctor, he had access to the cells of all prisoners and hoped to find me. All his friends shunned him, thinking he had become a Communist. To go around dressed in the uniform of the torturers is a much greater sacrifice than to wear the uniform of a prisoner.

"The doctor found me in a deep, dark cell and sent out word that I was alive. He was the first friend to discover me during my initial eight and a half years in prison! Due to him, word was spread that I was alive, and when prisoners were released during the Eisenhower-Khrushchev 'thaw' in 1956, Christians clamored for my release and I was freed for a short time. If it had not been for this doctor, who joined the secret police specifically to find me, I would never have been released. I would still be in prison—or in a grave—today.

"Using their position in the secret police, these members of the underground church warned us many times and were of tremendous help. The underground church in Communist countries has men in the secret police today who protect and warn Christians of impending danger. Some are high up in government circles, keeping their faith in Christ secret and helping us greatly. One day in heaven they can publicly proclaim Christ, whom they serve secretly now.

"Nevertheless, many members of the underground church were discovered and imprisoned. We had our 'Judases' too, who reported our activities to the secret police. Using beatings, druggings, threats, and blackmail, the Communists tried to find ministers and laymen who would report on their brethren."

• • •

The Lord does not look at the things man looks at. Man looks at the outward appearance, but the Lord looks at the heart.

(1 Samuel 16:7 NIV)

219

"Our Good Physician"

Hugh Laverick and John Aprice	England	1556

The two men, having refused to recant their faith, were led forward to the stakes. Hugh Laverick was a sixty-eight-year-old painter who had to walk with the aid of a crutch due to a crippled foot. The other, though spiritually enlightened by the truth of God's Word, was physically blind. The lord of London had sentenced them both to death during little more than an interruption to his dessert.

Laverick, in realizing that he would no longer need his crutch as the chains bound him to his stake, threw it away and turned to Aprice to rejoice together with him in their deliverance. "Be of good cheer, my brother; for my lord of London is our good physician; he will heal us both shortly—thee of thy blindness, and me of my lameness."

Both died in the flames to rise eternally healed in heaven.

• • •

You have this faith and love because of your hope, and what you hope for is kept safe for you in heaven.

Paul
(Colossians 1:5 NCV)

"I Have Never Separated Myself From Christ"

| John, Adolphus, and Aurea | Cordova, Spain | A.D. 850-856 |

Though John, Adolphus, and Aurea's father was a Muslim, they were raised devout Christians by their mother. Though untrained, John became a merchant in town and had some small success in selling things in the bazaar. When jealousy arose with another man, John was accused of deriding and reviling the Muslim prophet, Muhammad, so he was brought before the Moorish authorities in Cordova.

When the witness was found to have lied, his testimony contradicting itself, the judge had no grounds on which to execute John, but he required him to either deny Christ or suffer scourging.

"I will not forsake Christ even if you sentence me to die," John replied. "I am innocent of the charges. You should release me."

The conviction with which John spoke irritated the judge so much that he had him scourged. When John continued to hold to his faith, the judge demanded that the torture continue long past what a normal person could endure. John, receiving more than five hundred stripes, fell to the ground, apparently dead. When his torturers found that he was still breathing, they put him backward on a donkey and marched him through town, shouting, "This is what is done to any revilers of our prophet, and the ridiculers of our worship." John was then taken to jail and bound with heavy chains, where he died. History records that his brother, Adolphus, was also martyred.

His sister, Aurea, and her mother were able to escape to a convent, where they hid from their relatives, who would have turned them in to the Moorish authorities as well. Eventually, however, they were found, and Aurea was brought before a judge who was a relative of hers. Under his persuasion, the trauma of her brothers' deaths, as well as some of the other members of the convent, and under pressure of the trial, Aurea renounced Christ and was released.

Upon receiving her freedom, however, Aurea was stricken with guilt at her betrayal and began to attend church again, hoping that in the hearing of the Word of God her spirit might be strengthened against future persecutions and temptations.

When she was found out and returned before the judge, he again cajoled and threatened her as before. Yet this time in response she not only refused to deny Jesus, she even refused to acknowledge her first time before him as an abdication:

222

> I have never separated myself from Christ my God. I have never forsaken the religion of true godliness. I have never for one moment taken hold of your impious worship. Though I once, with my tongue, seemed to have rejected Christ, my heart was nevertheless far from it, and I have a firm confidence in my Lord Jesus Christ who has again lifted my contrite conscience by His consoling promise, "He that believes in me, though he were dead, yet shall he live." Though, with my words, I fell into the snare of denial, yet my heart was strengthened through the power of faith, for, as soon as I went away from you, I kept with heart and mind the faith, which I have practiced from infancy. Hence, there is nothing left, but to execute me with the sword, or else you must give me liberty to freely serve my Lord Christ.

Because of her resolve, she was returned to prison. The next day the decision came from King Muhammad I that she should be beheaded. The execution took place that same day. Her body was displayed with the thieves and murderers who had been executed, being hung upside down from the gallows. She was later buried with the criminals, their bodies being sunk into the river Betis.

• • •

Aurea admitted to having spoken against the name of Christ, but she was genuinely sorry for that act. Repentance and forgiveness are important concepts to understand. Just as God's forgiveness is genuine because He forgets forever what we repented of, so too our repentance must be genuine.

Not only is He the sole person to grant such forgiveness, but He is also the sole strength for true repentance. How can we afford to do anything else but turn to Him with all of our hearts?

I know all the things you do, and I have opened a door for you that no one can shut. You have little strength, yet you obeyed my word and did not deny me....

Because you have obeyed my command to persevere, I will protect you from the great time of testing that will come upon the whole world to test those who belong to this world. Look, I am coming quickly. Hold on to what you have, so that no one will take away your crown.

Jesus
(Revelation 3:8, 10–11 NLT)

Father, make us more like Jesus. Help us bear
difficulty, pain, disappointment, and sorrow,
knowing that in Your perfect working and design You
can use such bitter experiences to mold our
characters and make us more like our Lord.
We look with hope to the day when we will be
completely like Christ, because we will see
Him as He is…. My passions are crucified,
there is no heat in my flesh, and a stream flows
murmuring inside me—deep down in me saying,
"Come to the Father."

IGNATIUS
HIS PRAYER WHILE IN PRISON BEFORE
HE WAS DEVOURED BY LIONS
ROME
C. A.D. 111

The End of the Roman Persecutions

| Under Constantine | Roman Empire | c. A.D. 274–337 |

When Diocletian and Maximian abdicated the throne of the empire in A.D. 305, Constantius Chlorus and Galerius took over the rule of the Roman Empire. Constantius became emperor (or augustus) over the western Roman Empire (from roughly the Ionian Sea west, including the area along the northern coast of Africa), and Galerius became emperor over the eastern Roman Empire (basically Greece, Turkey, parts of eastern Europe, the Middle East, and the eastern part of northern Africa). During this time, the Roman soldiers set up Maxentius, Maximian's son, as their caesar in Rome. And while under Galerius and Maxentius the persecutions still went on for about eight years, Constantius had become a supporter of the Christians in his empire. Though this ended the persecution of Christians in the West, Galerius continued it in the East until his death in A.D. 311.

Constantius stayed in Britain, where he had been a ceasar (military leader or junior emperor) under Diocletian and governed the westernmost provinces of Spain, Gaul (France), and Britain. He remained western emperor only one year, however, and died in York in A.D. 306, with his son Constantine at his side. At his death, the Roman troops formerly under Constantius immediately proclaimed his son Constantine emperor in his father's place.

Meanwhile in Rome, infighting for the title of emperor erupted between Galerius, Maximian (who had been forced to abdicate the throne of emperor when Diocletian did), and Maximian's son Maxentius. Constantine managed to stay above the fray by making alliances with both Galerius—who gave him the title of caesar under Emperor Maxentius in A.D. 306 and

225

authority over the same provinces his father had governed as caesar (namely Spain, Gaul, and Britain)—and later with Maximian—who awarded him the title of augustus when Constantine married his daughter Fausta in A.D. 307. As things were, Maximian trusted neither his son Maxentius nor Galerius, and Galerius trusted neither of them. Meanwhile Maxentius also coveted the throne for his own and only used his relationship with his father to amass more power and allies.

After years of political and military actions to try covertly to unseat the other two, the strength of Galerius, Maximian, and Maxentius was greatly diminished as Constantine slowly strengthened his own position and forces in the far west. Constantine remained mostly undisturbed by events in Rome and the east until Maximian tried to assassinate Constantine in A.D. 310. For this, Constantine had him executed. Then in A.D. 311, Galerius died, and Constantine decided to travel to Rome to secure his title as augustus and rid himself of Maxentius.

Though Constantine was a soldier more than anything else, he had been taught by his father, Costantius, to believe in prayer. Constantius had passed on to his son his religion, the worship of Sol, the "unconquerable sun," as the only god, the supreme being who created all things and who governed all things.

Constantine was a man hungry to know his god. So on his way to Rome, as the troops had stopped at midday, Constantine could be found in his tent in fervent prayer. His prayer was simple, yet earnest. "Reveal to me who you are, your true nature ... and stretch forth your right hand to help me in these coming diffi culties."

As he continued praying, a ruckus began to grow outside. One of Constantine's servants then entered the tent and motioned for him to follow. When Constantine emerged, he saw his troops all gazing upward and pointing. When he followed their gaze, he too was awestruck by what they were looking at. It was the answer to his prayer, though he didn't know it at the time: There in the sky, shining brighter than the early afternoon sun, was a cross with the inscription beneath it, "Conquer by this." It was not the "unconquerable sun" who had answered, but the "Unconquerable Son."

Constantine pondered the meaning of this vision the rest of the day, attempting to make sense of its message. Yet that night, when he finally got to sleep, he had the answer: Jesus came to him in a dream with the same sign. "Make a likeness of this sign which you also saw in the heavens, and it will be a protection in all of your confrontations with your enemies." Thus the cross became the symbol that was carried before the armies of Rome wherever they went.

In a later dream as they approached more closely to Rome, it is also believed that Jesus again appeared to Constantine and instructed him to "mark the shields of your men with the heavenly sign of God." This sign was a melding of the Greek letters *Chi* (X) and *Rho* (P), the first two letters of the word "Christ."

Needless to say, Constantine obeyed these instructions and at the same time resolved that he would worship no other god than the One who had appeared to him. He thus marched into battle behind the sign of the cross and the name of Christ and won a decisive battle over Maxentius's troops at the Milvian Bridge outside of Rome in A.D. 312, which secured his place as emperor. When peace was made, Constantine took the title of emperor over the western half of the Roman Empire, overseeing the same territory his father had as emperor, and appointed Licinius emperor in the east.

He credited his success to the God of the Christians, as he soon came to understand that the symbols he had been given were Christian in origin. He sought out those who knew the doctrines of this religion and made them his advisors. He constantly questioned them on the nature of God and the possible meanings of these signs. At every opportunity they preached the Gospel to him and

answered his questions as carefully and fully as possible, explaining that God was the one true God and that salvation came through no other name than that of Jesus Christ.

Not long after this, Constantine met with Licinius in Milan, and there together in A.D. 313 they issued an edict granting all persons the freedom to choose whichever religion they wished. Despite this edict, however, Licinius later renewed the persecution of those who would not sacrifice to the Roman gods. This became part of a power struggle between Constantine and Licinius that eventually led to Constantine becoming the sole Roman emperor in A.D. 324.

Many other things also changed as Constantine learned more about Christianity and read more of the Holy Scriptures: Pastors became judges in civil lawsuits, courts and workshops were closed on Sundays, the branding of slaves and criminals on the face was forbidden, the crucifixion of slaves was abolished, gladiator games were prohibited, unwanted babies were no longer put to death, and sexual immorality became a crime in order to strengthen the institution of marriage. He also did a great deal to unify and organize the Roman Empire, bringing it to a standard of power and civic authority that was perhaps greater than in any other era of the Roman Empire.

Because of his power, Constantine also made himself the head of the church, and he presided over the first ecumenical council of the church at Nicea in A.D. 325. By the grace of God, he also presided over a number of controversies that threatened to deny the deity and person of Jesus Christ and settled them in the favor of Christ and the inspired writings Constantine had read.

In A.D. 326, he sought to further unify east and west by building Constantinople (which is today Istanbul, Turkey) on the site of the ancient Greek city Byzantium and moving the capital of the Roman Empire and church there. It remained the capital of the eastern Roman, or Byzantine, Empire until 1453. Around this same time, a dark shadow threw a question mark over the purity of Constantine's reign and Christianity: Crispus, the son of his first wife; Fausta, his second wife; and Licinian, the illegitimate son of Licinius, were all murdered at what was likely Constantine's command.

Constantine's mother, Helena, also greatly embraced the Christian faith and, with her son's blessings and financial support, preserved many of the historical Christian sites with churches and monuments. The Church of the Holy Sepulcher in Jerusalem and the Basilica of the Nativity in Bethlehem, which both still stand today, are examples of her efforts.

Constantine died on May 22, A.D. 337. According to the church historian Eusebius, though Constantine supported Christianity all of his reign, he had never been baptized until a few days before his death.

• • •

Though the reign of Constantine brought a newfound freedom to Christians, in it were also the seeds of pride that would later allow Christians to turn against their own brothers and sisters and persecute them. Also, as Christianity went from being persecuted to being fashionable, a trend was begun that still poses a challenge to believers today: cultural Christianity.

By uniting the power of the government and the power of the church into one head, expulsion from the church and accusations of heresy became political weapons to control others and hoard power. At the same time, the church became infected with the ways of government: It began to use torture and cruel executions to settle disputes. Thus when the Founding Fathers of the United States drafted their government, they made sure that freedom of religion was part of the Bill of Rights and that the powers of church and state were separate— not that the government would try to rule without the dictates of conscience and biblical morality, but that one denomination or religious group of the country would not be able to use the powers of the gov-

ernment to inflict their views and doctrines upon the rest of the nation.

During the reign of Constantine, the cost of being a Christian also dramatically changed. Whereas prior to Constantine's rule, deciding to acknowledge Jesus as Lord and Truth meant forsaking all, even life itself, now becoming a Christian was actually beneficial for advancement in society. Suddenly it became obligatory to be called a Christian in order to get a good position in the government. Being able to quote the correct phrases and dress the right way became the mark used to determine who was Christian and who was not—Christianity became an outward display for others to see. To become a Christian was suddenly an easy decision; there was no longer heartrending dedication required—it was just a matter of being born into the right culture or hanging out with the right crowd. Right doctrine became more important than correct moral behavior.

Christianity became an institution depending more on correct ritual, tradition, and memorization than heartfelt dedication to God. Christianity was melded with Roman culture to the point that they were indistinguishable, and the church lapsed from commitment to complacency. Heartfelt prayer was replaced with hollow repetition; spontaneous worship from a spirit overflowing with gratitude was replaced with songbooks and orders of service; intimacy with God was replaced with "playing the part" of a Christian for popularity's sake. There is another word for this type of play-acting: hypocrisy.

Because of all of this, Constantine is not included in this book as a Jesus Freak, but for his historical significance. He was dedicated to God for what God did for him; when the questions of obedience to the Scriptures or sacrifice on his own part came out, Constantine did as he wanted—he was emperor, he had the power, he could do as he pleased. He could enforce right doctrine on others, he could make laws that agreed with godly morality, but he could never ensure the change of heart needed to become a Christian in others, because he may not have experienced it himself until he was about to die.

This brings up some interesting questions for us today: If our

Christianity has cost us nothing, then how much is it really worth?

Knowing the correct password—saying "Master, Master," for instance—isn't going to get you anywhere with me. What is required is serious obedience—doing what my Father wills. I can see it now—at the Final Judgment thousands strutting up to me and saying, "Master, we preached the Message, we bushed the demons, our God-sponsored projects had everyone talking." And do you know what I am going to say? "You missed the boat. All you did was use me to make yourselves important. You don't impress me one bit. You're out of here."

These words I speak to you are not incidental additions to your life, homeowner improvements to your standard of living. They are foundational words, words to build a life on.

Jesus

(Matthew 7:21–23 THE MESSAGE)

232

*If the devil were wise enough and would
stand by in silence and let the Gospel be
preached, he would suffer less harm.
For when there is no battle for the Gospel it
rusts and it finds no cause and no occasion
to show its vigor and power.
Therefore, nothing better can befall the Gospel
than that the world should
fight it with force and cunning.*

MARTIN LUTHER
TRIED FOR HERESY, 1521
1483–1546

"Apostasy Is All They Require"

| Peter O'Higgins | Dublin, Ireland | 1641 |

Peter O'Higgins was led quietly to the scaffold in the courtyard of Dublin Castle before the large audience who had come to see him hanged. He had been charged with trying to seduce the Protestants from their faith, but having no solid evidence against him, he was told simply that if he recanted his Catholicism, he would be spared.

It was arranged that two documents would be sent as Peter mounted the gallows, one his warrant of execution, and one his document of pardon if he recanted. When they arrived, he took the pardon in his hand and held it up for all to see. There was a loud exclamation from the crowd at the apparent beginning of his rejection of the Catholic faith, but Peter's words were only for those in the crowd who shared his views:

233

> My brethren, God has so willed that I should fall into the hands of our relentless persecutors; they have not been able, however, to convict me of any crime against the laws of the realm. But my religion is an abomination in their sight; and I am here today to protest, in the sight of God and man, that I am condemned for my faith. For some time I was in doubt as to the charge on which they would ground my condemnation; but, thanks to heaven, it is no longer so; and I am about to die for my attachment to the Catholic faith. See you here the condition on which I might save my life? Apostasy is all they require; but, before high heaven, I spurn their offers, and with my last breath will glorify God for the honor he has done me, in allowing me thus to suffer for his name.

At this, he dropped the pardon to the ground and stepped forward to the executioner. When the rope was placed around his neck, and just before the trapdoor was sprung, those closest to the gallows could hear him thanking God with his last breaths.

• • •

While many would point to the times around the Reformation as proof of the fallacy of Catholicism because of their persecution of Protestants, few realize that once the Protestants took the upper hand, it was the Catholics who suffered for holding to what they believed. In some ways these battle lines are still drawn today, less obvious in some areas, while quite clear in places such as Northern Ireland.

To think that these differences can easily be put aside and a history of mutual murder and doctrinal differences easily forgotten is simplistic. But then, in the end the Gospel is quite simple and so is forgiveness. What are the key issues? Do you hold to Jesus and what He said above all else? Are you willing to set aside what you learned growing up if you don't find that it lines up with the Truth of what Jesus has said in God's Word? And then if we don't agree on how to interpret that, should we turn our energies into fighting each other while evil still runs free on the planet? Sure, one of us has to be wrong—though it is more likely that we both are in some way—but where does that leave us with respect to the greatest commandment: Love they neighbor as thyself? So there may be some debate between us when we get together to try to understand all that God has given us in His Word, which is just part of stretching ourselves to be more like Him, but when it is over, do we really have the time to walk away mad at one another when there is so much more we can do for God together?

Just as a revolutionary is not satisfied with the same old answers until they have proven them true, we can never expect someone's faith and beliefs to hold us up, no matter how good a person that person may be. Paul tells us in 1 Thessalonians 5:21–22 NAS, "Examine everything carefully; hold fast to that which is good; abstain from every form of evil." It is interesting how the next instruction, after he tells us to use our minds to determine what is good, is to beware of that analysis turning us toward evil.

It is significant to note that Jesus came to live in our hearts, not our minds. Paul thus tells us in this passage that there is no place for Jesus Freaks to throw their brains out the window, but those brains must always be ruled by Who is in their hearts.

> You can easily enough see how this kind of thing works by looking no further than your own body. Your body has many parts—limbs, organs, cells—but no matter how many parts you can name, you're still one body. It's exactly the same with Christ. By means of his one Spirit, we all said goodbye to our partial and piecemeal lives. We each used to independently call our own shots, but then we entered into a large and integrated life in which he has the final say in everything. (This is what we proclaimed in word and action when we were baptized.) Each of us is now a part of his resurrection body, refreshed and sustained at one fountain—his Spirit— where we all come to drink. The old labels we once used to identify ourselves—labels like Jew or Greek, slave or free—are no longer useful. We need something larger, more comprehensive.
> I want you to think about how all this makes you more significant, not less.
>
> Paul
>
> (1 Corinthians 12:12–14 THE MESSAGE)

235

"Honor Caesar as Caesar, but Fear God"

Speratus and Friends	Carthage	A.D. 180

The Proconsul Saturninus eyed the dissenters carefully. How could he bring these people back to their senses? "You can win the leniency of our lord the emperor if you return to reason."

Speratus answered for the group, "We have never done wrong. We have not taken part in any crime at all. We have never cursed. Even if we were ill-treated, we only gave thanks. Therefore we honor our emperor."

"We too are religious people," Proconsul Saturninus countered, "and our religion is simple. We swear by the genius of our lord the emperor and offer sacrifices for his well-being. You must do that too."

Speratus shook his head. "I do not recognize any empire of this present age. I serve that God whom no person has seen, or can ever see with these eyes. I have not stolen. On the contrary, when I buy anything I pay my taxes, for I know only one Lord, the King of kings, the Ruler of all nations."

Cittinus spoke up now: "There is no one whom we fear except the Lord our God who is in heaven."

Donata added, "Honor Caesar as Caesar, but fear God."

The Proconsul looked them over again. "Do you want some time to consider?"

Speratus replied, "In such a just cause there is nothing to consider."

Proconsul Saturninus read from his tablet: "Speratus, Nartzalus, Cittinus, Donata, Vestia, and Secunda, and the rest who confess that they want to live according to the Christian custom shall be executed by the sword, since they remain obstinate,

236

although the opportunity was offered them to return to the Roman tradition."

As the soldiers came to carry out the sentence, Nartzalus spoke for them all, "Today we are martyrs in heaven, thanks be to God."

• • •

Christian revolutionaries have a very different patriotic attitude. Though in all things they put God before country, that allegiance makes them better citizens for this, not worse. Because of their loyalty to God they can give themselves more wholeheartedly to following the laws of the state, knowing that the state has based its laws upon the statutes of the Bible and its moral code. When the laws of the land fall into conflict with those Biblical statutes, then they are better citizens for standing against them than they would be if they complied with ungodliness. Thus Christians, because of the conviction behind their stand for right and freedom, can be the most influential type of citizen there is.

This is also why they are the most feared, and why governments have been the greatest persecutors of Christians in the last two millennia.

Faith points to a moral law beyond man's law, and calls us to duties higher than material gain. Freedom of religion is not something to be feared, it's to be welcomed, because faith gives us a moral core and teaches us to hold ourselves to high standards, to love and to serve others, and to live responsible lives....

Life in America shows that liberty, paired with law, is not to be feared. In a free society, diversity is not disorder. Debate is not strife. And dissent is not revolution. A free society trusts its citizens to seek greatness in themselves and their country....

Tens of millions of Chinese today are relearning Buddhist, Taoist, and local religious traditions, or prac-

237

ticing Christianity, Islam, and other faiths.

Regardless of where or how these believers worship, they're no threat to public order; in fact, they make good citizens. For centuries, this country has had a tradition of religious tolerance. My prayer is that all persecution will end, so that all in China are free to gather and worship as they wish.

President George W. Bush
Speaking in China at Tsinghua University
February 22, 2002

Obey the rulers who have authority over you. Only God can give authority to anyone, and he puts these rulers in their places of power. People who oppose the authorities are opposing what God has done, and they will be punished. Rulers are a threat to evil people, not to good people. There is no need to be afraid of the authorities. Just do right, and they will praise you for it. After all, they are God's servants, and it is their duty to help you. If you do something wrong, you ought to be afraid, because these rulers have the right to punish you. They are God's servants who punish criminals to show how angry God is. But you should obey the rulers because you know it is the right thing to do, and not just because of God's anger.

Paul
(Romans 13:1–5 CEV)

The best government and highest sovereignty

you can attain to is to be subject to Him, that the

scepter of His Word and Spirit may rule in your heart.

The true glory of princes consists in advancing God's

glory, in the maintenance of true religion and the

Church's good; also in the dispensation of civil power,

with justice and honor to the public peace.

Above all, I would have you, as I hope you are

already, well-grounded and settled in your religion....

I would you have your own judgment and reason now

sealed to that sacred bond which education

hath written, that it may be judiciously your own

religion, and not other men's custom or tradition which

you profess.

239

CHARLES I
KING OF ENGLAND
1625–1649
IN A LETTER HE WROTE TO HIS SON, CHARLES II,
WHILE IN PRISON AWAITING HIS EXECUTION

The Illuminator

| Gregory | Armenia | A.D. 301 |

As Gregory walked up to the castle, he shaded his eyes from the brightness of the sun. Still, he could not resist admiring its brightness and squinted to take in the view of the countryside. It had been fourteen years since he had seen the sun and breathed fresh air. He was not sure he could stand it, but he took in as much of it as he could anyway. He remembered with awe the sight of Mount Ararat, which was the first thing that had greeted him as he left his prison of Khor Virap. He had never seen anything more lovely in his life.

As he was led by the guards through the halls of the castle, he was a strange sight in contrast to the wealth of the Armenian royal home that he was walking through. As he lingered near a tapestry, one of the guards looked him over again. His hair was long and unkept, as was his beard that nearly reached his waist. Though he was only a little older than forty, his hair was gray and he looked as if he were in his sixties. He was also gaunt, and the clothes he wore were no longer even suitable as rags.

Still, the guard thought, *the king's sister did call for him. We cannot waste time here*. "Come," he said to the man, "we are expected elsewhere."

Gregory followed compliantly without a sound.

When they entered a stateroom, the king's sister, Khosrovitookht, rose, crossed the room, and took the hands of the prisoner. Again the guard was struck by the harsh contrast between her royal person and this wraith of a prisoner. At the revulsion of it he took a step forward to intervene. Yet rather than welcoming the guard's concern, she turned to him and dismissed him.

"Brother Gregory, you have so often welcomed me in your

'home,' I am glad now that I can welcome you in mine," Khosrovitookht said, referring to her frequent secret visits to Gregory in the pit of Khor Virap, where her brother had imprisoned him some fourteen years before.

At this Gregory smiled, and for a moment she looked into his eyes. Despite his outward appearance, she would have never thought that this was a man who had just been released from so many years in a hole. He radiated peace like the sun radiated light.

"I have arranged for your release," she told him slowly. "My brother, the king ... he is not well." Then she went on to tell him the rest of the story. King Tiridates III, her brother, had grown more and more wild after Gregory's imprisonment in his attempts to stamp out the "heresy" of Christianity in Armenia, as she had already told him in her visits. Horrible things had happened since the last time she had seen him. Many had been killed and still more and more confessed Jesus as Lord. In the latest incident, Tiridates himself had gone to see to the execution of a group of Hripsimeyan nuns. She didn't know what had happened exactly, but whenever she asked people about it, a look of remorse crossed their faces and they said it was not the type of thing that a princess should have to hear about.

Upon Tiridates's return, he had shut himself up in his chambers and refused to let anyone see him. When a worried page finally entered the room with some food days later, he saw that the king had torn everything to pieces with his bare hands, and the page barely escaped with his life. "I am afraid he has been driven quite mad," the princess went on. "No one can enter his room for fear that he will kill them. I know this must be his reward for the evil he has done. But it has also allowed me to make arrangements for your release—"

"Take me to him," Gregory interrupted.

The princess looked at him in disbelief. "But have you not understood what I have said? This is the man who threw you in

241

that hole so many years ago! He will kill you! You of all people! You can't go in—"

Again Gregory interrupted. "Take me to him. As I have tried to teach you, God is not a God of madness, but of love. He has not cursed his majesty for my release, but rather brought me here for his majesty's sake."

At last the princess quieted her objections and did as Gregory requested. She offered him a bath and a change of clothes as well, but these, he said, could wait until after he had seen the king.

Khosrovitookht led Gregory to the king's chambers, opened the locked door to let him enter, and then locked it behind him. For a while there was a little ruckus and then quiet. She sat for some time waiting and praying outside the door. *Why is it so quiet?* she thought. *Has Tiridates killed Gregory? Is he now lying there dead on the floor as I sit here?*

Then she heard a knock at the door. She ran to open it slightly and was relieved to see Gregory's withered face appear from the other side. Yet even more to her amazement, her brother, now calm and sane, followed him.

Within the following weeks the king and all those in the castle were baptized as Christians, and Armenia became the first country to legalize Christianity, twelve years before Constantine's Edict of Milan endorsed Christianity in the Roman Empire.

For bringing the light of sanity and of Christianity to the king, and in the following years to the people of Armenia, Gregory became known as "Gregory the Illuminator" or "Enlightener."

• • •

The king's heart is in the hand of the Lord,
Like the rivers of water; He turns it wherever He wishes.

Solomon
(Proverbs 21:1 NKJV)

Civil Disobedience

Giorgi Vins and Gennadi Kryuchkox	U.S.S.R.	1966

It was like no protest the world had ever seen. In the news every day, we witnessed riots with slogans being yelled, signs and banners being waved, and even rocks being thrown at authorities as they tried to keep the angry mobs under control.

But on May 16, five hundred Soviet Baptists gathered in the courtyard of the Communist Central Committee and did not shout slogans or demands, but stood together praying and singing hymns. On their behalf, Georgi Vins and Gennadi Kryuchkov presented a petition to the Soviet government requesting the official recognition of their organization, a stop to governmental interference in church affairs, the release of imprisoned believers, and freedom for Soviet citizens to teach and be taught religious faith.

They stayed through the night and into the next day.

It was the culminating step of a peaceful movement for religious freedom in the Soviet Union that had begun in 1960. Vins, Kryuchkov, and others had then formed a committee to protest the tightening government restrictions on believers. In 1964, with the government's permission, they organized the first campaign for human rights in the Communist world. They distributed a list of 170 Baptists imprisoned for their faith in Christ to government leaders, international organizations, and others.

On the morning of May 17, soldiers and KGB officers surrounded the peaceful gathering. Around 1:00 P.M., a number of buses closed in and the soldiers attacked, beating the believers and forcing them toward the buses. No one fought back. Instead, the believers linked arms and started singing over the cries of pain from others being beaten and dragged to the buses. Once they were loaded onto the buses, they were taken to prison.

Yet even there they continued to pray and sing. The Communists had refused the pleas of these peaceful protestors, but they had not broken their spirits.

• • •

It took another twenty-five years, but eventually what was known as the Soviet Union was no more. Could it be that the example of these few helped to keep the flame of religious freedom lit? God doesn't always answer our prayers immediately or in ways that we expect, but He does answer. Every good work of the revolutionary Jesus Freak serves as a witness to the cause of Christ. Fearing God, not man.

244

Nonviolence is a powerful and just weapon ... which cuts without wounding and ennobles the man who wields it. It is a sword that heals.

Martin Luther King Jr.

You are the light of the world. A city set on a hill cannot be hidden; nor do men light a lamp, and put it under the peck-measure, but on the lampstand; and it gives light to all who are in the house.
Let your light shine before men in such a way that they may see your good works, and glorify your Father who is in heaven.

Jesus
(Matthew 5:14–16 NAS)

We need no rifles or pistols for our
battle, but instead, spiritual
weapons—and the foremost among
those is prayer…. Through prayer,
we continually implore new grace
from God, since without God's help
and grace it would be impossible for us to preserve the faith and
be true to His commandments….
Let us love our enemies, bless those
who curse us, pray for those who
persecute us. For love will conquer
and will endure for all eternity. And
happy are they who will live and die
in God's love.

FRANZ JÄGERSTÄTTER
BEHEADED FOR REFUSING TO SERVE IN THE
GERMAN ARMY DURING WORLD WAR II AFTER
THE ANSCHLUSS IN AUSTRIA
BERLIN, GERMANY
1943

A Face That Would Make You Forget Death

Joyce Lewes	England	1557

When Joyce Lewes witnessed the execution of Laurence Saunders in Coventry at the hands of the state church, she understood that he died for a righteous cause. She asked many questions about the reason for his death and what he believed, and came to realize the oppression that existed from the state church and what was the truth of God's Word concerning salvation through Jesus alone, not through the traditions set forth by the state church.

At length she sought out Mr. John Glover, who instructed her further in the Truth from God's Word and rebuked her devotion to the pleasures of this world at the cost of adhering to the Truth. She realized the folly of her lifestyle and turned wholeheartedly to Jesus for her salvation. Immediately Joyce began to despise the false teachings of the state church and began to speak out against its errors.

Her husband, Mr. T. Lewes, was still loyal to the Church of England and was unwilling to be taught by his wife. However, when a citation arrived for her arrest, he forced the bearer to eat it at the point of a dagger to his throat, then swallow it down. Then he sent the man away. This only turned the authorities' eyes on Mr. Lewes, and he was soon called for and brought before them. Admitting to his wife's contempt for their teachings, he was bound and fined until he could produce her before the court.

Joyce was heartbroken at her husband's confinement. However, Mr. Glover told her to hold fast for the sake of the Truth and promised that he would go to see her husband. When Mr. Glover met with Mr. Lewes, he urged him to forfeit the money he was bound in for the sake of saving his wife's life. Mr. Lewes would have none of this, though, and eventually Joyce was brought before the state church officials for judgment. She was promptly thrown in a horrid, dirty prison and brought time and time again before them for examination.

When she was presented with the traditions of the state church for acceptance, she was as firm in rejecting them as the early Christians were in refusing to sacrifice to the Roman gods. "If these things were in the Word of God," Mrs. Lewes testified before them, "I would with all my heart receive, believe, and esteem them."

Her judge, however, reproved her for this. "If thou wilt believe no more than what is warranted by Scriptures, thou art in a state of damnation!"

"How dare you speak thus of God's Word!" she threw back at him. "Your words are as impure as they are profane!"

Summarily she was sentenced to execution at the stake.

However, the local sheriff did not have the heart to kill her at the time, so she spent the next year in prison awaiting the fulfillment of her sentence. When a warrant for her death finally arrived from London to expedite the sentence, Joyce gathered her friends to her to discuss how she might make the spectacle of her death a testimony to the glory of God and the deceitfulness of those who opposed the truth of God's Word. In their discussions she told them, smiling, "As for death, I think but lightly of. When I know that I shall behold the amiable countenance of Christ my dear Savior, the ugly face of death does not much trouble me."

Her friends stayed with her through the night and comforted her with the Scriptures when she grew fainthearted or doubtful about her situation. With their encouragement she clung all the more to Jesus, who had died to take away the sins of the world that those who accept Him as Lord and Savior might have eternal life.

In the morning, around nine o'clock, the sheriff permitted her friends to walk with her to the place of her execution, something he was severely reprimanded for afterward. On the sight of the stake, she nearly fainted, but her prayer all the while was that England would be delivered from the falsehoods of the state church

and be free to worship Jesus according to His Word. Many sur-rounding her, including the sheriff, said "Amen" to this.

Before the stake, she prayed again and was then given a cup of water to refresh herself before her execution. She took it and said, "I drink to all them that unfeignedly love the Gospel of Christ, and wish for the abolition of the church hierarchy that loves itself more than God's Word." A good many in the crowd drank this toast with her, though they were marked and forced to repent of it later.

Though she had been a bit feeble in the approach, in the face of death she was bold. Her face shone with a cheerful spirit and rosy cheeks as she was bound to the stake. She extended her hands toward heaven until under the press of the flames she could no more. Mercifully the sheriff had, at the request of friends, prepared the fuel for the fire to be so much that she was engulfed quickly and died in only a matter of minutes.

At this sight, many found tears of pity in their eyes, and her cause won more supporters against the cruelty of her accusers.

• • •

We cannot be defined by weakness, if, in those times we feel weakest, we turn to His strength. For in this way we end in strength, and that strength leaves an even greater testimony to Him for our humility in turning to Him for assurance.

While Jesus was here on earth, he offered prayers and pleadings, with a loud cry and tears, to the one who could deliver him out of death. And God heard his prayers because of his reverence for God. So even though Jesus was God's Son, he learned obedience from the things he suffered. In this way, God qualified him as a perfect High Priest, and he became the source of eternal salvation for all those who obey him.

(Hebrews 5:7–9 NLT)

No one makes us afraid or leads us into captivity

as we have set our faith on Jesus.

For though we are beheaded and crucified

and exposed to beasts and chains and fire and all

other form of torture, it is plain that we do not

249

forsake the confession of our faith, but the more things

of this kind which happen to us the more

are there others who become believers and

truly religious through the name of Jesus.

JUSTIN MARTYR
SCOURGED AND BEHEADED
ROME
C. A.D. 165

More Than He Had Expected to Steal

| A Thief | Middle East | c. 1990 |

The van was parked at the village bazaar when the thief approached. Seeing the small leather folder sitting inside, he quickly snaked his hand in through the open window. In seconds the contraband was tucked into his coat and he was walking quickly away.

Later that night when he was safely home, he opened it. It wasn't a wallet. It was a book. There was no money inside. Frustrated, he wanted to throw it away, but instead he started flipping through the pages and then reading bits and pieces. Before long he was absorbed in the story.

The book told the story of a King who loved a far-off people so much that He sent His own Son to go and live among the people; to speak their language and learn their ways. By the time the man finished reading, he had grown to love that King. Was this story true? He had to find out.

Looking to the front of the book, he found the address of its owner. He went to the address, taking the book with him. He didn't know what to expect when he knocked on the door. *This is crazy!* he thought. *They will probably arrest me.* But he was willing to risk it to find out more about the King in the story.

"Hello and welcome," was the warm greeting from the man who opened the door. "Hey, you are returning my Bible!"

The "thief" was welcomed into a warm and loving church meeting. When he told the pastor how he had stolen his Bible thinking it was money, the pastor smiled. "It is a treasure greater than money."

The pastor helped the man to learn more and more about the

King of the story and about His Son, Jesus Christ, and the new life He offered. Before he left that night he had become the newest servant of the King in their congregation!

• • •

Today, that "thief" pastors a church of his own. The combination of the Word of God and a willing, open heart work consistent miracles. And there is no greater miracle than a heart that was dead to God coming alive to Him.

> For the word of God is full of living power. It is sharper than the sharpest knife, cutting deep into our innermost thoughts and desires. It exposes us for what we really are.
>
> (Hebrews 4:12 NLT)

251

*Against the persecution
of a tyrant the godly
have no remedy but
prayer.*

JOHN CALVIN
FRENCH REFORMER
1509–1564

*No one—imprisoned,
tortured, harassed, or
persecuted—should
escape the vigilance of the
praying church.*

WORLD COUNCIL OF CHURCHES
NAIROBI ASSEMBLY
1975

*Are you part of the
vigilant praying church?*

"I Die the King's Good Servant, but God's First"

| Thomas More | England | c. 1536 |

While some, like Luther and Tyndale, saw the need for such violent change in the church that they were willing to defy its authority in order to return to a truer, more biblical structure and practice in the church, others took a more moderate approach, believing that by staying within the church and only emphasizing the key points that needed reform, they would be performing a greater service to the entire body of Christ. One such man was Thomas More.

253

As had Luther, More began his career studying law. His hope, however, had been to join the priesthood from the beginning, joining a monastery soon after leaving law school. But after four years at the monastery, he left and joined himself to the English parliament. In this time, because of his wit and cheerful conversation, he made good friends with Henry VIII, Desiderius Erasmus, and John Colet. Because of his relationship with King Henry VIII, he found himself in various public offices, finally being named lord chancellor of England.

In this time, he wrote various discussions of church doctrine, which won him the title of "Defender of the Faith." Because of this, he was urged by the bishop of London to write arguments against the works of Luther and Tyndale. More was also involved in a lengthy and heated written debate with William Tyndale over aspects of doctrine and church authority, among other issues, on behalf of the established church and the crown of England. Because of such activities, More prospered greatly during the early part of King Henry's reign.

However, when Henry VIII decided to divorce Catherine of

Aragón to marry Anne Boleyn, More suddenly found he had more in common with Tyndale than he had thought. He and Tyndale, among others, opposed the king's divorce. This was also the beginning of King Henry's break with the established church and the eventual formation of the Church of England under leadership of the crown rather than a religious head who had come up from the ranks of the priests.

Thomas More eventually resigned his position as lord chancellor to return to private life and hopefully have nothing to say about Henry's political and religious policies. However, King Henry required an oath of allegiance from More and others, which included a pledge to acknowledge him as not only the king but also the head of the Church of England. While More did not believe in the absolute authority of the church hierarchy in its conduct, he could not support the crown as a better alternative either. He refused the oath and was imprisoned in the Tower of London.

254

More was accused of treason to the crown for opposing Henry's takeover of the church, which had much more to do with Henry's desire for power and control than his objections to the established church that were being voiced by the Reformers, though Henry tried to justify his actions by citing their objections to church authority. More was tried and condemned to death on the testimony of false witnesses and his unwillingness to take the oath of allegiance. In response to his sentence, he said,

I have nothing more to say, my lords, but that just as the blessed Apostle St. Paul, as we read in the Acts of the Apostles, was present and consented to the death of St. Stephen, and kept the coats of those that stoned him to death, and yet they are both together holy saints in heaven and shall continue to be friends there forever, so I truly trust, and shall right heartily pray, that though your lordships have now here on earth been my condemning judges, we may hereafter meet right merrily together in heaven and enjoy our everlasting salvations together. And thus I desire Almighty God to preserve and defend the King's majesty, and to send him good counsel.

Those in the church, including King Henry's new appointed bishop of London, Thomas Cranmer, opposed the verdict and sentence.

As More was led to the platform to be beheaded, he remained in good spirits. He joked with the master lieutenant on the way up and stood before the spectators with no air of remorse. When allowed to speak but a little from the platform, he asked for the prayers of those in the audience, requested that they should pray for the king, recited Psalm 51, and assured the crowd that he died "the king's good servant, but God's first."

He then turned to the executioner and said, "Today you will do me a greater favor than any other mortal man is able to do me; pluck up your spirit, man, and don't be afraid to do your duty. My neck is very short, so please take heed therefore to strike true." The executioner dispatched him with one stroke.

Thomas More was executed on July 6, 1536, by the order of the man he had fought so hard to defend most of his career, a date which was exactly three months before the execution under similar circumstances of the man he had opposed, William Tyndale.

• • •

There are no other revolutionaries like Christians who can pledge their loyalty to their persecutors in the same breath with voicing their defiance of them for which they are being executed. Only the love of God can do this. For Christians are never truly defiant as much as they are simply more loyal to a higher principle than that of man's rule.

This is the cutting edge of the love of God. While the world and modern psychology have tried to adapt the essence of the love of God for their use, calling it "unconditional love," the love of God is still

255

more powerful. "Unconditional love" will accept all activities and self-destruction that the object will get itself into, but only the love of God can love the sinner while hating the sin and standing firm to remove it from a person's life. It is this love that caused Jesus to rebuke the Pharisees, and sometimes the disciples, to try to wake them out of their traditional and Godless thinking. It is this love that knocked the soldiers down when they came to capture Jesus in the Garden of Gethsemane (see John 18:6), who then turned to heal the ear of the man Peter had attacked (see Luke 22:51). The love of God knows when to confront and when to comfort, it knows when to fight and when to forgive, through the guidance of its source: the Spirit of God.

This is something the world will never have until it knows God.

Have mercy on me, O God,
according to your unfailing love;
according to your great compassion
blot out my transgressions.
Wash away all my iniquity
and cleanse me from my sin.
For I know my transgressions,
and my sin is always before me.
Against you, you only, have I sinned
and done what is evil in your sight,
so that you are proved right when you speak
and justified when you judge.
Surely I was sinful at birth,
sinful from the time my mother conceived me.
Surely you desire truth in the inner parts;
you teach me wisdom
in the inmost place.
Cleanse me with hyssop, and I will be clean;
wash me, and I will be whiter than snow.
Let me hear joy and gladness;

let the bones you have crushed rejoice.
Hide your face from my sins
and blot out all my iniquity.
Create in me a pure heart, O God,
and renew a steadfast spirit within me.
Do not cast me from your presence
or take your Holy Spirit from me.
Restore to me the joy of your salvation
and grant me a willing spirit, to sustain me.
Then I will teach transgressors your ways,
and sinners will turn back to you.
Save me from bloodguilt, O God,
the God who saves me,
and my tongue will sing of your righteousness.
O Lord, open my lips,
and my mouth will declare your praise.
You do not delight in sacrifice, or I would bring it;
you do not take pleasure in burnt offerings.
The sacrifices of God are a
broken spirit;
a broken and contrite heart,
O God, you will not despise.
In your good pleasure make Zion prosper;
build up the walls of Jerusalem.
Then there will be righteous sacrifices,
whole burnt offerings to delight you;
then bulls will be offered on your altar.

David
After being confronted about his adultery
(Psalm 51 NIV)

You are indeed my lord,
but God is my Lord and yours.
It would be useful neither to you
nor to me if I were to neglect His will
in order to obey yours.
For on His fearful judgment day,
you and I will both be judged
as servants of one Lord.

THOMAS À BECKET TO HIS KING, HENRY II
SLAIN BY FOUR KNIGHTS WITH SWORDS
NEAR THE ALTAR OF CANTERBURY CATHEDRAL
CANTERBURY, ENGLAND
1170

"Ordained by the Pierced Hands of Jesus"

Young Russians	U.S.S.R.	1950s

"We met a young Russian who was a secret minister," wrote Pastor Wurmbrand. "I asked him who ordained him.

"He answered, 'We had no real bishop to ordain us. The official bishop would ordain nobody who is not approved by the Communist Party. So ten of us young Christians went to the tomb of a bishop who died as a martyr. Two of us put our hands on his gravestone, and the others formed a circle around us. We asked the Holy Spirit to ordain us. We are sure that we were ordained by the pierced hands of Jesus.'

"It is like the church in the first centuries. What seminaries did those attend who turned the world upside down for Christ? Did they all know how to read? And from where did they receive Bibles? God spoke to them."

. . .

Too many wait for some other recognition or degree before they serve God. If God has called you, then He has also ordained you to do it. Credentials from Bible schools or seminaries are wonderful if they are evidence of your growing closer to and becoming more knowledgeable about God, but you are really missing it if you think you must have their approval before you can touch lives for God. All you need in order to do that is obedience.

But when the Father sends the Counselor as my representative—and by the Counselor I mean the Holy Spirit—he will teach you everything and will remind you of everything I myself have told you.

Jesus
(John 14:26 NLT)

259

You have an anointing from the Holy One, and you all know. I have not written to you because you do not know the truth, but because you do know it, and because no lie is of the truth.

John
(1 John 2:20–21 NAS)

The Last Martyr of the Coliseum

Telemachus	Rome	A.D. 391

"Go to Rome."

Telemachus was a peace-loving monk who caringly kept his garden and lived in a small farming province in Asia. However, though he normally feared the hustle and bustle of large cities, when he heard God's voice tell him to go, he packed and left immediately. He prayed the entire journey for God's direction.

When he arrived, the city was in the midst of celebrating its victory over the Goths in the north. Troops marched through the streets laden with spoils and dragged behind them those prisoners taken in battle, some of whom were generals and kings. Young Emperor Honorius had paraded through the streets earlier in the car of victory headed for the Coliseum, though it was his general, Stilicho, who had actually guided the troops to victory. The main activities of the celebration were to take place there later that afternoon.

Swept along by the crowds, Telemachus soon found himself among the nearly eighty thousand spectators in the Coliseum. Though Constantine had put an end to the death of Christians in the Coliseum and barred gladiator games roughly seventy years earlier, Honorius had given in to the whims of the populace and retracted the prohibition against the gladiator contests.

As Telemachus made his way through the crowd, he looked onto the floor of the Coliseum to see two lines of young men armed with swords or three-pronged spears and nets. They stopped before the emperor's box and raised their weapons.

"*Ave, Caesar, morituri te salutant!*" ("Hail, Caesar, those about to die salute thee!")

Then, at some signal he had not seen, the two lines turned to face each other, pairing off, and they began to fight as bloody and fierce a contest as any on a battlefield. Telemachus was dumbstruck: *Four centuries after Christ and they are still killing each other for entertainment?*

Suddenly one young man with a sword was caught in a net and thrown to the ground. He was already badly hurt and unable to get back up. His opponent quickly pressed his advantage, taking his spear and resting it on the other's chest, preventing him from moving. He called out, *"Hoc habet!"* ("He has it!") and at some other unknown sign, the other gladiators stopped and stood aside.

Many in the audience began to stand, holding their thumbs down. A chant began, *"Recipe ferrum!"* ("Receive the steel!") A small group of officials from below made their way into the arena and stood by the men for a closer look. Echoing the crowd, they held their hands out with their thumbs down. To Telemachus's horror, the man simply nodded, then decisively drove the spear through the chest of his victim, whose death cry was lost in the cheers around him.

Then, as the officials made their way back to their seats, slaves came out with huge hooks and dragged the body of the fallen warrior across the sand, leaving a wake of blood. Others followed with more sand and rakes to refresh the floor of the Coliseum so the contests could continue.

Soon the other gladiators returned to their positions. However, before they could resume, a robed figure leaped the wall separating the crowds from the arena and ran to a position between the two fighters nearest the emperor's box. When he got there, Telemachus placed his hands on the chests of the two men to divide them, calling out, "In the name of Christ, stop! Don't despise God's mercy in turning away the sword of your enemies by murdering one another!"

The crowd was only stunned for a moment. "This is no place for preaching!" someone shouted. "The old customs of Rome must be observed—on gladiators!" came another. Then the roar rose again so that no voice was distinguishable from the others.

One of the gladiators hit the old man in the stomach with the handle of his sword, doubling Telemachus over and dropping him to his knees. Then they turned to recommence their fighting, but unexpectedly, Telemachus rose back to his feet quickly and stepped between them again, pushing them apart. "In the name of Christ, stop!"

"Get him out of there!" "Go away, old man!" "Let them continue!" "Sedition! Sedition! Down with him!" Then a chant arose: "Run him through! Run him through!" and people began throwing things into the arena—rocks, or whatever they could get their hands on, came soaring toward Telemachus.

One of the gladiators turned on him suddenly in the frenzy, driving his sword up to its hilt into the old man's stomach.

Suddenly the angry crowd hushed to an eerie silence.

Telemachus again sank to his knees, his blood flowing from his wounds into a growing pool of crimson in the sand. With his last breath, he again shouted out, "In the name of Jesus, stop!"

Then he fell to his face and did not move again.

No one else said a word. For a moment no one even stirred. Then one man got up and made his way out of the arena. Another man and his wife followed. Then more. Slowly the trickle grew until everyone had risen to their feet and all the spectators had made their way out of the Coliseum in a painful, guilty silence.

Never again were gladiator contests held in the Coliseum.

• • •

What does it take to stand against the crowd and cry out, "No, stop! This is wrong!" If we flow down the rivers of culture, even a "Christian" culture, that are based on people's desires and their traditions and not on truth, and never make a wave, are we truly living as a witness for Jesus?

Blessed are the peacemakers,
For they shall be called sons of God.
Blessed are those who are persecuted for righteousness' sake,
For theirs is the kingdom of heaven.

Jesus
(Matthew 5:9–10 NKJV)

If a man hasn't discovered something that he will die for, he isn't fit to live.

MARTIN LUTHER KING JR.
DETROIT, MICHIGAN
JUNE 23, 1963

A man really believes not what he recites in his creed, but only the things he is ready to die for. The Christians of the underground church have proved that they are ready to die for their faith.

RICHARD WURMBRAND
FOUNDER OF THE VOICE OF THE MARTYRS
SPENT FOURTEEN YEARS IN A COMMUNIST PRISON
ROMANIA
1940S, '50S, AND '60S

The Sweet Refreshing of the Spirit		
William Robinson, Marmaduke Stevenson, William Leddra, and Mary Dyer	New England	1659

On the day they were appointed to be hanged, the prisoners were marched to their gallows by a troop of approximately two hundred armed men and several horsemen, so much was the fear of a public uprising on their behalf. The four Quakers had been told to march in silence, but at the risk that they might try to speak and elicit sympathy from the crowd, a drummer was assigned to march before them, keeping a steady tempo, but to beat more loudly if the prisoners tried to speak.

The four prisoners, however, were not intimidated by all of this. They walked happily hand in hand to the place they were to suffer.

In 1658 a law had been passed in Boston banishing Quakers under the pain of death. The irony is that the ones who passed this law were the Puritans who had left Europe because of the religious persecution! The dispute between these religious groups was about the assurance of one's salvation.

"This to me is an hour of greatest joy," Mary Dyer exclaimed, adding that "No eye can see, no ear can hear, no tongue can utter, no heart can understand, the sweet refreshing of the Spirit of the Lord which I feel now."

Coming to the ladder of the gallows, they took tender leave of one another and yielded to their executioners.

Robinson's last words before the knot cut off his life were, "I suffer for Christ, in whom I live, and for whom I die."

Before his last breath, Stevenson said, "This day shall we be at rest with the Lord."

When it came William Leddra's turn to put his head in the noose, he remarked, "I commit my righteous cause unto Thee, O God." Then with his last breath he said, "Lord Jesus, receive my spirit!"

Last to be executed was Mary Dyer. At the sight of her mounting the scaffold, the crowd urged her to reconsider and come back down. But she refused them. "In obedience to the will of the Lord, I abide faithful unto death." She was straightaway hanged as the others had been.

. . .

Persecution alone does not make you a Jesus Freak. People do outlandish things out of their own selfish desires and are persecuted. Living in some parts of the world, simply belonging to a certain race or gender, or belonging to a certain group, will cause you to be persecuted. Persecution is never right. But people become Jesus Freaks because of their love for Jesus and willingness to give all for Him.

These early American settlers who fled Europe for the sake of gaining religious freedom became like the very people they fled from in too many instances. They loved believing they were right more than they loved being right. They loved gaining power more than they loved giving it away. They got set in their ways and beliefs and fell into the same traps that those fell into who made them want to leave Europe.

That is why Christianity is described more as a river and a walk than being a lake or a destination. Christianity is not truly alive unless it is moving and changing. That is also why it is not simply memorizing a list of do's and don'ts like the Ten Commandments, but is a life "in the Spirit" where daily actions are directed by the instructions we get from God in walking with Him every step of the way. This is also why we are instructed to "pray without ceasing" (1 Thessalonians 5:17 KJV). When water stands still and is not renewed, it begins to stagnate; so do we when we become so set in our ways that we think

we know it all already and have gone far enough on our journey with
God to be able to judge others.

> So I advise you to live according to your new life in the
> Holy Spirit. Then you won't be doing what your sinful
> nature craves....
> If we are living now by the Holy Spirit, let us follow the
> Holy Spirit's leading in every part of our lives.
>
> Paul
> (Galatians 5:16, 25 NLT)

> But I have this complaint against you. You don't love
> me or each other as you did at first! Look how far you
> have fallen from your first love! Turn back to me again
> and work as you did at first.
>
> Jesus
> (Revelation 2:4 NLT)

The Five Loves of a Jesus Freak

Love GOD

LOVE His Word

Love your ENEmies

LoVE your Neighbor
Love TRuth

A Foolish Waste of Lives?		
Jim Elliot, Peter Fleming, Ed McCully, Nate Saint, and Roger Youderian	Ecuador	1956

The missionaries looked from one face to another in the group around them, but in each they read the same quiet resolve. Everyone knew the danger was very real, and it seemed unlikely that all of them would come out unharmed. But no matter how deadly this tribe was considered, here was a group that had never heard the Gospel before. In the face of this, the risks were irrelevant—they had to do something to contact this people and tell them about Jesus.

"They aren't even called by their right name among the tribes we have already reached," Jim Elliot echoed again. "The Quichua call them 'Auca,' which means simply 'savages' in the Quichua tongue. Everyone seems to echo that they are deathly afraid of outsiders and will 'shoot first and ask questions later.' They will kill anyone for simply setting foot in their part of the forest."

All of those present nodded soberly, but it was Nate Saint who spoke what they were all really thinking: "Yes, we know all of that. That is not the issue we are here to discuss. We know the risk, what we need to know now is *how* do we get them the Gospel?"

In the coming weeks, they worked out a plan and began to implement it with the utmost patience and caution.

In their planning, they met with an area farmer who directed them to Dayuma, a woman who worked for him. She had once lived among the Auca, but escaped. From her they learned some helpful words and phrases in the language of these people. They also learned that they called themselves the *Huaorani* (literally "people" in their own tongue). "But," she also warned, "do not trust them. To you they might seem friendly for a while, but they will not stop short of killing."

In September 1955, Nate Saint and Ed McCully, two of the missionaries, had seen a cluster of Huaorani houses while flying in Nate's airplane. This had inspired them to use the plane to scout for Huaorani villages from the air and figure out some way to use it to make their presence welcome in the area before they made face-to-face contact with them.

The others agreed. "But," Jim reminded them, "if outside groups or the newspapers find out we're trying to reach the Huaorani, curious people might hurry in. That would scare off the Huaorani or get people killed. We must move slowly and keep our plan a secret."

271

More flights over the area showed several more Huaorani clearings. The first time Nate flew his plane low over the main clearing—which the missionaries nicknamed "Terminal City"— the Huaorani scattered in fright. But then the missionaries began dropping gifts tied to a rope. T-shirts, machetes, cloth, even pictures of the five men. Later, they were excited to see a few Huaorani waving at the plane, and others wearing their gifts.

Nate flew as low as he dared, and the missionaries leaned out of the plane, calling out in the Huaorani language, "I like you! I am your friend!" Then something exciting happened. As Nate slowly circled the Huaorani clearing after dropping the rope, the Huaorani tied on some gifts of their own: headbands of colorful feathers and even a parrot!

Three months went by as the missionaries tried to get the Huaorani people used to the small, yellow airplane flying over their villages. Finally in December, as Jim Elliot, Nate Saint, Ed McCully, Pete Fleming, and Roger Youderian got together to plan the next steps in Operation Huaorani, they made an

important decision. It was time to actually make the face-to-face meeting.

The plans for this meeting were made with even more care than the rest. First the five missionaries would land on a strip of beach on the river nearest "Terminal City." Then they would build a tree house for safety from jungle animals. They would wait for several days, letting the Huaorani get used to their presence, before attempting to make contact.

On Tuesday, January 3, 1956, it took pilot Nate Saint five trips to fly in all five men and their supplies. The landings and takeoffs on the beach were tricky, but their worst problem was the flying insects. The men got in touch with their wives each day, either by shortwave radio or with notes they sent with Nate in his plane. After a few days of camping on the beach, the men began calling out Huaorani phrases of welcome across the river. It was eerie, as they knew they must be under close surveillance, but they never saw a soul besides one another.

On Friday, however, they were finally rewarded. A Huaorani man and two women appeared on the opposite bank of the river. Jim Elliot waded out toward them, using all the Huaorani phrases he knew, to help lead them safely across. It was an exciting day. The missionaries took pictures of the visit and even took the man, whom they nicknamed "George," up in the plane for a ride over his village.

Saturday, Nate and Pete flew back to base camp to pick up supplies and report their progress. They returned to the beach on Sunday morning, January 8. When they landed, Nate radioed back to his wife: "Pray for us! We're sure we'll have contact again today! Will radio you again at four-thirty."

Elisabeth Elliot and the other wives gathered eagerly around their radio later that afternoon. But four-thirty came and went. Nothing. When they still had not heard from the men by Monday morning, they knew something was wrong. A search party made its way to the river camp. Five bodies were found in the river. The men had been killed by Huaorani lances.

• • •

This tragic story soon appeared in newspapers around the world. Some people thought the five men were foolish to try to make friends with such a savage Indian tribe. "A waste of lives!" they said. But others responded differently. In universities and churches around the globe, over a thousand young people volunteered to become missionaries in the place of these five brave men. In Ecuador, attendance by natives at mission schools and church services reached record levels, and the number of conversions skyrocketed. A member of another tribe, the Jivaro, followed the example of these men and went with the Gospel to another Jivaro tribe that had been at war with his for years. His visit brought peace between the two groups. Eventually Rachel Saint—Nate's sister—and Elisabeth Elliot lived among the very Huaorani who had murdered their family members. These women learned the Huaorani language and translated the Bible for them.

The questions still remained: How did these men die? What went wrong? When the relationship between the Huaorani and the missionaries was more solidified some time later, these questions were posed to one of the men who had been involved in the killing of the five men. He explained that up until that time, all of their contact with outsiders had involved killing or trying to kill one side or the other, and for this reason their fear of outsiders often prompted them to attack before the others attacked them. In the case of these five white men, the villagers had greatly wondered why they wanted to make contact with them—what profit did they hope to extract from their tribe? They instinctively feared a trap.

After the panic that ended in the murder of the five men, the tribe realized their mistake. In the attack, one of the missionaries had fired two warning shots from a revolver that had accidentally grazed one of the Huaorani. Because of this, they realized that the men had had weapons but refused to use them to harm any of the

273

villagers intentionally, even at the expense of their own lives. The Huaorani could not understand why anyone who could have killed them to save their own lives did not do so.

When others finally came in a similar way, they listened first before they attacked. When they heard the story of Jesus, how He had given His life to reconcile man to God, they immediately understood the actions of the first five missionaries.

It is very possible the Huaorani, and other subsequent tribes in their area, would never have been reached if these five "fools" had not acted just like Jesus. The Huaorani believed the Gospel preached, because they had seen the Gospel lived.

He is no fool who gives what he cannot keep to gain what he cannot lose.

Jim Elliot

We are fools for Christ's sake.

PAUL
(1 CORINTHIANS 4:10 KJV)

"Don't be a fool, Vitalus; sacrifice to the gods and live,"
the Judge Paulinus told the prisoner being
tortured on the rack before him.
Vitalus answered in gasps, but though his body was
exhausted from the strain, his spirit was still unyielding.
"You must have lost your reason to think that I
will be deceived by you and brought to eternal suffering
in soul and body, when all my life I have sought to
deliver others from the danger of such delusions."

VITALUS
BURIED ALIVE
RAVENNA, ITALY
C. A.D. 99

No Family Outside of Jesus

Irenaeus	Pannonia (probably modern Hungary)	c. A.D. 310

"You must obey the divine emperor's ordinances and sacrifice to the gods," Probus, the prefect of the region, demanded.

Irenaeus was a young man who was probably named after Irenaeus of Lyons, who had been martyred about a century before this. He was as calm and composed as his name, which means "lover of peace" in Greek, implied. "The person who sacrifices to the gods and not to the one true God shall be destroyed."

"But our gracious princes have ordered these sacrifices to be carried out or torture to be applied," Probus warned.

"And my gracious Prince of Peace has ordered me to submit to torture rather than to deny God and sacrifice to devils."

Probus stood from his seat at this. "You will sacrifice to the gods or I must have you tortured!"

"I will rejoice if you do, that I might share in my Lord's suffering."

At this, Irenaeus was severely beaten.

Probus still stood. "What do you say now, Irenaeus—will you sacrifice?"

"I am sacrificing—to my God with my good confession, as I have always done."

Then Probus commanded that Irenaeus's mother, father, wife, and friends be brought in before him. They pleaded with him to recant and sacrifice, that he was too young to die and that he should not choose such a path that would destroy his future.

"Let their tears wash away your madness, Irenaeus. Think of your youth and your future and sacrifice."

"I am. I am thinking of my eternal future, so I still refuse to sacrifice."

Probus then had Irenaeus thrown into prison, where he was tortured, starved, and allowed little sleep. When Probus thought he might have had enough, he called for him in the middle of the night to see if he might at last recant.

Probus addressed him again, "You must understand, I have my orders. If you do not sacrifice to the gods, I must have you executed most painfully."

"Do as you have been ordered, then, but don't expect me to sacrifice."

This time Probus had him beaten again with rods.

"Now what do you say?"

"I have God whom I have learned to worship since I was a child. I adore Him. He comforts me in everything, and to Him alone will I offer sacrifice—I cannot worship gods that are made with hands."

"What of your wife?"

"I have no wife."

"And your children?"

"I have no children."

"What about your father and mother?"

"I have no father and mother."

"Then who were these people I brought before you not long ago? Those who pleaded with you to leave this insanity and live?"

"One of Jesus' commandments says, 'He who loves father or mother, or wife or children or relatives, more than me, is not worthy of me.'"

Probus then had Irenaeus taken out to one of the bridges, where he stretched out his hands toward heaven and prayed, "O Lord Jesus Christ, who suffered for the salvation of the world, let your heavens open that your angels may receive the spirit of your servant Irenaeus, who suffers for your name and the name of your church. I ask your mercy, that you will receive me and confirm your faith in your church."

Then Irenaeus was struck down with a sword and his body tossed over the side of the bridge.

• • •

Then Jesus' mother and brothers arrived. Standing outside, they sent someone in to call him. A crowd was sitting around him, and they told him, "Your mother and brothers are outside looking for you."

"Who are my mother and my brothers?" he asked.

Then he looked at those seated in a circle around him and said, "Here are my mother and my brothers! Whoever does God's will is my brother and sister and mother."

Jesus and others
(Mark 3:31–35 NIV)

He Will Not Deny His Countrymen

Hezekiah	Laos	2001

Hezekiah's life had been so transformed that he had to tell someone. When he returned to the village he grew up in, he told the thirty-five relatives and villagers who met him and demanded to know why he had converted to Christianity, "Jesus is the only way I can be saved from my sins. Jesus is the only way I can have eternal life."

They didn't like this. As Hezekiah reasoned with them about the truths he had found studying God's Word and being discipled by other believers in the safe haven he had left to bring them the Gospel, tempers began to flare. Suddenly someone lunged out and grabbed Hezekiah. Others followed. They dragged him to the ground and beat him until he blacked out. Then they left him in the street, bruised and bleeding.

When the crowd had gone, a friend took Hezekiah to his own home, where he nurtured him back to health. It was four days before Hezekiah could raise himself off of the bed.

Hezekiah eventually left his village and to this day is still not welcome either there or in his family's homes. Instead, he now travels from village to village sharing what he has learned from the Bible and showing the way of salvation to as many as will let him. He said that he would not deny his countrymen the Good News.

Because of this, he has been beaten and thrown out of at least ten other villages. Some of the beatings were so bad that he thought he would not live through them—and some were so bad he wished he would not live through them. But his testimony remains strong: "As I have matured in my walk with Christ, I have more faith to endure these hardships. The trials I have gone

279

through have served to strengthen my faith, as I see God's faithfulness in delivering me. I thank God I have been able to bring thirty people to the saving knowledge of Jesus."

• • •

We often say we have school spirit or pride in our community, but how often are we willing to put our reputations on the line for others that they might also share the joy we have in Jesus?

I would gladly be placed under God's curse and be separated from Christ for the good of my own people.

Paul
(Romans 9:3 CEV)

"Why did you attract people to your
forbidden sect?" the Communist
judge demanded.
"Our aim," the Christian sister responded,
"is to win the whole world for Christ."

Methodically Following Jesus

John and Charles Wesley	England	1703–1791 and 1707–1788

Susannah Wesley was frantic as she gathered the children in front of the burning house. She counted heads quickly—someone was missing. "John! Where is John?!"

One of the other children pointed to an upstairs window. "There he is, Mother!"

Susannah ran toward the building. The flames were leaping quite high into the afternoon sky, and the roof groaned. "John! Jump! Quickly, son, just jump."

John leaped from the window into his mother's arms just seconds before the roof of the house collapsed, sending a stream of sparks high into the sky. Susannah, who had lost ten of her nineteen children before they reached the age of two, lay huddled on the ground with her six-year-old son, praising God through the tears flowing down her face.

The fire had been no accident. In 1662 a law had been passed in England that required all clergymen to adhere to the *Book of Common Prayer* over the Bible. Dissenters, such as Susannah's father and husband, were labeled "Nonconformists," and as many as five thousand of them died in English prisons. It was widely known that the Wesley family schooled their children at home, and someone who did not like their nonconformist stand had decided to try to save the government the trouble of jailing them.

Another time their barns had been burned, and her husband's own congregation had him arrested and imprisoned. Then while he was in prison, someone slashed the udders of their cow, denying the family much-needed milk for the children. Despite all this, the Wesleys refused to leave the state-sanctioned Church of England.

In 1729, John and Charles Wesley were both fellows of Lincoln College at Oxford, where they participated together with George Whitfield and others in a group called "The Holy Club." The group exercised great discipline in helping the sick and visiting prisons, so much so that other students labeled them "Methodists" for their methodical adherence to these works.

John and Charles went on to become missionaries in the state of Georgia after this, but Charles returned a year later because of ill health. A couple of years later, John also returned to England, discouraged because they felt his mission there had been a failure.

A popular doctrine of the day in the church was that of predestination, that the salvation of all people was determined before they were born, regardless of choices they made during their lifetimes. Yet through his time in the mission field and conversations with other Christians he had met during his trip, John had come to the conviction that the key to salvation was in a person's choice to follow after Jesus and accept him as Lord, and nothing else. This was a view that did not go well with the rest of his society at the time. He shared this with his brother Charles, who accepted it enthusiastically, but as they looked for openings to teach about the saving knowledge of Jesus Christ in churches, they found the doors were closed to them—no one would give them a pulpit to preach this truth from. Thus, being rejected by the established church, they took the Gospel to the streets. John traveled as many as five thousand miles a year preaching as many as five times a day to open-air gatherings in villages all over the British Isles. They were not always warmly received.

In nearly every part of England they were first met by a stone-throwing mob or with other attempts to wound or slay them. Seldom did they receive any protection from the local authorities. Yet the two brothers faced all these dangers with amazing courage and peacefulness. Though they were also openly slandered and mocked by the writers of their day, these refused to let any of this move them from their purpose of preaching the Gospel.

On one instance, Charles was preaching near Killyleagh, Ireland, when he had to flee before a growing mob. He literally ran for his life and took refuge in a nearby farmhouse. Jane Moore, the farmer's wife, hid the panting evangelist in the milk house.

A few moments later, some of the mob rushed to the house. Mrs. Moore tried to divert their attention by preparing refreshments. Fearful that they might search the premises and discover the evangelist, she went to the milk house on the excuse of getting a cold drink for her visitors.

"Quickly!" she said to Charles, "get out through the rear window and hide under the hedge."

He took her advice and climbed through the window. Outside he found a little brook flowing beside the hedge. The overhanging branches and the flowing water made for a safe and pleasant hiding place.

Yet Charles did not use the time to cower fearfully. Instead, he pulled a small piece of paper and pencil from his pocket and began writing down a song:

Jesus, Lover of My Soul

Jesus, lover of my soul, let me to Thy bosom fly,
While the nearer waters roll, while the tempest still is high.
Hide me, O my Savior, hide—till the storm of life is past;
Safe into the haven guide, O receive my soul at last!
Other refuge have I none—hangs my helpless soul on Thee;
Leave, ah, leave me not alone, still support and comfort me!
All my trust on Thee is stayed—all my help from Thee I bring;
Cover my defenseless head with the shadow of Thy wing.
Wilt Thou not regard my call? Wilt Thou not accept my prayer?
Lo! I sink, I faint, I fall—Lo! on Thee I cast my care;
Reach me out Thy gracious hand! While I of Thy strength receive,
Hoping against hope I stand, dying, and behold, I live.

Thou, O Christ, art all I want, more than all in Thee I find;
Raise the fallen, cheer the faint, heal the sick and lead the blind.
Just and holy is Thy name—I am all unrighteousness;
False and full of sin I am, Thou art full of truth and grace.
Plenteous grace with Thee is found, grace to cover all my sin;
Let the healing streams abound, make and keep me pure within.
Thou of life the fountain art—freely let me take of Thee;
Spring Thou up within my heart, rise to all eternity.

• • •

These two Jesus Freaks were both tireless workers for the Gospel, producing books and songs dedicated to Jesus that were widely distributed both during their lives and after. In fact, one of Charles's songs, "Hark! The Herald Angels Sing," is still a Christmas standard today. In his lifetime Charles wrote nearly seven thousand songs.

Having been raised in persecution, these two brothers were not ones to let popular opinions sway their testimonies. They had the courage to live beyond cultural Christianity and step out to say, "I don't care what people think, the important thing is Jesus."

Religion is nothing else than doing the will of God and not our own. Heaven or hell depends on this alone.

Susannah Wesley

Living a Martyred Life		
Leonides and Origen	Alexandria, Egypt	c. A.D. 202

In the previous months, because of the order of Emperor Septimus Severus, the Christians in the surrounding areas were brought into the capital city of Alexandria for their trials. Among these was Leonides, the father of Origen.

As he sat in prison, Leonides pined over his family and what would become of them. Had he instilled the faith in them that was needed to persevere in the coming days of difficulty for Christians? Would the emperor's orders quash the faith that was only newly growing in their hearts? What would become of them and their faith once he was gone?

It was about this time that he received a letter from his seventeen-year-old son, Origen. He read it through once, then returned to the words in an opening paragraph to read them again and again. In essence, they said,

> Father. Be strong in the Lord, and He will help you bravely face the suffering that must definitely await you. Do not grieve for us, your wife and my six younger brothers and sisters and myself. None of us could live with ourselves if, for the sake of thinking of us, you should forsake your faithful God and Savior and miss your eternal reward. If it were up to me, I would be with you except that Mother prevents me.

Leonides clutched the letter to his chest as the tears filled his eyes. He need not worry about his family.

Some days later, he was beheaded.

Origen
c. a.d. 254

Unknown to Leonides, Origen would very likely have joined him in Alexandria had his mother not taken away all of his clothes and left him in his room until he promised to stay with her and his brothers and sisters. But from that day forward, it seems Origen would live his life martyred to Christ's cause. Then, when their father was finally executed, the family lost everything when all of their possessions were confiscated by the emperor.

Origen went on to become a noted historian and teacher in the early church, many of his writings still being used today in the discussion of philosophy and correct biblical doctrine. If there were Christians in danger in the area, Origen would be there. He would be there at their trials and encourage them to hold on to Jesus no matter what, he would minister to them in prison, and he would even walk with them to their executions and bid them farewell, telling them he hoped to be along shortly. In the coming years he saw many of his brothers and sisters in Christ die for their faith, and then eventually many of his own disciples he had brought to the Lord and instructed in the Truth.

Somehow through all of this, Origen walked with a supernatural protection that brought him through several close calls, ambushes, and attempts to capture him.

In the end, when he was about sixty-four, in the midst of Emperor Decius's edict renewing Christian persecution in the empire, Origen was captured and cruelly tortured for his faith. He was cast into a dark pit they called a prison and had his neck weighed down with chains and his feet locked in stocks that spread out his legs four spaces so that they were constantly stretched in agony. He was poked with burning prods and tortured in various other ways, yet always he endured these with grace and patience. His torturers saw no reason for his execution, though, so they continued his torture indefinitely.

When Gallus became emperor at Decius's death, he forgot the Christians for a while in the wake of the war he was fighting in the north with the Goths. During this time, Origen was banished to Cesarea Statonis and then finally moved to Tyre, where he died a natural death at the age of sixty-nine.

• • •

Because of his father's example, Origen lived his life as a living sacrifice to God—a life that had already been crucified with Christ and therefore was no longer concerned for its own welfare or worldly desires. As a result of this, he lived a life without fear of what others could do to him, a life completely free of what others thought about or demanded of him, a life that was concerned with nothing else but spreading the kingdom of God.

Do you want real freedom? Real peace? Try living as though the only thing that keeps you going is the Word of God in your heart.

Live today as if you were going to die a martyr this evening.

Charles de Foucauld
Killed by Senussi rebels
Tamanrasset, Algeria
1916

Indeed, I have been crucified with Christ. My ego is no longer central. It is no longer important that I appear righteous before you or have your good opinion, and I am no longer driven to impress God. Christ lives in me. The life you see me living is not "mine," but it is lived by faith in the Son of God, who loved me and gave himself for me. I am not going to go back on that.

Paul
(Galatians 2:20 THE MESSAGE)

Wow! The Father is so wise and loving and good
to us. No wonder people can't understand Him or what
He's up to…. He's the source, guide,
and goal of everything that exists. Praise him! …
OK, sisters and brothers, because of all this,
and using God's loving-kindness in your lives
as a tool, give your whole selves back to Him.
What else is there for us to do, knowing what
He's done for us? Don't let the world system
squeeze you into its plastic mold. Instead,
bust out of it by letting God's Spirit give you
a brand-new mind. Then you'll be able to live
and enjoy the good and perfect life that God
wants you to have.

FROM LETTERS TO STREET CHRISTIANS
(A PARAPHRASE OF ROMANS 11:33, 36; 12:1–2)

"My Heart Seems Too Narrow to Contain His Joy"

A Japanese Prisoner and Others	Japan	1622

A Christian in Omura wrote the following in a letter from prison:

> Oh, if you taste the delights with which God fills the souls of those who serve Him, and suffer for Him, how would you condemn all that the world would promise! I now begin to be a disciple of Jesus Christ, since for His love I am in prison, where I suffer much.
>
> But I assure you, that when I am fainting with hunger, God has fortified me by His sweet consolations, so that I have looked upon myself as well recompensed for His service. And though I were yet to pass many years in prison, the time would appear short, through the extreme desire which I feel of suffering for Him, who even here so repays our labors.
>
> Besides other sickness, I have been afflicted with a continual fever a hundred days without any remedies or proper nourishment. Yet, all this time my heart was so full of joy that it seemed to me too narrow to contain it. I have never felt any equal to it, and thought myself at the gates of paradise.

Later, when he heard that he would be burned alive, he overflowed with joy. He constantly expressed his gratitude to God, for he felt himself unworthy of dying as a martyr for Jesus.

On September 2, he was taken with twenty-four others to Nangasaqui, where, only shortly before, fifty Christians had been executed for their faith. When they arrived near the city, they were taken to twenty-five stakes that were all in a row and tied to them. The wood had been set all around them with the farthest extremity about eight meters away. When the wood was lit at this point, it took about two hours for it to burn to those tied to the poles. The Christians stood all this time with their eyes toward heaven until the flames finally took them.

• • •

Not long after this, in 1623, the effort to exterminate Christians in Japan became law, and in 1629 the fumie was created to test whole villages to see who was Christian and who was not. Fumie means literally "picture to step on" and was initially a picture of a cross or the likeness of Jesus or some other religious picture taken from the art of the churches. Those suspected of being Christians were brought before the fumie and told to step on the image. If they did, they were let go; if they did not, they were executed. The use of fumies was not stopped until 1858.

291

We share in the terrible sufferings of Christ, but also in the wonderful comfort he gives. We suffer in the hope that you will be comforted and saved. And because we are comforted, you will also be comforted, as you patiently endure suffering like ours. You never disappoint us. You suffered as much as we did, and we know that you will be comforted as we were.

Paul

(2 Corinthians 1:5–7 CEV)

"A Witness to His Resurrection"

Matthias	Jerusalem	c. A.D. 70

"Judas must now be replaced among the twelve," Peter said to the disciples and other followers of Jesus gathered in the upper room. "The replacement must come from the company of men who stayed together with us from the time Jesus was baptized by John up to the day of His ascension, designated along with us as a witness to His resurrection."

In the discussion that followed, two men were nominated: Joseph Barsabbas, nicknamed Justus, and Matthias, both members of the seventy.

Then they prayed, "You, oh God, know every one of us inside and out. Make plain which of these two men you choose to take the place in this ministry and leadership that Judas threw away in order to go his own way."

Then they drew straws. The lot fell to Matthias, and he was counted one with the other eleven apostles.

Matthias ministered with the others in Jerusalem, preaching and teaching from house to house, until the apostles separated to take the Gospel to all nations as Jesus had instructed them to do. At this, Matthias penetrated to the interior of Ethiopia and reached a barbarous tribe with the light of the Gospel, making many converts among them. He then returned and took the Good News to Judea, Galilee, and Samaria, ministering to the Jews hungry for the truth about Jesus.

With the rest of the apostles elsewhere, the Jewish High Council singled out Matthias and brought him to trial, demanding that he deny Jesus and the power of His resurrection. When he would not, the high priest declared, "Then your blood is on your own head, for your own mouth has accused you."

Matthias was then hung on a cross and stoned. When this did not kill him, he was brought down and beheaded.

• • •

What Matthias had acquired by traveling with Jesus prompted him to continue sharing His Gospel despite the risks. What have your travels with Jesus prompted you to do?

The God of our ancestors chose you long ago to know his plan, to see the Righteous One, and to hear words from him. You will be his witness to all people, telling them about what you have seen and heard. Now, why wait any longer? Get up, be baptized, and wash your sins away, trusting in him to save you.

Ananias to Paul
(Acts 22:14–16 NCV)

293

294

Believe me! What you see happening before your eyes is no punishment; it will be over quickly, and doesn't take away life, but gives it. O happy souls who pass through this temporary fire to ascend into heaven to God, and, in the end, be saved from the fire that burns forever.

FRUCTUOSUS
BISHOP OF THE CHURCH OF TARRAGONA, SPAIN
TO HIS CONGREGATION AS HE STOOD BEFORE THE FLAMES
HE WAS SENTENCED TO DIE IN
C. A.D. 261

A Beloved Murderer

Richard and Sabina Wurmbrand	Romania	1940s

"In the concentration camp where I worked, I killed many Jews, even Jews with children in their arms," the man boasted to Pastor Wurmbrand. He had just come back from the front fighting for the Nazis and was proud of his accomplishments. He was glad to tell of them to anyone who would listen. Having heard the good German name Wurmbrand, the man must have had no idea that the pastor he spoke with was a Jew.

In response to being "privileged" with hearing of the man's barbarity and murdering, most Christians would have been at a loss for words. But not Pastor Wurmbrand. He promptly and affectionately invited the man to his home for dinner. The man loved music, and when Pastor Wurmbrand told him he would play the piano for him, he said he would be glad to come.

When the man arrived that evening, there were some other believers present, but his wife, Sabina, was feeling ill, so she stayed in her room. Pastor Wurmbrand played the piano for them all, and they had a wonderful evening together enjoying the music. After that they all had a long discussion into the night, further enjoying one another's company.

When it had grown quite late, Pastor Wurmbrand turned to the soldier and said, "Sir, I have to tell you something. You must promise me that you will listen for ten minutes quietly. After that ten minutes you can say whatever you would like."

The man was smiling broadly from all he had enjoyed that evening and said quite warmly, "All right, all right, you can speak to me even more than ten minutes. I promise that I will not interrupt you. You can say whatever you like."

"In the other room," the pastor began, "my wife is sleeping.

She is Jewish and I am Jewish too. Her family, which is also my family, perished in the big Nazi concentration camp where you boasted that you killed Jews with children still in their arms. So you are presumably the very murderer of my family.

"Now, I propose an experiment. We will pass into the other room and I will tell my wife who you are. I can assure you my wife will not speak one word of reproach to you, nor will she look angrily at you, but will smile at you as at every honored guest. She will go and prepare coffee and cookies for you. You will be received just like everyone else. Now, if my wife, who is only human, can do this, if she can love you like this, knowing what you have done, and can forgive you, then how much more will Jesus, who is love?"

The man began to tear at his jacket. "What have I done? What have I done? I am guilty of so much blood."

The pastor said, "Well, then, let us kneel down and ask for forgiveness from God."

They knelt. First Pastor Wurmbrand said a short prayer; then the man, who did not know how to pray, said again and again, "Jesus, forgive me. Jesus, forgive me. I believe that you will forgive me." There were many tears, and then he and the pastor embraced.

"I have promised you an experiment. Now we will go to see my wife."

Sabina had heard nothing while sleeping in the other room far away in the house from the main room where they had been speaking. They went to her and Pastor Wurmbrand woke her. "Do you know this man?" Pastor Wurmbrand began.

"No," she replied sleepily.

So he introduced the man. "This is the murderer of your sisters, your brothers, and your parents. But now he has repented and he is our brother in the Messiah, our brother in faith. What do you have to say to him?"

She fell around his neck and they both wept together.

• • •

By this we know that we love the children of God, when we love God and observe His commandments. For this is the love of God, that we keep His commandments; and His commandments are not burdensome. For whatever is born of God overcomes the world.

John
(1 John 5:2–4 NAS)

God authorized and commanded me to commission you: Go out and train everyone you meet, far and near, in this way of life, marking them by baptism in the three-fold name: Father, Son, and Holy Spirit. Then instruct them in the practice of all I have commanded you. I'll be with you as you do this, day after day after day, right up to the end of the age.

Jesus
(Matthew 28:18–20 THE MESSAGE)

What Can Separate Us?

If God is for us, who can ever be against us? Since God did not spare even his own Son but gave him up for us all, won't God, who gave us Christ, also give us everything else?

Who dares accuse us whom God has chosen for his own? Will God? No! He is the one who has given us right standing with himself. Who then will condemn us? Will Christ Jesus? No, for he is the one who died for us and was raised to life for us and is sitting at the place of highest honor next to God, pleading for us.

Can anything ever separate us from Christ's love? Does it mean he no longer loves us if we have trouble or calamity, or are persecuted, or are hungry or cold or in danger or threatened with death? (Even the Scriptures say, "For your sake we are killed every day; we are being slaughtered like sheep.") No, despite all these things, overwhelming victory is ours through Christ, who loved us.

And I am convinced that nothing can ever separate us from his love. Death can't, and life can't. The angels can't, and the demons can't. Our fears for today, our worries about tomorrow, and even the powers of hell can't keep God's love away. Whether we are high above the sky or in the deepest ocean, nothing in all creation will ever be able to separate us from the love of God that is revealed in Christ Jesus our Lord.

PAUL
(ROMANS 8:31–39 NLT)

from this day forward ...

- I will make a difference.
- Jesus, I thank you that you suffered and died for me on the cross to pay for my sins.
- Father, I thank you that you raised Jesus from the dead to be my living Lord and Savior.
- Holy Spirit, I thank you that you will lead me to do the right thing and change my world.
- Today, Lord, I want to make you a promise.
- I will not be ashamed of your name or your Gospel.
- I will do what I can for those who are persecuted and pray for them.
- I will look enemies in the eye and love them with your love.
- I will pray for them and love them—no matter what the consequences.
- I will follow your voice wherever you lead me, unafraid, for I know you will be with me.
- If I should stumble, if I should fall, if I should deny your name, if I should feel guilty that I did not pray or forgot to do something you asked me to do, I will not quit. I will not wallow in guilt. I will turn back to you, confess my sin, and do what you called me to do, because that is why you died for me.
- I will stand with you and my brothers and sisters around the world, because no matter what happens, no matter what I face or how it looks, in the end, we will be victorious—we will inherit eternity and heaven with you.
- I can do nothing else, because...

... I am a Jesus Freak.

299

_____   _____

How Do I
BECOME a
Revolutionary?

TeN RULES for RevolU T I o n a r i e s

1.

Live the FiVE LOVeS

Jesus replied: "'Love the Lord your God with all your heart and with all your soul and with all your mind.' This is the first and greatest commandment. And the second is like it: 'Love your neighbor as yourself.' All the Law and the Prophets hang on these two commandments."

JESUS
(MATTHEW 22:37–40 NIV)

Love your enemies, bless those who curse you, do good to those who hate you, and pray for those who spitefully use you and persecute you.

JESUS
(MATTHEW 5:44 NKJV)

By living the Five Loves of a Jesus Freak through the power of God's love, you walk in the supernatural constantly. Be willing to pull this spiritual weapon out at any time and be a catalyst for making heaven on earth. (See page 269 for the list of Five Loves.)

2.

AlWays Go DirECTLY to the Source

Then you will call upon Me and come and pray to Me, and I will listen to you. And you will seek Me and find Me, when you search for Me with all your heart.

GOD

(JEREMIAH 29:12–13 NAS)

Jesus said to his disciples: I am the true vine, and my Father is the gardener. He cuts away every branch of mine that doesn't produce fruit. But he trims clean every branch that does produce fruit, so that it will produce even more fruit. You are already clean because of what I have said to you. Stay joined to me, and I will stay joined to you. Just as a branch cannot produce fruit unless it stays joined to the vine, you cannot produce fruit unless you stay joined to me. I am the vine, and you are the branches. If you stay joined to me, and I stay joined to you, then you will produce lots of fruit. But you cannot do anything without me. If you don't stay joined to me, you will be thrown away. You will be like dry branches that are gathered up and burned in a fire. Stay joined to me and let my teachings become part of you. Then you can pray for whatever you want, and your prayer will be answered. When you become fruitful disciples of mine, my Father will be honored.

JESUS

(JOHN 15:1–8 CEV)

Go to God regularly through prayer and His Word. Jesus is our primary Source for all we need in life. Verify everything you have learned through His Spirit and the Word. Go to Him for strength to live and love to give. He is our life. Without His life flowing through us, we bear no better fruit than those who despise His name.

Cultivate the spiritual fruit in your life. God has given you these things for your success. Get rid of things in your life that bear bitter fruit or don't bear any fruit at all. In all that you do, let your spirituality be evident to others in being as much like Jesus as you can.

Also avoid living your life on hearsay or secondhand information. Ignore rumors. Verify things from firsthand sources whenever possible, or don't make too much out of them until you do.

3.
GET Connected—
You Are Not Alone

Let us be concerned for one another, to help one another to show love and to do good. Let us not give up the habit of meeting together, as some are doing. Instead, let us encourage one another all the more, since you see that the Day of the Lord is coming nearer.

(HEBREWS 10:24–25 TEV)

We will hold to the truth in love, becoming more and more in every way like Christ, who is the head of his body, the church. Under his direction, the whole body is fitted together perfectly. As each part does its own special work, it helps the other parts grow, so that the whole body is healthy and growing and full of love.

PAUL
(EPHESIANS 4:15–16 NLT)

Plug into a good church where they will help you be accountable to God. Though your relationship to God is first, we often make mistakes without the good counsel of ministers and friends who have more experience following God than we do or who are trying to walk the same narrow road. We are a body, and though we all play a different part in it, if we do not work together, we will never accomplish all we are called to do.

God designed us as different parts that fit together with one another. His goals on the earth cannot be accomplished by one person working alone—or else God could have left Jesus here to do it all by himself. Each of us is integral to His plan for the earth, but not if we don't work together and submit to one another's gifts in love. This is why He has called us a "body." (See 1 Corinthians 12.)

Plug into and support ministries that are reaching out into areas you feel called to help in. Learn about them and keep up to date about what they are doing. Pray for them and their missions. Stay informed about what is happening in your world. Pay attention to events that affect you and your brothers and sisters around the world. This will help you know what to pray for and how to help others who are in need. (See page 310 and 311 for the list of world-changing organizations you can hook up with and get information from.)

4.
ADOpt Transformational ThINkING

Do not conform any longer to the pattern of this world, but be transformed by the renewing of your mind. Then you will be able to test and approve what God's will is—his good, pleasing and perfect will.

PAUL
(ROMANS 12:2 NIV)

Don't become so well-adjusted to your culture that you fit into it without even thinking. Instead, fix your attention on God. You'll be changed from the inside out. Readily recognize what he wants from you, and quickly respond to it. Unlike the culture around you, always dragging you down to its level of immaturity, God brings the best out of you, develops well-formed maturity in you.

PAUL
(ROMANS 12:2 THE MESSAGE)

Don't think like the world thinks, but be ready to see God's will done in every situation and let Him guide you in how to accomplish it. Those who walk closely with God are always innovative. That is why all things are possible with God. When others have already given up, you may be just getting started if you are willing to get God's guidance on the situation.

5.
LIve It, DON't Just SAY It

Meanwhile, live in such a way that you are a credit to the Message of Christ. Let nothing in your conduct hang on whether I come or not. Your conduct must be the same whether I show up to see things for myself or hear of it from a distance. Stand united, singular in vision, contending for people's trust in the Message, the good news, not flinching or dodging in the slightest before the opposition. Your courage and unity will show them what they're up against: defeat for them, victory for you—and both because of God.

PAUL
(PHILIPPIANS 1:27–28 THE MESSAGE)

Actions speak louder than words. St. Francis once said, "Go and preach the Gospel. Use words, if necessary." Others notice more about who you are than what you say.

Jesus' model is that we are first to be His disciple before we can disciple others. How much we follow Him comes out in how we walk out our lives. If we *live* the Gospel, then when we *share* the Gospel it will have weight.

On the other hand, are we truly *living* the Gospel if we never *share* it? Can Jesus' love really have changed us if we are never willing to tell anyone else about it? Are you always ready to answer anyone who questions the hope you have in Christ? (See 1 Peter 3:15.)

6.

MeSS Up

So let us not become tired of doing good; for if we do not give up, the time will come when we will reap the harvest.

PAUL

(GALATIANS 6:9 TEV)

You will make mistakes in trying to obey God and do good things. We are all human. We often don't learn unless we make mistakes. Just accept that. People may get mad at you. Rejoice! You touched a nerve. You touched their consciences. Not everything you do will go the way you planned, but that is all just part of the adventure. Some of your mistakes may even be opportunities for good.

Sure, the closer you walk with God, the fewer mistakes you will probably make, but even Paul failed at times. Did he do the right thing in refusing to take John Mark with him on his second missionary journey? Did he ever get arrested and found guilty? Did he ever try to go someplace and God told him he was wrong in trying to go there? (See Acts 16:6–7.) But what we see as a failure is not always what God sees as a failure. Like a baby taking its first steps, no one sees it as a failure if the baby falls down a few times before getting it right. And doesn't the Bible say that those who are like little children will be the greatest in the kingdom of God? (See Matthew 18:1–4.)

7.
DON'T Accept FAce VaLUE

God deliberately chose things the world considers foolish in order to shame those who think they are wise. And he chose those who are powerless to shame those who are powerful.

PAUL
(1 CORINTHIANS 1:27 NLT)

I planted the seed, Apollos watered it, but God made it grow. So neither he who plants nor he who waters is anything, but only God, who makes things grow. The man who plants and the man who waters have one purpose, and each will be rewarded according to his own labor. For we are God's fellow workers; you are God's field, God's building.

PAUL
(1 CORINTHIANS 3:6–9 NIV)

Things are not always what they seem. What you may see as a failure in one instance may have actually moved another person or situation farther along God's path toward himself or His will. This is the beauty of working with a Master Planner—we don't have to lose heart if we don't do it all ourselves. We just have to do our part. Should a plumber be upset if, once he puts in the plumbing in a brand-new house, it is not ready to live in yet? Of course not. He has done his part the best he can, but it is up to someone else to come in and finish the walls, install the electricity, put in the flooring, etc., before the house is finished.

Sometimes what God tells you to do will look crazy. Do good to those who do evil? Turn the other cheek? Bless those who curse you? But your obedience to Him may be just what is needed to release the kingdom of heaven in someone else's life.

8.
STAND Up for WHAT You Believe

Preach the Good News. Be ready at all times, and tell people what they need to do. Tell them when they are wrong. Encourage them with great patience and careful teaching, because the time will come when people will not listen to the true teaching but will find many more teachers who please them by saying the things they want to hear. They will stop listening to the truth and will begin to follow false stories.

PAUL
(2 TIMOTHY 4:2–4 NCV)

Do people even know you are a Christian? Have you ever brought your faith into a philosophical classroom discussion? Do people even know that your opinions on many issues are grounded in the Word of God?

When you enter into debates, do it in a spirit of love. Be informed. Learn. Open your mind to new ideas without forsaking the Truth. Avoid disputes that arise just for the sake of arguing, but listen intently as a seeker of truth so that you can understand other viewpoints and argue for truth. If you grow confused, pull away and go back to the Word and your trusted Christian advisers, who can help you through it. Don't just be intrigued with something because it is interesting, but be a sincere seeker of truth. The truth will keep you free, and your understanding of other viewpoints and of the truth will help you set others free as well.

9.
ReMEMber the B.A.S.I.C.s

Remember the Lord's people who are in jail and be concerned for them. Don't forget those who are suffering, but imagine that you are there with them.

(HEBREWS 13:3 CEV)

B.A.S.I.C.s stands for Brothers And Sisters In Chains. Don't forget those who are suffering around the world for their faith in Jesus. Be informed about what is happening and help where you can. Imagine what you would want someone to do for you if you were there, and then do it for them.

So then, rid yourselves of all evil, all lying, hypocrisy, jealousy, and evil speech. As newborn babies want milk, you should want the pure and simple teaching. By it you can grow up and be saved.

PETER
(1 PETER 2:1–2 NCV)

Also, stick to the basics of your faith. Don't act like an expert in areas you know little about. Don't major in minor issues. If there are other areas you feel led to study, make sure you have the first principles in the proper place.

10.
"Your Mission, Should YOU Choose to Accept It ..." ACCept It.

"I knew you before I formed you in your mother's womb. Before you were born I set you apart and appointed you as my spokesman to the world."

GOD

(JEREMIAH 1:5 NLT)

309

In all the body of Christ there is only one you. That is no mistake, and you are not an extra part that is not needed. God has a unique calling for your life. Watch for it. When it comes you will know it.

Then walk in it and change your world.

A SHORT List of
WoRLd-Changing ORGanizations

THE VOICE OF THE MARTYRS
P.O. Box 443
Bartlesville, OK 74005
U.S.A.
Telephone: (800) 747-0085
e-mail: **thevoice@vom-usa.org**
Web site: *www.persecution.com*

THE RELIGIOUS PRISONERS CONGRESSIONAL TASK FORCE
Web site: *www.house.gov/pitts/rights.htm*

COMPASS DIRECT NEWS SERVICE
P.O. Box 27250
Santa Ana, CA 92799-7250
U.S.A.
Telephone: (949) 862-0314 / Fax: (949) 752-6536
e-mail: **compassdirect@earthlink.net**
Web site: *www.compassdirect.org*

KESTON INSTITUTE
38 St. Aldate's
Oxford
OX1 1BN
UNITED KINGDOM
Telephone: + 44 (0)1865/79 29 29
Fax: + 44 (0)1865/24 00 42
e-mail: **keston.institute@keston.org**
Web site: *www.keston.org*
or U.S. address:
Keston Institute
P.O. Box 426
Waldorf, MD 20604
U.S.A.

OPEN DOORS WITH BROTHER ANDREW
P.O. Box 27001
Santa Ana, CA 92799
U.S.A.
Telephone: (949) 752-6600
Web site: *www.opendoorsusa.org*

FREEDOM HOUSE
Center for Religious Freedom
1319 18th Street NW
Washington, D.C. 20036
U.S.A.
Telephone: (202) 296-5101 / Fax: (202) 296-5078
Web site: *www.freedomhouse.org/religion/*

JUBILEE CAMPAIGN, U.S.A.
9689-C Main Street
Fairfax, VA 22031
U.S.A.
Telephone: (703) 503-0791 / Fax: (703) 503-0792

CHINASOURCE
P.O. Box 4343
Fullerton, CA 92834
U.S.A.
Telephone: (714) 449-0611 / Fax: (714) 449-0624
Web site: *www.chinasource.org*

WORLD EVANGELICAL FELLOWSHIP
Web site: *www.worldevangelical.org*

ADVOCATES, INTERNATIONAL
9691D Main Street
Fairfax, VA 22031
U.S.A.
Telephone: (703) 764-0011 / Fax: (703) 764-0077
Web site: *www.advocatesinternational.org*

For a more current list, check out *www.jesusfreaks.net*

A Brief History of MARTYRdom and CHRISTianity

See notes at the end of the chart for the definitions of terms and headings.

PERIOD OR EVENT	RULER OR CHIEF PERSON	PLACE	YEAR(S)
Jesus' crucifixion, resurrection, and ascension	Pontius Pilate (A.D. 26–36)	Jerusalem	A.D. 33
First Roman persecution	Nero	Roman Empire	A.D. 64–68
First missionaries to Armenia	Astyages (A.D. 66)	Armenia	c. A.D. 66–97
First Jewish rebellion	Various Jewish Leaders (A.D. 66–73) Vespacian (A.D. 69–79)	Judea	c. A.D. 70
Second Roman persecution	Domitian (A.D. 81–96)	Roman Empire	A.D. 91–96
Third Roman persecution	Trajan (A.D. 98–117)	Roman Empire	A.D. 104–117
Persian persecution	Artaxerxes (c. A.D. 110)	Armenia	A.D. 110–125

The history of Christian martyrdom is, in fact, the history of Christianity itself; for it is in the arena, at the stake, and in the dungeon that the religion of Christ has won its most glorious triumphs.

WILLIAM BRAMLEY-MOORE
EDITOR OF AN 1869 EDITION OF FOXE'S BOOK OF MARTYRS

SOME KEY MARTYRS (DATE)	EST. # OF MARTYRS	OTHER NOTES
Jesus	1	
Paul (64), Peter (64), Evodius of Antioch (64), John Mark (68), Andrew (69)	5,000	
Judas Thaddaeus (66), Bartholomew (68), Zakaria (76), Atirnerseh (c. 97)	1,000	
	10,000	Christianity scattered; the Temple is destroyed by Titus's troops (A.D. 70); the siege of Masada (A.D. 70–73)
Flavius Clemens (91), Antipas (91), Manius Acilius Glabrio (95), Timothy (97), Clement (97)	2,000	Domitian assumes divine honors, commanding others to consider him lord and god (c. A.D. 87); John exiled (c. A.D. 95)
Simeon (108), Ignatius (111), Rufus and Zozimus (115)	1,500	
Oski, Soukias, and others (110), Acacius and Militiamen (125)	14,000	

313

PERIOD OR EVENT	RULER OR CHIEF PERSON	PLACE	YEAR(S)
Jewish revolt	Hadrian (117–138)	Cyprus and Libya	A.D. 115
The Old Testament is translated into Greek	Aquila (c. A.D. 128)		c. A.D. 128
Second Jewish rebellion	Bar-Kochba (Jewish leader) Hadrian (117–138)	Jerusalem	A.D.132–135
Fourth Roman persecution	Marcus Aurelius Antoninus (A.D. 161–180) Lucius Verus (A.D.161–169)	Roman Empire	c. A.D. 163–180
Fifth Roman persecution	Septimus Severus (A.D. 193–211)	Roman Empire (northern Africa)	A.D. 200–211
Sixth Roman persecution	Maximus (A.D. 235–238)	Roman Empire	A.D. 235–238
Shapur I's persecution	Shapur I (A.D.241–272)	Armenia	A.D. 241–272
Seventh Roman persecution	Decius (A.D. 249–251)	Roman Empire	A.D. 249–251
Eighth Roman persecution	Valerian (A.D. 253–260)	Roman Empire	A.D. 257–260

SOME KEY MARTYRS (DATE)	EST. # OF MARTYRS	OTHER NOTES
	10.000	
		Aquila is a kinsman of the emperors; he first turns Christian, then turns to Judaism
	30,000	Hadrian rebuilds Jerusalem and names it Aelia Capitolina
Carpus, Papylus, Agathonica, Justin Martyr and companions (165), Felicity (165), Polycarp (168), Marcellus (178), Matyrs on the Rhone River (France) (c. 178), Speratus and companions (180)	4,000	The Thundering Legion help Marcus Aurelius to victory in Germany (c. A.D. 174)
Perpetua, Felicitas, and Saturus (202), Leonides (202), Irenaeus in Lyons (202), Potamiaena (202), Basiliades (202)	40,000	
Hippolytus (235), Demetrius (235), Pontian (235)	3,000	
	10,000	
Fabian (250), Babylas (250), Cornelius (253), Stephen I (255)	120,000	
Cyprian (258), Sixtus II (258), Novatian (258), Denys (258), Montanus (258), Lucius (258), Fructuosus (261)	150,000	

315

PERIOD OR EVENT	RULER OR CHIEF PERSON	PLACE	YEAR(S)
Ninth Roman persecution	Aurelian (A.D. 270–275)	Roman Empire	A.D. 274–5
First Persian persecution	Varahran II (A.D. 276–293)	Persia	A.D. 276–293
Coptic Era of Martyrs	Local Roman Officials Under **Diocletian** (A.D. 284–305)	Egypt	A.D. 284–311
Martyrs of Agaunum	**Maximian** (Marcus Aurelius Maximian) (A.D. 286–305)	Gaul (France)	A.D. 287
Armenian persecution	Tiridates III (A.D. 287–330)	Armenia	A.D. 287–301
Tenth Roman persecution	Diocletian (Marcus Valerius Diocletianus) (A.D. 284–305) Maximian (Marcus Aurelius Maximian) (A.D. 286–305) Galerius (Gaius Valerius Galerius Maximinianus) (A.D. 293–305) Caesar Augustus (A.D. 305–311)	Roman Empire	A.D. 301–311
Edict of Milan	**Constantine** (A.D. 307–337)	Roman Empire	A.D. 313

SOME KEY MARTYRS (DATE)	EST. # OF MARTYRS	OTHER NOTES
Marina (278)	5,000	
Mani (275), Candida (286)	4,000	
Menas (305), Peter I Ieromartyros (311)	450,000	
Theban Legion (287), Maurice (287), Urs (287), Victor, Exuperius (287), Candidus (287)	5,000	
Gayane (287), Hripsime (287), 37 virgins (287), Theodore Salahouni (287)	20,000	**Tiridates III converts to Christianity in c. A.D. 301 and becomes the first Christian king**
Anthimus of Nicomedia		Diocletian and Maximian served as co-emperors (Augusti) (A.D. 286–305); Constantius and Galerius were junior emperors (caesars) (A.D. 293–305); when Diocletian abdicated in 305, Maximian lost power as well—Constantius was emperor in the west, Galerius in the east; Constantius was never one to persecute the Christians, so he avoided it; this was the bloodiest period of Roman Persecution
		Christianity legalized in the Roman Empire

PERIOD OR EVENT	RULER OR CHIEF PERSON	PLACE	YEAR(S)
Licinius's persecution	Licinius (A.D. 312–324)	Eastern Roman Empire	A.D. 316–324
Persecution of the Donatists	Constantine (A.D. 307–337)	Northern Africa	A.D. 317
Great (Second) Persian persecution	Shapur II (A.D. 309–379)	Persia	c. A.D. 333–377
Visagoth War with Rome	Theodosius I (A.D. 379–395) Honorius (A.D. 395–423)	Roman Empire	A.D. 390–410
Books of the Bible set	**Council of Hippo**	**Hippo (North Africa)**	**A.D. 393**
The Latin Vulgate	Jerome (c. 347–c. 419)	**Bethlehem**	**A.D. 405**
Third Persian persecution	Bahram V (A.D. 420–438)	Persia	A.D. 420–424

SOME KEY MARTYRS (DATE)	EST. # OF MARTYRS	OTHER NOTES
Blaize (316), The Thundering Legion (320)	2,000	
	10.000	
Simeon Barsabae and 100 clergy (341), Shahdost (342), Brbashmin (346), Pusak and 100 clergy (346)	120,000	
Telemachus (391), Marcella (410), M. Flavius (c. 420)	10,000	
		Council follows outline of Augustine for which holy writings would make up accepted biblical canon
		Jerome makes first full translation of the Bible into the common language of the day– Latin. Up until this point there were New Testaments in Latin, Syriac, and Coptic. The version met much criticism and was not collected together as a whole until the sixth century and not approved by the church until 1546
Hormisdas (422), Chouchanik (422), Suenas (422), James (422), Peroz (422), Benjamin (c. 423)	90,000	

PERIOD OR EVENT	RULER OR CHIEF PERSON	PLACE	YEAR(S)
Attila the Hun	Attila the Hun A.D. 433–453	Western Europe	A.D. 433–453
Under Arian Vandals	Gaeseric (A.D. 428–477) Huneric (A.D. 477–484)	Northern Africa	A.D. 439–?
Anglo-Saxon invasion	Anglo-Saxon tribes	England	A.D. 442–472
Fourth Persian persecution	Yazdegerd II (A.D. 438–457)	Persia	A.D. 448–454
Ethiopian persecution	Local Rulers	Ethiopia	c. A.D. 450
During the time of Roman Empire		**World**	A.D. 33–500
Islam founded	**Muhammed (c. A.D. 570–632)**	**Arabia**	A.D. 610–632
Persian invasion	Khusro II (A.D. 591–628)	Palestine	A.D. 615
Islamic persecution	Arab Factions	Northern Africa	A.D. 700–797
Islamic persecution	caliph Omar II (A.D. 717–720)	Middle East	A.D. 717
Viking raids	Vikings	Europe	A.D. 807
Byzantine persecution of Paulicians	Michael III (A.D. 842–867) Theophilus II (A.D. 867) Basil I (A.D. 867–886)	Cilica	A.D. 842–874

SOME KEY MARTYRS (DATE)	EST. # OF MARTYRS	OTHER NOTES
Auraeus (434), Ursula & virgins (434), Gereon (434), Livarius (451)	200,000	
	10,000	
	20,000	
10 bishops at Kirkuk (448), Vardan Mamikonian and 1,035 troops (451), Atom and his legion (451), Hovsep I (454)	178,000	
Kharitas and companions (450)	11,000	
	2,101,751	
Zacharias (615)	90,000	
	80,000	Tangiers Christians massacred (A.D. 707)
	60,000	Demanded conver- sion to Islam or death
	20,000	68 monks killed in Ionia; 6,000 believ- ers killed in Spain and Italy
Chrysocheir (873)	100,000	

PERIOD OR EVENT	RULER OR CHIEF PERSON	PLACE	YEAR(S)
Moorish persecutions	Abderamene II (A.D. 822–852)	Cordova, Spain	A.D. 850–859
The Dark Ages			**A.D. 500–950**
Copts persecuted	caliph al-Hakim (A.D. 996–1021)	Middle East	A.D. 996
The Great Schism	**Michael Cerularius (Patriarch of Constantinople) (1043–1058) Leo IX (Bishop of Rome) (1049–54)**	Europe and Middle East	1054
Turkish persecution	Seljuk Turks	Armenia	1064
Norman Conquest of British Isles	**William I (1066–1087)**	**British Isles**	1066
First Crusade	**Urban II (1088–99) and a few nobles and lesser barons**	**Holy Lands**	1095–1099
Second Crusade	**Eugenius III (1145–53) Conrad III (1138–52) Louis VII (1137–1180)**	**Holy Lands**	1144–1148
English persecution	Henry II (1154–1189)	Europe	1166
Muslim recapture of the Holy Lands	Saladin of Egypt (1167–1193)	Nubia	1173

SOME KEY MARTYRS (DATE)	EST. # OF MARTYRS	OTHER NOTES
Flora (850), Mary (850), John and Adolphus (850), Nunilo and Alodia (851), Columba (853), Pomposa (853), Eulogius (853), Aurea (856)	50	
	792,810	
Ghabrial (996)	50,000	
		The Universal Church divides into the Roman Catholic Church (West) and the Greek Orthodox Church (East)
	100,000	Capital city of Ani destroyed with 1,001 churches
		Captured Jerusalem and held it until 1187
Thomas à Becket (1170)	2,000	
	130,000	

PERIOD OR EVENT	RULER OR CHIEF PERSON	PLACE	YEAR(S)
Third Crusade	Clement III (1187–91) Richard I (1189–1199) Philip II (1180–1223) Frederick I (1152–90)	Holy Lands	1190–1192
Fourth Crusade	Innocent III (1198–1216) and other European leaders	Asia	1199–1204
Raids of Genghis Khan	Genghis Khan (1211–1227)	Uzbekistan and Afghanistan	1214
Raids of Genghis Khan	Genghis Khan (1211–1227)	Persia and Iraq	1220
Mongol persecutions	Mongols	Turkestan	1221
Inquisition	Begins under Gregory IX (1227–1241)	Europe	1231–1531
Mongol invasion of Russia	Ogodei Khan (1235–1241)	Russia and Hungary	1237–1241
Mongol persecutions	Hulagu Khan (1256–1265)	Iraq	1258
Mameluke persecutions	Mamelukes (1250–1517)	Egypt and Syria	1301–c. 1400

SOME KEY MARTYRS (DATE)	EST. # OF MARTYRS	OTHER NOTES
		The expedition never made it to the Holy Land, but ended by sacking Constantinople; other crusades following this had even less support and success
	5,000,000	Christian strongholds of Bokhara, Samarkand, Tashkent
	150,000	
	600,000	Mongols destroy Seljuk, capitol of Merv, and Khwarizm
	10,000	
	313,000	Mongols destroy Moscow, Suzdal, Vladimir, and Kiev; Krakow attacked (1241)
	1,100,000	End of Abbasid dynasty; Aleppo and Antioch destroyed
	80,000	Copts and Jacobites suffer systematic persecution

PERIOD OR EVENT	RULER OR CHIEF PERSON	PLACE	YEAR(S)
Muslim persecutions	Kurds and Arabs	Iraq	1310
Muslim persecutions	Muslims	India	1310
Mongol persecutions	Mongols (1279–1368)	China	1339
The Black Death (Bubonic Plague) hits Europe	**Various European leaders**	**Europe**	**1348–1349**
Resurgence and advancement			**950–1350**
Persecutions under Tamerlane	Tamerlane (1370–1405)	Asia, Georgia, Middle East, Egypt, and Caucasus	1358–c. 1400
Wycliffe's English translation of the Bible	**John Wycliffe** (c. 1330–1384)	**England**	**1382**
Dissidents executed	Boniface IX (1389–1404) Innocent VII (1406–06) Gregory XII (1406–1415)	Europe	1393–1416

SOME KEY MARTYRS (DATE)	EST. # OF MARTYRS	OTHER NOTES
	150,000	Arbela destroyed
	180,000	Muslims conquer southward to Vindhya mountains
Richard (1339)	100,000	Massacre of Christians in Mongol capital, Almalik
		Nearly a third of the population dies in the plague
	8,919,792	
Saleeb (1400), Ileya (1400), Sidrak and 5 monks (1400), Arsenius (1400), Abu'l Farag and 4 priests (1400)	5,079,000	Catholic Apostolic Church of the East persecuted across Asia; 700 Georgian towns destroyed and all the churches in the capital of Tiflis destroyed; Jacobite churches and monasteries from Asia Minor to Persia destroyed; Copts persecuted; Baghdad and Sevauss sacked
		First English translation; it was translated from the Latin Vulgate
John of Nepomuk (1393), John Huss (1415), Jerome of Prague (1416)	5,000	

327

PERIOD OR EVENT	RULER OR CHIEF PERSON	PLACE	YEAR(S)
Lollard persecutions	Henry IV (1399–1413) Henry V (1413–1422)	England	1399–1418
Witch trials	Various leaders	Europe	1400–1700
Printing press invented	Johannes Gutenberg (c. 1400–1468)	Germany	1443
Gutenberg Bible printed	Johannes Gutenberg (c. 1400–1468)	Germany	c. 1453
Columbus discovers America	Christopher Columbus (1451–1506)	America	1492
Pre-Reformation			1350–1500
Luther posts his Ninety-five Theses	**Martin Luther (1483–1546)**	**Wittenberg, Germany**	**October 31, 1517**
American persecutions	Native American Tribes	Mexico	1519–1536
Turkish invasion of Hungary	Suleiman I (1520–1556)	Hungary	1526
Muslim persecutions	Ahmed Gran (1527–1541)	Ethiopia	1527–1542
State persecutions	Henry VIII (1509–1547)	England	1528–1547
First Dutch Bible printed	Jacob van Liesveldt	Holland	1534
Luther publishes a copy of the Bible in German	**Martin Luther (1483–1546)**	Germany	1534

SOME KEY MARTYRS (DATE)	EST. # OF MARTYRS	OTHER NOTES
W. Sawtrey (1401), J. Badby (1410), John Oldcastle (1418)	100	Lollards persecuted
	500,000	Many tried as witches were innocent churchgoers
		First printed Bible; was a copy of the Latin Vulgate
	5,583,700	
	1,000,000	Nearly 6 million Amerindians had been baptized during this period
	50,000	
	100,000	
J. Frith (1533), J. Fisher (1535), Thomas More (1535), William Tyndale (1536)	300	

PERIOD OR EVENT	RULER OR CHIEF PERSON	PLACE	YEAR(S)
Coverdale Bible printed	**Miles Coverdale (c. 1488–1569)**	**England**	**1535**
Missionaries killed	Native American Tribes	America	1542–1597
Waldenses massacred in Vaudois	Francis I (1515–1547)	France	1545
Dissidents executed	Henry II (1547–1559)	France	1547–1559
Missionaries killed	Native American Tribes	Florida	1549–1597
Reign of Mary I	Mary I (1553–1558)	England	1553–1558
Spanish Inquisition	Charles V (Holy Roman Emperor) (1519–1558)	Spain	1558
The Geneva Bible is printed		**England**	**1560**
Spanish conquistadors	Philip II (of Spain) (1556–1598)	Mexico	c. 1560
Huguenots persecuted	Charles IX (1560–1574)	France	1562
Huguenot colony	Philip III (of Spain and Naples) (1598–1621)	Florida	1562

SOME KEY MARTYRS (DATE)	EST. # OF MARTYRS	OTHER NOTES
		First complete English Bible printed
Avila y Ayala (1672)	350	Mainly in New Mexico, Arizona, Illinois, and Texas
	3,000	
Anne du Bourg (1559)	10,000	Many burned at the stake for "heresy"
P. Martinez (1566)	100	
T. Cramner (1553), N. Ridley (1553), H. Latimer (1553), J. Hooper (1553)	300	Many burned at the stake for "heresy"
	300	Many burned at the stake during this year
		First Bible dividing the Scriptures into verses; it was the Bible of the Pilgrims
	2,200,000	As many as 15 million Amerindians killed; many were baptized Christians
	3,000	Charles IX became king at the age of ten; his mother, Catherine de Médicis, rules from behind the throne; Massacres in Vassy, Toulouse, and elsewhere
	200	Spaniards massacre colony of French Huguenots

PERIOD OR EVENT	RULER OR CHIEF PERSON	PLACE	YEAR(S)
Life of William Shakespeare	**Elizabeth I (1558–1603) James I (1603–1625)**	**England**	**1564–1616**
Dissidents executed	Elizabeth I (1558–1603)	England	1565
St. Bartholemew's Day Massacre	Charles IX (1560–1574)	France	1572
The Kirishtan Holocaust	Began under Toyotomi Hideyoshi (Taikosama) (1582–1598) and Tokugawa Ieyasu (1543–1616)	Japan	1596–1637
King James Bible published	**James I (1603–1625)**	**England**	**1611**
Thirty Years' War	Involved most of the countries in Western Europe	Europe	1618–1648
Waldenses massacred in Tirano, Lombardy	Philip II (of Spain) (1556–1598)	Italy	1620
Pilgrims land at Plymouth Rock	**Miles Standish (1620–1649)**	**America**	**1620**
Missionaries killed	Local non-Christian religious authorities	Tibet	1624–1630

SOME KEY MARTYRS (DATE)	EST. # OF MARTYRS	OTHER NOTES
J. Hamilton (1556)	400	Church of England (headed by Elizabeth) persecutes dissenters
Gaspard de Coligny (1572)	72,000	August 24, 1572; Catherine de Médicis influences her son, Charles IX, to have the Huguenots massacred in an ambush
26 martyrs of Nagasaki (1597), Simon Yempo (1623), T. Tsuji (1627), R. B. Gutierrez (1632), J. K. G. Tomonaga (1633), M. Kurobiove (1633), W. Courtet (1637)	175,120	Christians were persecuted in Japan fairly consistently until 1873; as many as one million Christians may have died for their faith over this time
		First authorized English translation
Liborius Wagner (1631)	15,000	Fought mainly in Germany
	1,000	July 11, 1620; area was under Spanish rule
A. de Andrade (1624)	400	By the end of this period all of the missionaries who had entered Tibet were dead

PERIOD OR EVENT	RULER OR CHIEF PERSON	PLACE	YEAR(S)
English Civil War	Oliver Cromwell (1640–1660)	England	1640–1660
Massacre of 1641	Family of the O'Neals and followers	Ulster, Ireland	1641
The Kirishtan Holocaust (continued)	Tokugawa Shogunate (1603–1867)	Japan	1649–1697
Waldenses persecuted in Piedmont	Philip IV (of Spain, Naples, and Sicily) (1605–1665)	Piedmont, Italy	1655
Covenanters and Quakers persecuted	Charles II (1660–1685)	Scotland and England	1660–1688
Edict of Nantes revoked	Louis XIV (of France) (1643–1715) Innocent XI (1676–1689)	France and Italy	1685–1686
Dissidents executed	Louis XIV (1643–1715)	France	1702
English governor destroys Capuchin missions	Anne (1702–1714)	Florida	1704
Reformation and Expansion			**1500–1750**

SOME KEY MARTYRS (DATE)	EST. # OF MARTYRS	OTHER NOTES
William Laud (1645), Charles I (1649), T. Venner (1661)	700	
C. Plunkett (1649)	7,000	Main day was October 23, 1641; financial support and manpower provided by the French minister, Cardinal Richelieu
	61,000	
	2,000	
James Gunthrie and A. Campbell (1661), Margaret Wilson (1661), Mary Dyre (1662), D. Cargill (1680), J. Renwick (1688)	3,500	
Louis de Marolles (1685), I. Le Fevre (1685)	13,000	The Edict of Nantes had promised certain religious freedoms to minority Christian groups such as the Huguenots and the Waldenses; its revocation led to massacres and expulsions
	15,000	12,000 executed in Languedoc
	400	Missionaries and 300 Apapachee converts killed; 1,000 enslaved
	4,513,701	

PERIOD OR EVENT	RULER OR CHIEF PERSON	PLACE	YEAR(S)
Ottoman persecutions	Osman III (1754–1757) Mustafa III (1757–1774) Abd al-Hamid I (1774–1789) Salim III (1789–1807)	Ottoman Empire	1754–1795
United States declares independence from England		**U.S.A.**	**1776**
French Revolution	Various revolutionary governments	France	1789–1799
First major slave rebellion	John Adams (1797–1801)	U.S.A.	1800
Missions and revival			1750–1815
Slave rebellion	James Monroe (1817–1825)	U.S.A.	1817
Slave rebellion	Andrew Jackson (1829–1837)	U.S.A.	1831
Great Heavenly Kingdom members persecuted	Hung Hsiu-Ch'üan (1853–1864)	China	1862
Final Great Persecution	Taewon'gun (1864–1873)	Korea	1866
Commune of Paris uprising	Commune of Paris (1871)	France	1871

| --- | --- | --- |
Nicholas (1754), Damascenus (1771), Polydorus the Cypriot (1794), Theodore (1975)	30,000	
		July 4, 1776
J. M. Du Lau (1792), L. A. Expilly (1794), C. Carnus (1794)	5,000	Carmelite martyrs of Compiegne (1794)
Gabriel Prosser (1800)	300	A Christian army of 10,000 African-American slaves was involved
	153,243	
	350	Denmark Vessy leads the largest U.S. slave insurrection ever
Nat Turner (1831)	800	Turner and many other followers were hanged; others massacred
	1,000,000	Based in Nanking
S. F. Berneaux and M. A. N. Daveluy (1866), R. J. Thomas (1866), Peter Cho (1866)	10,000	7 priests, many catechists, 10,000 other believers killed
G. Darboy (1871)	300	

PERIOD OR EVENT	RULER OR CHIEF PERSON	PLACE	YEAR(S)
Suppression of Bulgars, Armenians, Manorites, and others	Abdul-Aziz (1861–1876) Murad V (1876) Abdul-Hamid II (1876–1909) Mehmed V (1909–1918)	Bulgaria, Turkey, Persia, and Lebanon	1872–1916
Persecution of Salvation Army members	Local authorities, the Skeleton Army, and others	England	1880–1885
Racial violence	Various white racist groups	U.S.A.	1882–1922
North China Boxer Revolt	Boxers (1900–1901)	China	1900
National Revolution	Various revolutionary leaders	Mexico	1910–1929
The Greatest Century of Christian Expansion (Missions)			1815–1914

SOME KEY MARTYRS (DATE)	EST. # OF MARTYRS	OTHER NOTES
John Papizian (1894), 176 priests (1894), 25 pastors (1894)	1,185,000	In Adana, largest city of Cilicia, further massacre of Armenians, including Armenian Evangelical Union at their annual conference; 50,000 killed in Urmia in Persia (1914); 600,000 killed in Anatolia (1915); 600,000 more deported from Turkey, many dying by roadside or in Syrian desert (1915); 22% of Maronite population (100,000) killed in Lebanon (1916)
	50	660 brutally attacked and thrown into prison
	2,300	Numerous Christian leaders lynched among 3,437 African-Americans between 1882–1922; roughly 100 a year continue to die until 1963
Wang Ten Ren (1900), C. and E. Price (1900)	49,000	5 bishops, 31 priests, 188 missionaries, 48,000 Chinese converts
M. Pro Juarez (1927)	70,000	
	2,275,433	

PERIOD OR EVENT	RULER OR CHIEF PERSON	PLACE	YEAR(S)
World War I	Various world leaders	Europe	1914–1919
Bolshevik (Early Soviet Communists) Persecutions	Russian Revolution (1917) Vladimir Lenin (1922–1924) Joseph Stalin (1922–1953) Nikita Khrushchev (1953–1964) Leonid Brezhnev (1964–1982)	U.S.S.R. and Georgia	1917–1980
Tulsa Race Riot	White racist groups	U.S.A.	1921
Roman Catholic Church	Joseph Stalin (1922–1953)	U.S.S.R.	1925–c. 1950
Soviet persecution in the Ukraine	Joseph Stalin (1922–1953)	Ukraine	1927
Chinese Civil wars	Bandits and guerrillas	China	1927–1948
Autocephalous Church exterminated	Joseph Stalin (1922–1953)	Belorussia	1927–1943
Lutherans persecuted	Joseph Stalin (1922–1953)	U.S.S.R. (Russia specifically)	1927–1953

SOME KEY MARTYRS (DATE)	EST. # OF MARTYRS	OTHER NOTES
	100,000	
Kirion (1918), Nasaire (1923)	16,060,000	78 bishops, 12,000 priests killed (1917–1926); 8,100 priests killed (1922); Christians die in prison camps, including 30,000 clergy and 250 bishops, also pastors, evangelists, catechists (1921–1950); total clergy killed 200,000 (1917–1980)
	200	White mobs torch 35-block Black business district, burn churches, burn or lynch 250 African Americans
L. Fedorov (1935), C. Abrikosov (1936)	1,200,000	Soviets attempt to liquidate entire Roman Catholic Church
N. Bretzkiy (1927)	500,000	34 bishops, 2,000 priests, 20,000 lay officers
W. E. Simpson (1932), Y. C. Liu, J. and B. Stam (1934), F. V. Lehhe (1940)	200,000	
Filaret of Bobruisk, Mikhail of Slutsk, Ioann of Mozyr (1927–1938); Nemantsevich (1943)	120,000	
	600,000	One million German-origin Lutherans across Russia are executed, churches destroyed

PERIOD OR EVENT	RULER OR CHIEF PERSON	PLACE	YEAR(S)
Orthodox persecuted; the Terror-Famine (1929–1937)	Joseph Stalin (1922–1953)	Ukraine	1928–1953
Nazi persecutions of Confessing Church and Roman Catholics	Adolph Hitler (1933–1945)	Germany	1933–1945
Persecution of the "Catacomb Church"	Joseph Stalin (1922–1953)	U.S.S.R.	1935–1953
Spanish Civil War	Francisco Franco (Leader of revolution, 1936–1939; Leader of Spain, 1939–1975)	Spain	1936–1939
Gypsies persecuted	Adolph Hitler (1933–1945)	Germany	1936
Italian conquest	Benito Mussolini (1922–1943)	Ethiopia	1937
The Holocaust	Adolph Hitler (1933–1945)	Europe	1937–1945
Final attempt to liquidate Orthodox Church	Joseph Stalin (1922–1953)	Russia	1937–1945

SOME KEY MARTYRS (DATE)	EST. # OF MARTYRS	OTHER NOTES
I. Pavlivsky (1936), M. Boretsky (1937), V. Lypkivsky (1938)	3,000,000	95% of all Orthodox parishes destroyed, 19 bishops killed; 14.5 million Orthodox peasants killed or starved to death
B. Lichtenberg (1933), M. J. Metzger (1944), J. Schmidlin (1944), D. Bonhoeffer (1945)	125,000	
I. E. Voronaev	1,000,000	
L. Isla (1936), J. Valenti (1936), T. Sitjar (1936)	107,000	13 bishops, 4,254 priests, 2,489 monks, 283 nuns, and 100,000 laypersons executed or assassinated
	50,000	Hitler orders city of Berlin "cleaned up" by rounding up and massacring thousands of Sinti and Romani Gypsies
Mikael Petros (1937)	500,000	Scores of priests and monks massacred, churches razed
Edith Stein (1942), Max Jacob (1944)	1,000,000	Nazis kill 5 million religious Jews and 1 million Jewish Christians
	120,000	85,300 clergy shot (1937); 21,500 clergy shot (1938); 900 shot (1939); 100 more each year (1939–1945)

PERIOD OR EVENT	RULER OR CHIEF PERSON	PLACE	YEAR(S)
Gypsy Holocaust	Adolph Hitler (1933–1945)	Europe	1938–1945
Invasion of Poland during World War II	Adolph Hitler (1933–1945)	Poland	1939–1945
Others martyred during World War II	Axis Powers and Soviets	World	1939–1945
Invasion of Greece during World War II	Axis Powers	Greece	1940–1945
Invasion of Balkans during World War II	Axis Powers and Soviets	Baltic states	1940–1945
World War II in Yugoslavia	Croats, Nazis, and Civil War	Yugoslavia	1941–1945
World War II and aftermath in Lithuania	Axis Powers and Soviets	Lithuania	1941–1944

SOME KEY MARTYRS (DATE)	EST. # OF MARTYRS	OTHER NOTES
Joseph Horvath (1938)	350,000	Nazis exterminate 500,000 Gypsies across Europe in the Porajmos (Gypsy Holocaust), mostly Christians
M. Kolbe (1941)	1,000,000	Nazis execute 6 bishops, 2,030 priests, 173 brothers, 243 nuns
T. Brandsma in Dachau death camp (1942)	200,000	Out of 55 million killed in World War II, about 6 million total died as martyrs for their Christian faith
	21,000	German, Italian, Bulgarian troops murder 350 priests
	150,000	200,000 deported; 10,000 bishops, clergy, nuns shot or killed in prison by Soviets; 41 pastors killed
J. Simrak (1945), 270 priests (1945)	450,000	In Croatia, 350,000 Serbian Orthodox massacred by Croats—3 bishops, 220 priests; Nazis and civil war also kill vast numbers of other clergy and laity
V. Litaunieks (1941), M. Reinys (1953), P. Ramanauskas (1959)	100,000	Nazis kill 200,000; Soviets kill 300,000 (1944)

PERIOD OR EVENT	RULER OR CHIEF PERSON	PLACE	YEAR(S)
World War II in Belorussia	Axis Powers and Soviets	Belorussia	1941–1945
La Violencia civil war	Various leaders	Colombia	1944–1958
Ukrainian Catholic Uniates Persecuted	Joseph Stalin (1922–1953) Nikita Khrushchev (1953–1964)	Ukraine	1945–1959
Soviet Persecution in Romania	Joseph Stalin (1922–1953) Nikita Khrushchev (1953–1964) Leonid Brezhnev (1964–1982)	Romania	1948–1970
Post–World War II Persecutions in Russia	Joseph Stalin (1922–1953) Nikita Khrushchev (1953–1964) Leonid Brezhnev (1964–1982)	U.S.S.R. (Specifi cally Russia)	1948–?
During the periods of World War and their aftermath/ the rise of Communism		**World**	**1914–1950**
Communist pressure in Vietnam	Communist leaders	Vietnam	1950–1953
Korean War and aftermath	Kim II Sung (1948–1994)	North Korea	1950–1960

SOME KEY MARTYRS (DATE)	EST. # OF MARTYRS	OTHER NOTES
	550,000	A million Christians, clergy, bishops, killed (1) by Stalin "eliminating all Belorussian enemies of the state," (2) by occupying Nazis, then (3) by returning Soviets
Juan Coy (1944)	120,000	300,000 Christians killed
Kocylowskyj (1946), T. Romza (1947), A. Kherie and many priests (1959)	70,000	Soviets attempt to destroy 3.5 million strong Ukrainian Catholic Uniates
Afteinie, Frentiu, and Suciu, (1948), J. Hossu (1970)	50,000	Uniate churches destroyed: many priests killed; 500 priests die in prison
	500,000	MGB (ex NKVD) begins to destroy true Orthodox Church (3 million underground Russians)
	31,724,520	**Nearly half of all those martyred for their faith (45.7%) during these 36 years**
Nguyen (1950), Phan Long (1950), Thien Thi (1950)	28,000	
Tong-Sin (1950), Sung Du (1950), P.T. Brennan (1950), P.J. Byrne (1950)	800,000	Mass slaughter of Christians: troops massacre 150 priests and 500 pastors

PERIOD OR EVENT	RULER OR CHIEF PERSON	PLACE	YEAR(S)
Liquidation of churches	Zhou Enlai (1949–1976)	China	1950–1980
"Churches of Silence" liquidated in 8 countries	Communist leaders	Eastern Europe	1950–80
Muslim and Hindu retaliation	Various factions	India	1950–1999
More Soviet persecutions	Joseph Stalin (1922–1953) Nikita Khrushchev (1953–1964) Leonid Brezhnev (1964–1982)	U.S.S.R.	1950–1980
Chinese Independent Churches persecuted	Zhou Enlai (1949–1976)	China	1952–1955
Aftermath of Castro's Communist revolution (1952–1958)	Fidel Castro (1959–present)	Cuba	1959
Great Leap Forward	Zhou Enlai (1949–1976)	China	1959–1962
Civil wars	Guerilla groups	Latin America	1960–present
Muslim resurgence	Muslim groups	West Irian (Indonesia)	1962–mid 1990

SOME KEY MARTYRS (DATE)	EST. # OF MARTYRS	OTHER NOTES
Wang Ling-Tso (1950), Tsiang Beda (1950)	500,000	800 Chinese priests killed (1950–1954)
Iuliu Maniu (1953), Pavol Gojdic (1960)	900,000	
Rani Maria (1995)	400,000	Over 10,000 Christians, evangelists, workers killed each year due to mobs, infuriated relatives, etc.
M. Ostapenko (1974), N. Rozanov (1974)	5,000,000	Christians die in prison camps
Watchman Nee arrested (1952), dies in prison	74,000	
	15,000	Expels 590 priests, 970 brothers, 2,400 nuns, executes many who die shouting "Long live Christ the King!"
H. H. Lin (1960)	300,000	Communists kill 25 million peasants, workers, pastors, priests
Camilo Torres (1966), H. Gallejo (1966), A. Navarro (1977)	300,000	
	70,000	Genocide: 150,000 West Papuans killed by Muslim troops, 1962–1982; by 1995 total killed reaches 200,000

PERIOD OR EVENT	RULER OR CHIEF PERSON	PLACE	YEAR(S)
Sudanese Civil War	Northern Arabs vs. Black Africans in the South	Sudan	1963–present
Great Proletarian Cultural Revolution	Zhou Enlai (1949–1976)	China	1966–1969
Biafra Civil War	Odumegwu Ojukwu (1967–1970)	Nigeria	1967–1970
Communist persecutions	Khmer Rouge	Cambodia	1970–1977
Unregistered churches targeted by KGB	Leonid Brezhnev (1964–1982)	U.S.S.R.	1970–1980s
Amin persecutions	Idi Amin (1971–1979)	Uganda	1971–1979
Communist persecution	Le Duan (1969–1986)	Vietnam	1975–1985
Lebanese Civil War	Various factions	Lebanon	1975–1995

SOME KEY MARTYRS (DATE)	EST. # OF MARTYRS	OTHER NOTES
G. Adwok (1963)	660,000	Northern Arabs kill 64 missionaries and 600,000 Black Christians (1962–1972); 500,000 Southern Black Christians driven into deserts and starved to death through deliberate diverting of famine relief food by Islamic state bureaucrats (1993)
Li Xinsheng was imprisoned (1969), tortured, and eventually died in prison (1989)	400,000	Churches razed, 2,500,000 believers imprisoned
	200,000	One million killed, including massacre of 150,000 Ibos by Muslims; also 10,000 Ogoni Christians slaughtered
	50,000	
V. A. Shelkov (1980), S. Bakholdin (1980), N. P. Khrapov (1982)	60,000	
J. Serwanika (1973), Janani Luwum (1977)	200,000	
	50,000	Churches closed, pastors executed; 65,000 butchered in 1984
A. Masse (1987)	25,000	200,000 killed; thousands of Christians kidnapped and killed

PERIOD OR EVENT	RULER OR CHIEF PERSON	PLACE	YEAR(S)
Communist persecutions	Khmer Rouge	Cambodia	1975–1979
UDT–Fretilin Civil War	Revolutionary Front for an Independent East Timor (Fretilin)	Timor	1975–2000
Indian persecutions	Indira Gandhi (1966–1977 and 1980–1984)	India	1980
Government persecutions	Ferdinand Marcos (1965–1986)	Philippines	1985
Hutu Massacre	Hutu Tribe	Rwanda and Burundi	1993–1995
Christianty's Surge in the Third World/ The Cold War			1950–2000
Total Since Jesus			A.D. 33–2000

SOME KEY MARTYRS (DATE)	EST. # OF MARTYRS	OTHER NOTES
P. Tep Im (1975), J. C. Salas (1976), B. C. Chunsar (1976)	42,000	Khmer Rouge take over Cambodia in 1975 and rename it Democratic Kampuchea; they slaughter 2 million, execute 80% of all city dwellers including known Christians by 1979; in 1979 Khmer Rouge is overthrown
	90,000	200,000 Timorese (70% being Christians) killed; military kill 270 Christian youths at a funeral in Santa Cruz massacre (1991)
	240,000	In Nagaland, Indian Army continues 50-year genocide against 2 million Nagas; many churches destroyed
T. Favali (1985), A. Romero (1985), N. Valerio (1985), R. Romano (1985), M. Beling (1985)	40,000	
I. Havugimana (1994), T. Gatwa (1994), J. Rutumbu (1994), G. Bimazubute (1993), J. Ruhuna (1996)	560,000	Hutus massacre Tutsis; fifth wave of violence since 1961; 200,000 Hutus killed by Tutsi army; clergy targeted; 3 bishops, 101 priests, 64 nuns killed
	13,356,280	
	69,421,230	

Notes:

1) Because of differences in the historical record, all dates are approximated—the earlier dates more than the latter. Those marked with a "c." for circa indicate periods where no dates were found or dates found varied widely.

2) Key historical events (other than periods of martyrdom) and totals are in boldface type.

3) People listed under "Rulers or Chief Person" for historical events are related to the events and were not necessarily rulers during the period listed. Those listed as rulers during the period were mostly responsible for the martyrdoms, though some merely had jurisdiction over the area, while other lesser officials or groups were responsible for the killings.

4) For the sake of this chart and its estimates, the following definition is used for martyr: "a believer in Christ who loses his or her life prematurely, in a situation of witness, as a result of human hostility." For this chart, this includes villages or areas that were ransacked by groups for the Christian faith of the people there (non-Christians killed in such raids are not part of the estimates), Christians who stood up for biblical truth (civil rights, opposition of persecution of other people, etc.), Christians killed in churches (cases where church doors were barred and the building burned to the ground, armed people came into the church meetings and killed those present, etc.), as well as all those executed after trial who refused to reverse their beliefs for the sake of remaining alive.

5) These periods listed in this chart have been chosen either because of their magnitude (greater than fifty-thousand martyred) or their historical significance (mainly to Western culture). They do not represent the largest periods of persecution of all time. (For a complete list of "The 500 major martyrdom situations in history," see World Christian Trends a.d. 30–a.d. 2200, pages 238–246.)

The above information included in this chart, as well as the definition of *martyr*, was mostly taken from David B. Barrett and Todd M. Johnson's *World Christian Trends* A.D. 30–A.D. 2200: *Interpreting the Annual Christian Megacensus*. (Pasadena, CA: William Carey Library, 2001), 225–264. All rights reserved. Used by permission. Other dates and information were taken from *Microsoft® Encarta® Encyclopedia 2000* (Redmond, WA: Microsoft Corporation, 1993-1999), various Internet sites, and other sources listed under "Where we got our information...."

Top Ten Persecuting Groups Since Jesus

RANKING	NAME OF GROUP	NUMBER OF MARTYRS UNDER THIS GROUP FROM A.D. 33 TO 2000
1	State Ruling Powers	55,871,000
2	Atheists	31,689,000
3	Muslims	9,121,000
4	Pagan Religions	7,469,000
5	Other Christians	5,539,100
6	Quasi-religious Groups	2,712,000
7	Buddhists	1,651,000
8	Hindus	676,000
9	Zoastrians	384,000
10	Jews	60,100

Notes:

The totals above overlap (i.e., a martyr killed under an atheistic state ruling power would be counted under both "State Ruling Power" and "Atheists," etc.). The definition for martyr remains the same as it was for the previous chart.

The above information included in this chart was taken from David B. Barrett and Todd M. Johnson's *World Christian Trends A.D. 30–A.D. 2200: Interpreting the Annual Christian Megacensus*. (Pasadena, CA: William Carey Library, 2001), table 4–5, page 230.

Endnotes

Lord, Show Me the Truth

Dave DiSabatino, "Chapter III: The Jesus People Movement (1967–1973)." Online at *http://caic.org.au/biblebase/cog-family/jesusmovementhistory.html*.

No Greater Honor

"Anti Christian Edicts," from *Kodansha's Encyclopedia of Japan*, Kodasha Ltd., 1993. Online at *www.baobab.or.jp/~stranger/mypage/edicts.htm*.

Billy Bruce, "Christians Recall Japan's 'Holocaust.' " *Charisma* magazine, April 1997. Online at *www.charismamag.com/april97/ca197112.htm*.

Diego R. Yuki, "On Martyrs Hill." Online at *www.baobab.or.jp/~stranger/mypage/martyr.htm*, *www.baobab.or.jp/~stranger/mypage/pulpit.htm*, and *www.baobab.or.jp/~stranger/mypage/conquer.htm*.

"The San Felipe." Online at *www.baobab.or.jp/~stranger/mypage/urado.htm*.

Philip Yancey, "Japan's Faithful Judas: Shusaku Endo's Struggle to Give His Faith a Japanese Soul." From *Christianity Today*, 1995. Online at *www.baobab.or.jp/~stranger/mypage/endo.htm* and *www.baobab.or.jp/~stranger/mypage/endo2.htm*.

Profitable for the Ministry

2 Timothy 4:11, paraphrased.

Preaching in the Russian Army Barracks

Richard Wurmbrand, *Tortured for Christ* (Bartlesville, OK: Living Sacrifice Books, 1967, 1998), 20–21.

"Revolutionaries of the Spirit" Quote

Eberhard Arnold, *The Early Christians: In their Own Words* (Farmington, PA: The Plough Publishing House, 1997), 20.

Not-So-Blind Chang
James and Marti Hefley, *By Their Blood: Christian Martyrs of the Twentieth Century* (Grand Rapids, MI: Baker Books, 1996), 39–41.

General William Booth Quote
General William Booth, *The War Cry*, January 20, 1881, quoted in *The Founder Speaks Again* (London: Salvationist Publishing and Supplies, 1960), 100–101.

The Conqueror's Heart
Richard Wurmbrand, *Tortured for Christ* (Bartlesville, OK: Living Sacrifice Books, 1967, 1998), 113.

The Hiding Place
David Wallington, "The Secret Room." *www.soon.org.uk/true_stories/holocaust.htm*. Updated March 1999.

Faithful to the End
Luke 1:3–4 NAS; 2 Timothy 4:9–11 NIV; Acts 4:12, paraphrased.

Underground and Undercover
Richard Wurmbrand, *Tortured for Christ* (Bartlesville, OK: Living Sacrifice Books, 1967, 1998), 31–32.

A Foolish Waste of Lives?
Dave and Neta Jackson, *Hero Tales: A Family Treasury of True Stories from the Lives of Christian Heroes*, Vol. 2, (Minneapolis: Bethany House Publishers, 1997), 45-55.
John Mark Ministries, *"Nate Saint and other Martyrs of the Ecuador Mission."* Online at *www.pastornet.net.au/jmm/afam/afam0097.htm*.

"A Witness to His Resurrection"
Acts 1:22, 24–25 THE MESSAGE.

Where Do I Find Out More About Such World-Changers?

WHERE WE GOT OUR INFORMATION ...

Arnold, Eberhard. *The Early Christians: In Their Own Words*. Farmington, PA: The Plough Publishing House, 1997.

Barrett, David B., George T. Kurian, and Todd M. Johnson. *World Christian Encyclopedia: A comparative survey of churches and religions in the modern world*. Vols. 1,2. New York: Oxford University Press, 2001.

Barrett, David B., and Todd M. Johnson. *World Christian Trends* A.D. *30–*A.D. *2200: Interpreting the Annual Christian Megacensus*. Pasadena, CA: William Carey Library, 2001.

Burke, Carl F. *God Is for Real, Man*. New York: Association Press, 1966.

Cave, William. *The Lives of the Primitive Fathers*. London: Rose and Crown, 1682.

"Christianity In Japan." from *Kodansha's Encyclopedia of Japan*, Kodasha Ltd., 1993.
www.baobab.or.jp/~stranger/mypage/chrinjap.htm.

Douglas, J. D. *Who's Who in Christian History*. Wheaton, IL: Tyndale House, 1997, 1992.

Fox, John. *Fox's Book of Martyrs*, Edited by William Byron Forbush.
www.ccel.org/f/foxe_j/martyrs/home.html. Grand Rapids, MI: Christian Classics Ethereal Library of Calvin College. Updated May 24, 2000.

Foxe, John. *Foxe's Christian Martyrs of the World*. Uhrichsville, OH: Barbour Publishing, Inc., 1989.

Hanks, Geoffrey. *70 Great Christians: The Story of the Christian Church*. Fearn, Scotland: Christian Focus Publications Ltd., 1992.

Hefley, James C. and Marti. *By Their Blood: Christian Martyrs of the Twentieth Century*. Grand Rapids, MI: Baker Books, 1979, 1996.

Jackson, Dave and Neta, *Hero Tales: A Family Treasury of True Stories from the Lives of Christian Heroes, Vol. 2.* Minneapolis: Bethany House Publishers, 1997.

John Mark Ministries, *"Nate Saint and other Martyrs of the Ecuador Mission."* Online at *www.pastornet.net.au/jmm/afam/afam0097.htm.*

Martyr, Justin. "The First Apology of Justin." *www.ccel.org/fathers /ANF-01/just/justinapology1.html#Section2.* Grand Rapids, MI: Christian Classics Ethereal Library of Calvin College. Updated: September 27, 1996. *Microsoft® Encarta® Encyclopedia 2000.* Redmond, WA: Microsoft Corporation, 1993–1999.

Van Braght, Thieleman J. *Martyrs Mirror.* Scottdale, PA: Herald Press, 1660, 1886, 1950.

Ricciotti, Abbot Giuseppe. *The Age of Martyrs: Christianity From Diocletian* (A.D. *284) to Constantine* (A.D. *337).* Rockford, IL: Tan Books and Publishers, 1959, 1999.

The Voice of the Martyrs monthly newsletters (formerly known as *Jesus to the Communist World*). Issues ranging from 1968 to 2002.

Ten Boom, Corrie et al. *The Hiding Place.* Fairfax, VA: Chosen Books, 1971.

Thigpen, Thomas Paul. *Blood of the Martyrs: Seed of the Church.* Ann Arbor, MI: Servants Publications, 2001.

Two brothers from Berkley. *Letters to Street Christians.* Grand Rapids, MI: Zondervan Publishing House, 1971.

Voice of the Martyrs, The. *Extreme Devotion.* Nashville: W Publishing Group, 2001.

Water, Mark. *The New Encyclopedia of Christian Martyrs.* Hampshire, UK: John Hunt Publishing Limited, 2001.

Wurmbrand, Richard. *Tortured for Christ.* Bartlesville, OK: Living Sacrifice Books, 1967, 1998.

Wurmbrand, Sabina. *The Pastor's Wife.* Bartlesville, OK: Living Sacrifice Books, 1970.

OTHER SUGGESTED TITLES ...

Bergman, Susan. *Martyrs: Contemporary Writers on Modern Lives of Faith.* Maryknoll, NY: Orbis Books, 1996.

Bonhoeffer, Dietrich. *The Cost of Discipleship.* New York: Simon and Schuster, 1959, 1976.

Brackin, Ron. *Sweet Persecution.* Minneapolis: Bethany House Publishers, 1999.

Brother Andrew, with John and Elizabeth Sherrill, featuring Jars of Clay. *The Narrow Road: Stories of Those Who Walk This Road Together.* Grand Rapids, MI: Fleming H. Revell, 1967, 2001.

Companjan, Johan. *Please Pray for Us.* Minneapolis: Bethany House Publishers, 2000.

Companjan, Anneke. *Hidden Sorrow, Lasting Joy: The Forgotten Women of the Persecuted Church.* Wheaton: Tyndale House Publishers, Inc., 2001.

Johnstone, Patrick. *Operation World.* Carlisle, Cumbria, U.K.: Paternoster Lifestyle, 2001.

Royal, Robert. *The Catholic Martyrs of the Twentieth Century: A Comprehensive World History.* New York: The Crossroads Publishing Company, 2000.

Alphabetical Index

I

J

Chronological Index

Scripture Index

About dc Talk

TOBY MCKEEHAN MICHAEL TAIT KEVIN MAX

In 1987 three college friends formed a little band called dc Talk that reflected both their deep spiritual commitments and their diverse interest in rock, rap, and pop music.

Now with the release of the *dc Talk Solo* projects, two things have become blatantly obvious. First is how far Toby McKeehan, Michael Tait, and Kevin Max have come in their artistic evolution that has been demonstrated by a string of acclaimed gold and platinum albums, sold-out high-energy concert tours, and a growing collection of Grammy, Dove, and *Billboard* magazine awards.

But equally amazing is how three friends who met at Virginia's Liberty University have transformed the Christian entertainment world. They've introduced Christian music to untold numbers of new listeners and to mainstream critics at publications like *Rolling Stone* and *Entertainment Weekly* while at the same time maintaining their commitment to their faith. One example of that is their first book, *Jesus Freaks: Martyrs*. The book has sold over one million copies to date and chronicles the suffering and persecution of Christians around the world. With *Jesus Freaks: Revolutionaries*, dc Talk once again challenges readers to question their standards of faith and dedication.

Discography
2001   TobyMac: Momentum
2001   Kevin Max: Stereotype Be
2001   Tait: Empty
2001   dc Talk Solo; Grammy Award
2000   Intermission: The Greatest Hits
1998   Supernatural—certified platinum
1997   Welcome to the Freak Show Live—certified gold;
       Grammy Award
1995   Jesus Freak—certified double platinum; Grammy Award
1992   Free at Last—certified platinum; Grammy Award
1990   Nu Thang—certified gold
1989   dc Talk

379

Videography
1999   The Supernatural Experience—live video
1999   Consume Me
1998   My Friend (So Long)
1997   Welcome to the Freak Show—live video; gold
1997   Colored People
1996   Just Between You and Me
1995   Jesus Freak
1994   Narrow Is the Road—long-form video; gold
1993   The Hard Way
1993   Jesus Is Still Alright
1992   Walls

About The Voice of the Martyrs
Serving the persecuted church since 1967

The Voice of the Martyrs is a nonprofit, interdenominational organization dedicated to assisting the persecuted church worldwide. VOM was founded thirty years ago by Pastor Richard Wurmbrand, who was imprisoned in Communist Romania for fourteen years for his faith in Jesus Christ. His wife, Sabina, was imprisoned for three years. In the 1960s, Richard, Sabina, and their son, Mihai, were ransomed out of Romania and came to the United States. Through their travels, the Wurmbrands spread the message of the atrocities that Christians face in restricted nations, while establishing a network of offices dedicated to assisting the persecuted church. The Voice of the Martyrs continues in this mission around the world today through the following five main purposes.

1. To give Christians Bibles, literature, and broadcasts in their own language in Communist countries and other restricted areas of the world where Christians are persecuted.

2. To give relief to the families of Christian martyrs in these areas of the world.

3. To undertake projects of encouragement to help believers rebuild their lives and witness in countries that have suffered Communist oppression.

4. To win to Jesus Christ those who are opposed to the Gospel.

5. To inform the world about atrocities committed against Christians and about the courage and faith of the persecuted.

The Voice of the Martyrs publishes a free monthly newsletter giving updates on the persecuted church around the world and suggesting ways you can help.

To subscribe, call or write:
The Voice of the Martyrs
P.O. Box 443
Bartlesville, OK 74005
(800) 747-0085
e-mail address: thevoice@vom-usa.org
Web site: www.persecution.com

Permissions

Put Down My Name (pp. 34–35)
Encyclopedia of 7700 Illustrations by Paul Lee Tan
Copyright © 1979 by Paul Lee Tan.
Published by Bible Communications. All rights reserved. Used by permission.

Martin Luther King Jr. (p. 44)
Simpson's Contemporary Quotations, compiled by James B. Simpson
Copyright © 1988 by James B. Simpson
Published by HarperCollins Publishers Inc. All rights reserved. Used by permission.

Revolutionaries of the Spirit (p. 69)
The Early Christians by Eberhard Arnold
Copyright © 1997 by Plough Publishing House of the Bruderhof Foundation.
Published by The Plough Publishing House. All rights reserved. Used by permission.

Not-So-Blind Chang (pp. 77–79)
By Their Blood by James C. and Marti Hefley
Copyright © 1996 by James C. and Marti Hefley.
Published by Baker Books. All rights reserved. Used by permission.

The Hiding Place (pp. 103–108)
70 Great Christians by Geoffrey Hanks
Copyright © 1992.
Published by Christian Focus Publications, Ltd. All rights reserved. Used by permission.

Jim Elliot (p. 126)
Encyclopedia of 7700 Illustrations by Paul Lee Tan
Copyright © 1979 by Paul Lee Tan.
Published by Bible Communications. All rights reserved. Used by permission.

More Straight Talk to Challenge Your Faith

Learn about some of the biggest Jesus Freaks of all time: those who stood out from the crowd enough to be called martyrs. If Jesus was willing to give His life for me, and if these people, these martyrs, were willing to give up their lives for Him, how much does it take for me to truly dedicate my days on earth to Him?

Jesus Freaks by dc Talk and The Voice of the Martyrs

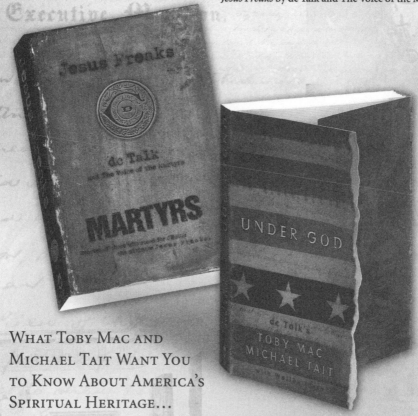

What Toby Mac and Michael Tait Want You to Know About America's Spiritual Heritage...

Unflinching and inspiring, *Under God* looks at the triumphs and tragedies of our spiritual legacy and asks "What Part Will You Play?" in shaping our nation's future. With our nation at a crossroads, your answer has never been more important.

Under God by TOBY MAC and MICHAEL TAIT